100 SOLUTIONS
FOR ACHIEVING
HIGH NET WORTH

# ROSENTRETER'S RULES

## kurt rosentreter, C.A.

Prentice
Hall
Canada

A PEARSON COMPANY

TORONTO

**Canadian Cataloguing in Publication Data**

Rosentreter, Kurt
     Rosentreter's rules : 100 solutions for achieving high net worth

ISBN 0-13-033339-5

1. Investments. 2. Finance, Personal. I. Title.

HG4512.R776 2001 330.024'01     C2001-901237-3

ISBN 0-13-033339-5

Editorial Director, Trade Division: Andrea Crozier
Acquisitions Editor: Nicole de Montbrun
Managing Editor: Tracy Bordian
Art Direction: Mary Opper
Cover Design: Carol Moskot
Interior Design: Mary Opper
Author Photograph: George Whiteside
Production Manager: Kathrine Pummell
Page Layout: Dave McKay

1 2 3 4 5  WEB  05 04 03 02 01

Printed and bound in Canada.

This publication contains the opinions and ideas of its author and is designed to provide useful advice in regard to the subject matter covered. The author and publisher are not engaged in rendering legal, accounting, or other professional services in this publication. This publication is not intended to provide a basis for action in particular circumstances without consideration by a competent professional. The author and publisher expressly disclaim any responsibility for any liability, loss, or risk, personal or otherwise, which is incurred as a consequence, directly or indirectly, of the use and application of any of the contents of this book.

ATTENTION: CORPORATIONS
Books are available at quantity discounts with bulk purchase for educational, business, or sales promotional use. For information, please email or write to: Pearson PTR Canada, Special Sales, PTR Division, 26 Prince Andrew Place, Don Mills, Ontario, M3C 2T8. Email ss.corp@pearsoned.com. Please supply: title of book, ISBN, quantity, how the book will be used, date needed.

Visit the Pearson PTR Canada Web site! Send us your comments, browse our catalogues, and more. **www.pearsonptr.ca**

A Pearson Company

*Dedicated to the love of my life.*

# ACKNOWLEDGEMENTS

I would like to take a moment to thank those people who have assisted me in finalizing this book. Peter Kortenaar, Karen Silvester, and Ian Thompson took time from their busy schedules to provide valuable review of the content, and their assistance is very much appreciated. I am proud to call them all friends and associates.

# A Quick Quiz

*Rosentreter's Rules* will help you answer many of the following questions about your personal finances and start you on the road to finally achieving peace of mind about your finances.

| Test your personal financial savvy | Yes, I'm OK | Help! |
|---|---|---|
| Do you know whether you should buy mutual funds, individual stocks and bonds, pooled funds, index funds, seg funds, wrapped investment products, protected seg funds, build an individually managed portfolio, or use discretionary management for your investment needs? | | |
| Do you know whether you should hire a bank, a trust company, an investment counsellor, a broker, a financial advisor, a financial planner, a wealth management specialist, a portfolio manager, a mutual fund specialist, a private wealth consultant, or an insurance agent to give you financial advice? | | |
| Do you know how to differentiate the following credentials on a financial advisor's business card: CFP, PFP, RFP, CA, LLB, BA, CIM, FCSI, CIMA, CMC, CHFC, CLU, ABC, XYZ, and so on? | | |
| Rather than just shooting for the highest possible returns, do you actually know what returns you need as a minimum to achieve the future lifestyle or financial goals you want? | | |
| Do all investments you own everywhere fit together in a logical, disciplined way that is tax effective, risk managed, value priced, coordinated according to your changing needs, while their progress is still easy to measure? | | |
| Is your investment portfolio organized to maximize after-tax returns, not the pre-tax returns you see in the newspapers? What tax-smart strategies have you implemented to maximize after-tax returns and leave more money in your pocket? | | |
| Are you completely confident you are doing everything possible to minimize the tax you pay? Have you had a tax planning opportunity review from a qualified professional recently? | | |
| Do you know if you have done all you can to minimize income taxes and probate fees payable on your death? | | |
| Do you know if you have the right amount of insurance and the right type for your needs and situation? | | |
| Have you ever had a comprehensive financial review of your current and future financial needs, objectives, and resources to determine if you are missing opportunities to enhance your situation? | | |
| Do you have complete comfort with, and control over, your personal finances? | | |

# THE RULES

# CONTENTS

## RULE 3

**Evaluate the correct types of products for your needs before you shop for specific brand names.  43**

## RULE 7

## RULE 8

## RULE 9

### Explore insurance carefully for effective net worth preservation and enhancement.   169

## RULE 10

### Factor your children into your net worth growth.   179

## RULE 11

### Re-engineer your retirement finances today for a better tomorrow.   187

## RULE 12

### Optimize retirement cash flow to enjoy the golden years.   197

## RULE 13

### Carefully explore using debt to grow your net worth.   225

# RULE 14

**Understand what wealth management means and whether it is right for you.   233**

Have you visited the financial section of your local bookstore lately? You can see that thousands of books now exist to teach you about investing, taxes, and other personal finance topics. Many of these books appear similar and serve as a perfect example of how confusing the investing marketplace has become. I sympathize with Canadians trying to find value, understanding, and peace of mind financially in a sea of overwhelming choice.

On a regular basis I will sit down with people who are frustrated with money matters to help them understand the investment world that exists in Canada today. There are no specific types that I tend to work with—there are people of all ages, all wealth levels, from all walks of life. There is only one characteristic they have in common when they end up on my doorstep: They are all overwhelmed by the rapidly changing financial landscape in Canada.

Some of these people have had bad experiences with previous financial advisors, and no longer trust anyone. Some are novice investors and don't know where to start. Some are do-it-yourselfers looking for a second opinion. But in each case, I hear statements like these:

- I am confused by the number of investment products now available....
  I don't really know how to evaluate what is best for me.
- I am intimidated by the sheer number of financial advisors in the yellow pages—so many different types of advisors, different credentials, and all have varying opinions on what I should do. I can't begin to understand the differences and fear hiring someone who doesn't know what they are doing.
- I don't know what questions to ask when I shop around for products, services, and financial advisors.
- How do I know if I am progressing towards my goals?

If you are having doubts about whether this book is for you, take the test on the inside cover. Your test results can be used as a gauge of your need for the financial advice provided in this book.

This is my second book. I wrote it because I know that the financial landscape in Canada today is intimidating and scary. It's a land where most investors and taxpayers are in the dark about how to invest, how to minimize taxes, what investments to buy, and whether they are getting any value from their current financial advice providers. I hope this book will act as your boat rudder, as you sail through the never-ending sea of investments, advisors, institutions, and personal finance issues.

In this book I have no products to sell you—only advice to give. I'm going to be honest—over and over again, on many of the financial issues that may be keeping you up at night. My advice in this book is based on analytical thinking and common sense, and it is explained in easy-to-follow, plain language as much as possible rather than complicated financial talk.

In this book, I will share my personal finance experiences and opinions with you, and hopefully you will benefit from my endeavours in the marketplace. Over time, I have had the opportunity to experience much of the financial landscape that you may come across, and I'll teach you how to find the right solutions. In the end, I hope you will feel a lot more comfortable—even empowered—in dealing appropriately with your personal finances, particularly your investments.

If you have been feeling "in the dark" about your personal finances and investments, I hope this book will "turn on the light" for you and lead you to a more prosperous and informed financial future.

Kurt Rosentreter, CA, CFP, CIMA, TEP, B.Comm.
1-866-ASK-KURT
kurtrosentreter@hotmail.com
www.kurtrosentreter.com

# RULE 1

**Set goals and integrate all aspects of your finances to manage your big picture long before you buy products.**

What is the one thing that is common to every aspect of your personal finances? Cash flow. Cash in and cash out, after tax, plays a role in every financial decision you make. That's because spending and saving are a result of cash flow. Here are some examples of how cash flow is at the heart of every financial decision you make:

- If you had more cash flow, you could contribute more to your RRSP and retirement savings.
- If you had more cash flow you could purchase more life insurance to protect your dependants.
- If you had more cash flow you could use your credit card less, and pay down your mortgage faster.
- If you had more cash flow you could live in a nicer house.

The tradeoffs you make when deciding how to use your cash flow are the most relevant factors. These tradeoffs are determined by your goals and your priorities. Every day you face tradeoff decisions that require financial evaluations of how your cash flow is best utilized. But all of these decisions are linked by your cash flow, and it quickly becomes apparent that financial decisions cannot be made in isolation. Cash flow, taxes, your goals and priorities, and the different areas of your personal finances (investing, retirement, estate, insurance, children, employment) are all related. Any key decision must be made only after giving thought to the bigger picture of your finances.

For example, should you spend your tax refund on a vacation, pay down your mortgage, contribute to your RRSP, or contribute to your child's RESP? Or should you use your year-end bonus cheque to buy a new car, save for retirement, pay off your credit card, buy into your company's group RRSP, or lend the money to your brother for school?

## Don't forget about taxes!

Tax planning is a high priority that touches every aspect of your finances and cash-flow decision making. From minimizing taxes on your paycheque to how to structure a tax-effective RRIF income flow, tax planning is essential. Focusing on sources and uses of cash flow must be evaluated on an after-tax basis, since that is the real money left for spending. Tax minimization should always be a primary goal in your financial big picture.

## Process is more important than product

Ask many Canadians about investing and they start talking about their latest mutual fund purchase. This first section is about process, not product, and how you need a foundation for your personal finances first, long before you explore products. This foundation must include a review and analysis of your cash flow sources, needs, and tradeoffs. Only by paying attention to how your cash flow is utilized across your entire financial spectrum can you effectively plan to meet your goals.

## Get to a higher level first

Cash flow, taxes, your goals and priorities, and the different areas of your personal finances (investing, retirement, estate, insurance, children, employment) are all related. None of these areas can be evaluated without giving consideration to the others at the same time. Your investment program must be built according to the interrelationships of these and other factors.

This first section starts off by getting you to set the parameters for your new professional investment program. While this section will go in many directions, it is founded in one common principle throughout each question: Cash flow affects all areas of your finances. It is important to recognize that integrated planning is essential to ensure effective, comprehensive financial planning.

# 1

## When I think about investing, I immediately think about products. Is that the right way to start?

Before we go on a vacation, we decide where we want to go, budget how much to spend, shop around for the best deals, and compare tour packages. We do all this because we want to end up with a positive experience at a fair price.

Many Canadians, however, do not follow a similar process with their finances. Many people think that investing is buying a product, then another product, and another, and that nothing else matters. Unfortunately, the first thing some financial advisors do when they meet you is show you a product, educate you about their products, and sell you a product. Placing product ahead of planning is inappropriate. As with a vacation, how do you know what to buy without having a blueprint first?

A discussion about what products to buy shouldn't even creep into discussions with your financial advisor until after a disciplined process of defining your personal goals, examining needs and resources, examining your financial big picture issues, and setting parameters around your plans. Once you know what you need your investment portfolio to generate for you annually, then you can select investment products that will match your needs. Building an investment portfolio by rushing out to buy products first without a plan is like buying a last minute plane ticket to a vacation spot picked by someone else—it's fun initially, but if it doesn't match your needs and preferences, you are headed for disappointment.

Use the steps listed in the Investment Management Consulting Process chart (p. 6) and described below to help you towards a professional investment program. Each of these steps is discussed in detail within Rosentreter's Rules 1–7 in this book. As you can see, the specific product discussion doesn't even come up until step 4.

## How to build a professional investment program

**STEP 1: GOALS.** Define and prioritize your financial and nonfinancial goals over the short term and long term. This first step helps to refine your overall expectations for your personal finances.

**STEP 2A: FINANCIAL PLAN.** Examine your financial big picture before getting into details. For example, review the taxes you pay, current and future savings levels, annual spending, desired retirement plans, estate goals, children's costs, and insurance needs. Each of these areas will affect your investment program. For example, reducing your annual tax bill leaves more money for savings or insurance; increasing your insurance premiums leaves less money for children's savings or your estate wishes. All of the aspects of your finances are tied together and must be collectively evaluated before deciding on investments.

**STEP 2B: CASH FLOW FORECAST.** Examining the big picture means looking at your current and future cash flow needs—the money that is coming in and going out. It is critical to stay on top of this to ensure that your money is being used effectively on a continuous basis.

**STEP 3: SIP&G.** Prepare a Statement of Investment Policy and Guidelines. It serves as a blueprint to your investment profile, summarizing your risk tolerance, cash flow needs, target returns, liquidity needs, tax situation, and time horizon for investing. The information obtained from this policy statement will provide a roadmap to your investment product needs. Simply put, this document defines who you are as an investor and how to invest in order to move towards your goals.

**STEP 4A: MACRO INVESTMENT ANALYSIS.** Examine the appropriate types of investment products suitable to your situation. Long before you consider specific brand names of products, assess what is the right type of product for your needs (for example, funds versus wrap programs versus stocks). This macro analysis looks at the financial services industry overall to determine where you fit in.

**STEP 4B: MICRO ANALYSIS.** Only now do you start to examine specific products. Once a blueprint is drawn, and it is determined that you belong in a specific product type according to logical conclusions, then it is time to talk product.

**STEP 4C: REBALANCING.** After a draft plan is put in place and specific products are selected, the next step is to develop a transition plan to move towards your new portfolio as set out in your SIP&G. This rebalancing plan requires a cost/benefit analysis of your current portfolio in order to decide how quickly you can move to the new plan.

Up to this point, the steps show how to build a professional investment program according to a logical and disciplined process. The remaining steps represent the ongoing work of maintaining the plan.

**STEP 5: PROACTIVE MONITORING AND ANALYSIS.** Regularly measure and monitor the ongoing quality of your investments. Your financial advisor should be acting as a watchdog over the people who manage your money and should also be monitoring your financial lifestyle to ensure that your investment program continues to reflect your financial needs.

**STEP 6: PROACTIVE REVIEW.** Typically once a year, it is worthwhile to fully review the integrity of your financial solutions and to integrate any new issues. Review the big picture in all areas of your finances together with your financial advisor. Review your tax planning, insurance levels, cash flow modeling and forecasts, and so on. Adjust your investment program according to this information.

As you can see, I believe that investing is a lot more about process and planning than it is about product. Today most financial advisors can sell the same products. Their real value is in the quality of the advice they provide around the products. The steps outlined above provide a good example of a professional consulting process that brings logic and discipline into the creation of a professional investment program.

# Investment management consulting process

| Step 1 | Step 2 | Step 3 | Step 4 | Step 5 | Step 6 |
|---|---|---|---|---|---|
| **Getting to know you** | **Evaluating your big picture** | **Building your financial blueprint** | **Implementing your blueprint** | **Keeping you informed** | **Keeping you on track** |
| **Objectives** | **Objectives** | **Objectives** | **Objectives** | **Objectives** | **Objectives** |
| Goal focusing and prioritization | Cash flow optimization and financial integration | Liquidity reserves calculation | Macro portfolio design | Proactive annual monitoring and analysis | Proactive annual review and update |
| | | Constraints assessment | Micro portfolio design | | |
| **Process** | **Process** | Tax analysis and minimization | Investment search and selection | **Process** | **Process** |
| Assess financial and nonfinancial needs | Cash flow forecasting and "what if" analysis | Volatility profiling | **Process** | Ongoing measuring and monitoring of financial solutions for continued effectiveness | Complete annual review and analysis of all plan aspects and personal finances in general for continued applicability and effectiveness |
| Clarify goals, constraints, and preferences | Integration of investments with overall personal finances | **Process** | Determine appropriate types of investments for you | Constant behind-the-scenes money manager due diligence | |
| **Results** | Regular monitoring of progression towards integrated objectives | Suitable after-tax optimization of your financial profile | Evaluate current investments against up to ten criteria | | **Results** |
| Establish expectations | | **Results** | Rebalance requirements (short term and long term) | **Results** | Regular review of your plan to measure its progress and its ability to meet your changing needs |
| | **Results** | Development of a written Personal Financial Blueprint (called "Statement of Investment Policy and Guidelines"), serving as the infrastructure to your investment plan | New money manager search and selection process | Regular personalized reporting | Identify new opportunities |
| | Cohesive, multi-layered gameplan where opportunities are maximized across your entire personal financial spectrum | | **Results** | Proactive personal contact and communication on results, value, progress, and new opportunities | |
| | | | Action plan to move to a desired investment policy over an agreed upon period of time | | |

Achieve objective

Financial peace of mind

Initial plan — Ongoing work

# 2

**I want to make sure that my financial dreams and wishes are fulfilled. What is the best way to set goals and to measure my progress towards them?**

We all have dreams and objectives—some more far-fetched than others—so goal setting is something that comes naturally to most of us. But sometimes we forget or fail to prioritize our goals according to importance and timelines.

For example, if a middle-aged couple with teenage children were to set some financial goals, they may look like this:

- Save for a fruitful retirement.
- Pay off the mortgage.
- Buy a new car.
- Retire early.
- Fund the children's university education.

But listing these goals is only the first step. The next step is to attach time lines in which to accomplish those goals. So the list could be expanded as follows:

- Save enough to start a fruitful retirement in 20 years.
- Pay off the mortgage by the end of this year.
- Buy a new a car next year.
- Retire in 15 years instead of 20.
- Fund the children's university education starting in five years.

With defined timelines, the goals are starting to take shape. But what if there isn't enough cash available to achieve all of them? Divide the goals into essential and non-essential ones.

**ESSENTIAL:** New car, university funding, and retirement planning.
**NON-ESSENTIAL:** The quick mortgage payoff, and early retirement.

Now the couple has a clearly defined set of goals that are prioritized. The next step would be to examine cash flow resources and needs, and then strategize to ensure that at least the essential goals are achieved.

## Specific Financial Goals

The starting point of all effective investment planning is to understand your goals. These goals can be long term, such as saving for your retirement, or short term, such as minimizing your taxes. Some goals can be of greater or lesser significance to you and, of course, these goals can change over time.

Here is a list of some goals shared by many people. Please identify your goals according to the time frame that you have in mind to achieve each goal. Add any other goals that may be relevant to you.

| | Relevant Time Frame | | | |
|---|---|---|---|---|
| | Short Term (0–1 year) | Medium Term (1–5 years) | Long Term (5–10 years) | Greater than 10 Years |
| Adequate retirement income | ❏ | ❏ | ❏ | ❏ |
| Saving for your child's education | ❏ | ❏ | ❏ | ❏ |
| Purchasing a home | ❏ | ❏ | ❏ | ❏ |
| Taking a vacation | ❏ | ❏ | ❏ | ❏ |
| Lower taxes | ❏ | ❏ | ❏ | ❏ |
| Purchasing a vacation home | ❏ | ❏ | ❏ | ❏ |
| Purchasing a car | ❏ | ❏ | ❏ | ❏ |
| Providing for survivors in event of your death | ❏ | ❏ | ❏ | ❏ |
| Protecting against inflation | ❏ | ❏ | ❏ | ❏ |
| Taking early retirement | ❏ | ❏ | ❏ | ❏ |
| Starting a business | ❏ | ❏ | ❏ | ❏ |
| Other | ❏ | ❏ | ❏ | ❏ |

## What types of goals should I set?

Having no goals or vague goals leaves you with nothing to strive for, and may result in insufficient resources. If you spend more time deciding on your next vacation than you do planning your financial future, you may wind up with a financial shortfall later in life.

Many Canadians use investment returns as their goals. I'm sure you've heard someone say, "I expect to earn 12% a year from my investment portfolio." It's pretty easy to fall into this mindset when we see so much advertising that tells us that mutual funds can provide huge returns. We want to strike it rich too!

But chasing big returns blindly is the wrong way to plan. First of all, big returns come and go, and are rarely consistent year to year. Second, along with the potential for big returns comes higher risk. When there is the possibility of a 30% return, there is often also the potential to lose 30%. That might be okay if you can weather the ups and downs in a long-term investment, but you won't want to take that risk if your goals are closer at hand. In some years, it is easy to get caught up in the hype surrounding monster investment returns. But sooner or later these returns are replaced by more normal returns, and if you have invested heavily in one sector, it may leave you exposed to more loss than you can handle or a shortage in reaching your goals.

The most important question to ask yourself about investment returns is "What annual return do I need to earn in order to achieve my financial goals?" You may be pleasantly surprised to learn that you don't need to earn 15% a year to hit a financial home-run. You may only need 6% to easily reach your financial goals. Sure, shooting for 6% a year isn't as much fun as dreaming about getting 15%, but it's safer and may be all you need. Remember that it is just as important to preserve your wealth as it is to enhance it.

## How do I measure my success?

It is critical that you regularly monitor progress towards your goals so that you can adjust your plans and strategies when necessary (for example, when unexpected—and expected—changes happen in your lifestyle and finances). For some goals, like saving for a child's education, it is easy to evaluate the progress of your savings. Simply compare accumulated savings against anticipated future costs and adjust as necessary. Many simple financial planning software tools or financial calculators can help you to accurately evaluate financial progress, or you can enlist a financial advisor to do this for you.

There is also a way to evaluate all financial goals together. I call it the *net worth approach* to goal evaluation. Most people tend to evaluate their wealth according to income levels. Instead, you should evaluate your wealth by preparing a net worth statement of your personal finances each year (or more often). On this statement list all your assets at fair market value and then subtract the value of your debts to arrive at your net personal worth.

Your net worth is the best number for evaluating your success with your personal finances. Logically, your worth will rise when you pay off debts, buy assets, grow your investments, and accumulate savings of any kind. By preparing a net worth statement you can examine all aspects of your finances on one page, linked together, for a fair evaluation of how you are doing. Your investments can be listed one by one for a comparison, year over year. In my opinion, if your net worth isn't growing at 5% a year, you need to change things to make this happen. Perhaps you are spending excessively, carry too much debt, or have insufficient savings. Keep in mind too that some of your assets (such as cars) will lose value, so take this into account when planning how to grow your net worth.

Consider using this net worth approach as a gauge to your financial success. Only under a net worth approach are you given a snap shot of your wealth values that can be constantly re-evaluated and compared.

# Your Personal Net Worth

| | Current Value | | |
|---|---|---|---|
| | **You** | **Spouse** | **Joint** |
| **Assets** | | | |
| **Liquid Assets** | | | |
| Cash, chequing, and savings accounts | $ _____ | $ _____ | $ _____ |
| Treasury bills, term deposits | _____ | _____ | _____ |
| Canada Savings Bonds | _____ | _____ | _____ |
| Other | _____ | _____ | _____ |
| **Investments** | | | |
| Bonds | _____ | _____ | _____ |
| Stocks | _____ | _____ | _____ |
| Mutual funds | _____ | _____ | _____ |
| Real estate (income property) | _____ | _____ | _____ |
| Business assets | _____ | _____ | _____ |
| Retirement plans (RRSP, RPP) | _____ | _____ | _____ |
| Other | _____ | _____ | _____ |
| **Personal Assets** | | | |
| Principal residence | _____ | _____ | _____ |
| Recreational property | _____ | _____ | _____ |
| Other | _____ | _____ | _____ |
| **TOTAL ASSETS** | $ _____ | $ _____ | $ _____ |
| **Liabilities** | | | |
| **Current debt** | | | |
| Personal loans outstanding | _____ | _____ | _____ |
| Credit cards | _____ | _____ | _____ |
| Other | _____ | _____ | _____ |
| **Long-term Debt** | | | |
| Mortgage—Principle residence | _____ | _____ | _____ |
| Mortgage—Recreational property | _____ | _____ | _____ |
| Other | _____ | _____ | _____ |
| **TOTAL LIABILITIES** | $ _____ | $ _____ | $ _____ |
| **TOTAL NET WORTH** | | | |
| **TOTAL ASSETS MINUS TOTAL LIABILITIES** | $ _____ | $ _____ | $ _____ |

# 3

## What is a cash flow forecast, and how can it help me with my investments?

A cash flow forecast is an important step towards building a disciplined professional investment program. This is because cash flow—or money in and out with your daily spending and savings—is the lifeblood of your personal finances. Focusing on your cash flow binds together all the different areas of personal finance and forces you to evaluate them as an integrated package. Often tradeoffs are involved in your daily cash flow decisions: Is your money better spent investing in an RRSP or paying down your mortgage? Should you save for your children or your own retirement? Should you buy life insurance or a new car? Better cash flow decisions can be made when they are evaluated on a combined basis using a cash flow forecasting model.

A financial advisor can assist you in completing a cash flow forecast, or you can do it yourself using a software package or a financial calculator. Use the forecast to determine whether you will have enough money to achieve your short-term and long-term financial goals. In the case of planning for retirement, you would examine your current savings and compare this to how much money you would like to live on each year during your retirement. In the calculation you need to account for inflation, additional savings, unusual cash flows, and the time value of money; you also need to assume an annual investment rate of return and calculate the impact of taxes. It sounds hard to do, but this exercise can be completed in a few hours using the right tools. At the end of this exercise, you'll have several important bits of information:

- You will be able to conclude whether your current savings levels are adequate to reach your future goals.
- By re-doing the calculations using different investment returns, inflation rates, and savings levels you can examine several "what if" scenarios to determine how you can improve your chances of reaching your goals.
- You will end up with several simple targets to make your future plans work, such as a target annual rate of investment returns or a minimum level of savings you need to accumulate each year.

Unfortunately, some people prefer to head towards their financial goals with their eyes closed rather than prepare a cash flow forecast of their finances to see what their financial future looks like. They hope to live on whatever they accumulate until retirement and top it up with government benefits. But these people often find out that because of their poor planning they have to live their retirement years in a constant cash crunch situation—perhaps living on a third or less of what they had been earning. They can no longer afford to take vacations or buy a new car.

If you are wondering if you are headed down this disastrous road to retirement, ask yourself these questions: Do I know if I will have adequate funds to live the retirement lifestyle I want, based on my current course? Do I know what I need to earn annually from my investments to ensure this future lifestyle? If you don't know the answers, I strongly urge you to find out. Review this information annually, and adjust your spending to stay on track.

## The many uses of cash flow forecasting

Almost every aspect of your finances can benefit from a cash flow review and forecast. Here are some examples:

- Someone in their pre-retirement years should forecast to see if they are progressing towards the amount of money they envision needing in retirement.
- A retired person can use cash flow forecasting to structure their retirement income to be maximized on an after-tax basis.
- A student can use cash flow forecasting to structure a debt repayment schedule that will erase their student debt or their mortgage over time.
- A business owner can use forecasting to integrate their personal cash flow with their business cash flow for optimal effectiveness.

# 4

## What is the best way to use a cash flow forecast for planning?

There are a lot of people today who do their own financial planning or utilize financial advisors. This is a great step towards organizing your personal finances, assuming that you can properly complete the financial plan or that it is done by someone appropriately qualified. One shortcoming of many financial plans is the lack of forecasting for different possible scenarios. Some financial advisors show consumers only a very positive cash flow forecast; for example, a 12% or more annual rate of return. And many people purchase investment products based on these optimistic forecasts. However, it is always prudent to examine what the outcome will be like if not-so-wonderful investment returns result.

A cash flow forecast should examine not only the best-case scenario, but also the worst-case and mostly likely scenarios. I call this balanced examination *sensitivity analysis*. It involves examining a series of different situations and results by adjusting the variables involved for possible outcomes. It makes sense to know what your financial future will look like if the markets don't return 12% a year forever, because it is unlikely that they are going to!

So, if you are forecasting to see how much money you will have accumulated by age 65, you should estimate your total savings based on annual returns of 10%, 8%, 6%, and so on, to better understand the range of possible results. In this way, you are in a better position to know when to adjust your plan along the way to improve the likelihood of achieving the results you want. Further, this form of analysis may leave you pleasantly surprised to see that you don't need to earn 12% a year to hit a financial home run—that you can still live the lifestyle you want with a compounded rate of return of only 4%, for example, and as a result, can build a less aggressive portfolio that will let you sleep better at night. Ultimately, performing sensitivity analysis on your cash flow forecasts will help you to determine the minimum annual rate of return you need to earn, help you to set a target rate of return, and let you dream about the possibilities by examining the best possible returns.

Sensitivity analysis is a risk management technique that can help you to determine what you really need from your money, and then incorporate financial strategies that include only as much risk as you need to take in order to get you where you want to go. Think of this technique as a risk-managed approach to investing and your personal finances.

If you have never examined what it will take to reach your goals according to a variety of scenarios, it is a good idea to work with a financial advisor now to become better informed about the factors that impact your financial future.

# 5

## I like to shoot for the highest possible investment returns. Why do I need a target rate of return for a goal?

It is not surprising that we want to shoot for the highest possible investment returns. It's exciting to roll the dice and hope we'll end up with 30% returns each year, and everyone wants a little fun in their life, right? Additionally, we are conditioned to want the highest possible returns. Everyday, in the media, we hear about only the best and highest returns an investment has generated in the past. It's no wonder we are lured by the possibility of getting some of that for ourselves.

I'm not saying that you shouldn't have some of your savings invested in products that have the potential to generate big returns. But I don't think you should bet the farm either. Often what is forgotten when investing aggressively is that increased returns usually mean increased investment volatility as well. More specifically, the potential to earn 30% a year from an investment can typically mean you also have the danger of losing 30%. And you may not be in a position to be able to lose that kind of money even if it is only short term.

By doing some basic financial planning and cash flow forecasting, you should be able to generate a target rate of return for your investments that is based on your financial circumstances and goals. A target return is a return that you hope to earn each year from your investments. It is the return you need to achieve in order to reach your financial goals, and it is based on mathematical logic derived from your cash flow forecasts. Earn less, and you face financial failure or the need to make changes to your plan. Earn more, and you have a possible financial cushion for the future.

Having a target rate of return for your investment portfolio, as well as doing some sensitivity analysis around this return to examine worst-case and best-case scenarios, is a process that I call *risk-managed investing*. A desire for higher investment returns is typically followed by more investment volatility and more sleepless nights worrying about your money. A more disciplined approach of setting a target return and custom building an investment portfolio to match the target exposes you only to risks you prefer to tolerate while ensuring the portfolio matches your long-term financial plan. So instead of buying only hot equity investments hoping you'll earn 20% next year, you might calculate a necessary target return of, say, 9% compounded annually over 20 years to reach your financial goals. Your portfolio can then be structured to include cash, Canadian fixed income, international fixed income, Canadian equity, U.S. equity, and international equity in proportion to their expected returns in each asset class in a way that will add up to equal at least 9% return annually. While this may not be desirable to everyone, it is definitely a disciplined and integrated approach to managing your investments.

# 6

## What does it mean to "fragment" and "integrate" my personal finances? Which is best?

*Fragmenting* your finances means several things: maintaining several investment portfolios at different institutions without coordinating them; failing to integrate your investment portfolio with other areas of your finances such as taxes and cash flow; and maintaining several different financial advisors without telling each one about the others. *Integrating* your finances means getting a sense of all of the separate elements of your portfolio and other personal finance issues and incorporating that information into a cohesive financial plan.

### Breaking a portfolio into small pieces

Many Canadians fragment their personal finances by spreading money around among several different institutions and financial advisors, perhaps because they don't want any one institution to know about everything they have. But, generally, you are far better off having one main financial advisor and purchasing a variety of products through that advisor. In this way you still get broad product choice, and that one person can help you to build an overall plan.

By fragmenting your finances among institutions you are shortchanging yourself in several ways:

- Each institution you deal with can provide advice only on the portion of information that it knows about, and it will be unable to see the big picture. This can be financially dangerous, and definitely leaves you with an incomplete financial game plan.
- Each quarter you receive piles of investment statements from many institutions. This makes it difficult to coordinate your investments and to see how well you are doing overall.
- You may be paying more fees than necessary, and you may be restricting yourself from accessing some of the best investments around. Many products today are priced according to the amount of money you invest in them, with lower fees applicable to larger investments. As well, some investment programs require high minimum investment amounts to access them.

If you hire a life insurance agent, a couple of investment institutions to manage your money, an accountant to do your taxes, a lawyer for estate planning, a banker, a mortgage lender, and you also make your own investments, consider restructuring the number and type of financial advisors you have in order to get control and integration of your personal finance issues. If you do hire more than one financial advisor, at the very least it makes sense to let one of them know about all of your investments so they can manage your financial big picture.

## Focusing only on investments

Some people zero in on investments and fail to think about all the other parts of their personal finances. But when investments are examined without considering the other aspects of your financial life, you end up making decisions without fully considering all the variables.

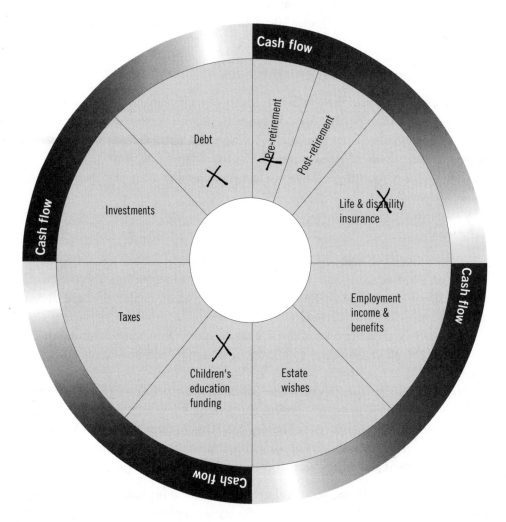

Above, you will see a wheel with a summary of many of the aspects of a personal financial picture: Sometime in your life, some or all of these different aspects of your finances will be important. Some of them, such as taxes, you interact with everyday. Others, like life insurance, you focus on only at certain times in your life. However, they all fit together to form your financial picture and all must be integrated to properly maximize your opportunities. All of these areas are bound together by cash flow, which as I said earlier, is the lifeblood of your finances. Daily cash flow is directed in different places as your priorities shift, making it essential that your financial picture be examined as a whole, not in pieces.

Overall, it is critical to examine your financial big picture, when at least once a year you look over your entire financial situation and examine whether it is all hanging together appropriately, whether you are integrating goals and resources between different areas of importance, and whether you are progressing towards your goals in the different sections of your personal finances. Only by taking an integrated—rather than fragmented—approach, can you ever truly hope to take full advantage of all opportunities in front of you.

# 7

## What is financial planning and a financial plan?

In Canada today, many financial advisors will use the term "financial plan" when they describe the services they can offer you. The problem is that many financial advisors define financial planning differently. Let's examine exactly how financial planning should be defined, so that you will finally have a standard to compare against.

Financial planning and financial plan are defined in the glossary at the back of this book. Briefly, if a financial advisor is offering to prepare a financial plan for you, you should be offered financial advice on *all* aspects of your personal finances. Alternatives and decisions are integrated with other financial decisions that must be made at the same time.

Here are some key characteristics that help to define financial planning:

- A financial advisor who provides advice on investing only is not providing a comprehensive financial plan, nor is any financial advisor providing advice on only a single area of your finances.
- Financial planning is best defined by the Canadian Association of Financial Planners: In order for a financial advisor to be a practising member of the CAFP, the financial advisor must follow the six steps of financial planning as outlined in their bylaws. These six steps involve collection of a client's financial information, prioritizing client goals and issues, analyzing the alternatives the client has for meeting goals, providing recommendations on what the client should do, assisting with implementation once decided, and following up with the client to ensure progress towards his or her goals. This practice of due diligence over a client's finances is applicable to investments, cash flows, retirement, estate, insurance, pre-retirement, children's finances, and all other areas of the client's finances.
- A financial planner is a guardian and advice provider over clients' entire financial picture. In some areas, the financial planner will provide expert advice, and in other areas will work with experts on your behalf.
- A financial plan is a written document summarizing your personal information, objectives, and financial issues, alternatives analyzed, recommendations made by the financial advisor, implementation of an action plan, and follow-up results. A financial plan is usually prepared at the end of an engagement on your financial issues and then updated annually for new events and results.
- Financial planning is conducted annually. The financial advisor will regularly check on your progress towards goals and seek to provide additional advice and strategies relevant to your finances.

- There are two different types of financial planning engagements: segmented and comprehensive. A segmented plan is a financial plan for a specific topic (e.g., a financial planning assignment to explore the possibility of early retirement). A comprehensive financial plan covers several areas of your finances together (investing, insurance, retirement, cash flow, etc.).
- It is important for you and for the advisor to have an engagement letter as a form of contract over your relationship. An engagement letter outlines parameters of your advisory relationship, fees, services to be provided, key dates, legal liability, and other variables. The engagement letter is signed by you as client and is updated annually. The engagement letter can provide comfort to clients and to advisors in clarifying your advisory relationship. Engagement letters should be carefully crafted by financial advisors and carefully reviewed by clients.
- A true practising financial planner should be governed by a code of ethics and a set of practise standards, should follow a professional financial planning process, and should belong to an association like the CAFP, which holds practising financial planners to a high standard.

## Dangers of financial planning

There are many financial advisors in Canada who are providing documents called financial plans to clients. Here are some things you should know as you search for a financial advisor.

- Be cautious about a financial plan created for you by a fancy software program. Financial planning software has become quite sophisticated today, often providing overwhelming reports that few clients need or understand. Most people can be well served with only a basic analysis, drawn up with as little as a pen, paper, and calculator. Further, many financial advisors believe that their financial planning software is the value they provide to you, but they are *wrong:* the software is no more than a tool, and technical abilities are the value that your financial advisor should provide. Beware a financial advisor who hides behind software!
- Ask to see a financial advisor's financial planning practice standards. These are the controls behind the scene to ensure the quality of what you are given. Here are some examples of what you may wish to see:
  - The engagement letter governing your relationship.
  - Membership in a financial planning association. If it is the CAFP, is the advisor a practitioner member?
  - Names of those who supervise and review the financial plan provided to you.
  - Confirmation that the financial advisor is subject to practice audits each year
  - The code of ethics that your advisor follows.

## The cost of a plan

Financial planning is never free. Some financial advisors charge hourly fees, flat fees, or asset-based fees to draft a plan for you. In such cases, you clearly see what fee you are being charged.

In other cases, the financial plan is provided at what appears to be no charge. That is not the case. Many financial advisors earn enough compensation through the products they sell you to pay for the plan they may also provide. So you do pay for the financial plan, just indirectly. Paying a separate fee for the financial plan is preferable. This way the financial advisor is less likely to be biased in favour of a product offered to you.

Separate your financial plan from your product purchases. Pay for them separately to preserve objectivity.

## Do you need a financial plan?

Everyone needs a financial plan. In essence, this entire book is about financial planning, because it covers many of the important areas that usually make up a financial plan. A financial plan is essentially advice on your personal finances. Everyone would benefit from continuing organization of their finances.

However, not everyone needs an exhaustive plan right now. Some financial advisors will provide a comprehensive financial plan the first time they meet you. Stop. The amount of advice you need should be based on an evaluation of your financial issues. Not everyone needs a full plan today. Personal finance issues come and go throughout life, and it is more important that the financial advisor recognize this and provide proactive advice regularly over time.

# RULE 2

## Build a disciplined investment infrastructure that will stand the test of time.

Before you can decide which investments to buy, you need a master plan, or blueprint, to follow. Your investment program should be custom made to match your financial needs. Only after the creation of this financial blueprint can you start to examine the investment products needed to fill it in.

In many ways, investing is similar to building a new house and furnishing it. You may hire an architect (financial advisor) to design your home (investment program). Both your home and your investment program are built according to your preferences, needs, and objectives. When building a home, much thought and time are spent on the framework and layout, before the furniture is purchased. All aspects of the building are typically discussed and decided among all family members. The design for the house is written down. The design for your investment program should also be written down in a Statement of Investment Policy and Guidelines.

Once a house is built, furnishing commences based on the finished home's needs. With an investment program, it should be the same way: investment products are purchased to match the professional investment program that you have designed with your financial advisor. Products are the equivalent of your house furnishings: You should plan thoroughly, shop around, and then make a purchase. Your investment products should match the specifications laid out in your plan.

Investing is about process, not product. It's about hiring experts to help with the design of your program. It's about integrating your program with all aspects of your finances including cash flow. It's about staying the course and updating your program as needed. It's about assessing progress towards your goals on a timely basis and tweaking the program as needed. It is about assessing and selecting specific investment products when the time is right and after all the planning is done: products that play a specific role within your program, a role that fits with your needs. Does your current investment portfolio have this kind of logic built into it? Are there sound reasons to own the products you own?

This next section will help you to develop the infrastructure of your investment program. In many ways this section is the most important one of the investing process. It helps you to formulate strategy, and it is the part of the program that will set the stage for the easy part—picking investments.

# 8

## What is strategic capital allocation, and why do you call it the backbone to any investment program? How do I complete a Statement of Investment Policy and Guidelines?

*Strategic capital allocation*, or SCA, is the process of building an investment program according to each investor's personal financial situation. The key document of the investment program based on SCA is called a *Statement of Investment Policy and Guidelines* (SIP&G), and it should serve as the infrastructure for your investment program and the guideline for the purchase of investment products.

The SIP&G consists of three parts, all of which are written down: a financial profile summary, a breakdown of recommended asset classes, and signatures. An SIP&G is prepared long before you consider buying any investment products. After all, how can you buy anything without knowing what you need?

**Part one** is a summary of your personal financial characteristics and risk profile. In this section, define your personal net worth, investing time horizon, marginal tax rate, needs for ongoing cash flow from investments, risk tolerance for investing, liquidity needs from your investments, and any other notable factors about your personal finances. Also include your determination of a target rate of return from your portfolio (based on a cash flow forecast of your current assets matched against your financial goals). All of this information matters in the construction of your portfolio. For example, if you want to buy a new car two years from now, then you will want to treat the money for it in a special way in your portfolio. You might purchase a two-year bond to ensure that the funds will be available for that specific purpose.

**Part two** is a listing of all the major asset classes and the recommended percentage of your investable wealth that should be invested in each asset class according to your personal profile from section one. Studies have shown that it is far more important to invest in the right asset class (bonds, equity, real estate, foreign equity, cash, etc.) than it is to own one particular stock over another, or a particular mutual fund over another.

The table below differentiates between the major asset classes according to some key variables.

As you can see, each asset class has significantly different characteristics. A portfolio should never be put together without serious consideration of the characteristics of each asset class and how they fit with an investor's SIP&G. When I look at investors' portfolios, I ask them how they decided to put a certain amount of money in a particular asset class. Often, investors don't have a clear answer. But there should be exact and specific reasons for why and how much you have invested in a particular asset class. And that's what having an SIP&G is all about.

# Characteristics of Major Asset Classes

| Investor Criteria | Cash | Cdn. Fixed Income | Int'l. Fixed Income | Cdn. Equity | U.S. Equity | Int'l. Equity (blue chip only) |
|---|---|---|---|---|---|---|
| Risk of loss of principal | Almost none | Can happen with certain interest rate changes and bond defaults | Can happen with certain interest rate changes, foreign currency fluctuations and bond defaults | Can be significant with stock market fluctuations over the short term only | Can be significant with stock market fluctuations and foreign currency fluctuations over the short term only | Can be significant with stock market fluctuations and foreign currency fluctuations over the short term only |
| Good for short-term liquidity | Yes | Yes | No | No | No | No |
| Can provide monthly income | Yes | Sometimes | Sometimes | Minimal or no | Minimal or no | Minimal or no |
| Tax effective | No | No | No | Yes | Yes | Yes |
| Possible to get high returns | No | Remote | Remote | Yes | Yes | Yes |
| Minimum investment time required to smooth volatility | 1 day | 1 day to 5 years | 7 to 10 years | 10 years | 10 years | 10 years |
| Complexity of Investment | Simple | Easy to monitor | Harder to monitor | Harder to monitor | Harder to monitor | Harder to monitor |
| Type of income generated by investment | Interest | Interest and capital gains/losses | Interest and capital gains/losses | Dividends and/or capital gains/losses | Dividends and/or capital gains/losses | Dividends and/or capital gains/losses |

The percentage of an investor's overall portfolio that is invested in each asset class must be determined based on an evaluation of some key circumstances. Ask yourself the following basic questions:

- What is your investment time horizon for this money?
- Do you have a need to keep a lump sum aside for a short-term purchase or need?
- Do you require an annual income from this portfolio?
- What is your tax bracket, and do you have taxable and nontaxable investments?
- Are you married and, if so, does your spouse have investments that should be included in this program?
- What is the level of your investment knowledge?

- What is your risk tolerance? Can you tolerate short-term investment losses and, if so, how much?
- What is the target investment return from your cash flow plan that you need in order to meet your financial goals?

Once you have formulated answers to these questions and others, you and your financial advisor will be able to put the major asset classes together in proportions that best suit your situation. The sum of these proportions should add up to 100%, and one plan should incorporate all of your investment accounts—taxable and nontaxable—as well as those of your spouse. This is the only correct way to build a portfolio, in my opinion.

Once the percentages are assigned to each asset class, some financial advisors will go further and assign ranges around these percentages to allow for some variation in what is assigned. For example, if any investor assigns 20% of their money to be invested in U.S. equity investments, a range of 18% to 22% may be tolerable. These ranges are included for two reasons: one, to allow for some minor market timing if you can't give up the thrill of market chasing completely; and two, as a re-balancing mechanism. As the markets rise and fall, the percentages you originally invest in each asset class will change. Setting acceptable ranges of variation can serve as an automatic trigger for you to rebalance the portfolio back to the target policy by selling investments in asset classes that are too high compared to the policy, and buying those too low (in other words, outside of the set ranges). Another nice thing about setting ranges is that the rebalancing keeps your risk tolerance in check and forces you to sell high and buy low—a proven winning investment strategy.

**Part three** of the SIP&G consists of signatures. The SIP&G can serve as a written contract between you and your financial advisor, you and your money manager, or just for your own records. Once a client of mine even wrote an SIP&G into their will and estate plan. The signatures bring accountability to the parties involved. You, as the client, sign it and all other parties involved sign it as well. In many cases, failure to follow an established SIP&G can be grounds for legal action.

## Sample Statement of Investment Policy and Guidelines

| Investment Objectives | Characteristics |
|---|---|
| Financial situation | Max and Eleanor are both retired. Max receives pension income of $180,000. Max and Eleanor require approx. $100,000 pre-tax each year to live on. They have no outstanding debt. Their net worth is $1.5 million, with $1 million investable wealth. |
| Time horizon | Max and Eleanor have a long-term time horizon for this portfolio. This money, as needed, should be available for the rest of their lives, which is expected to be another 25 years. |

| | |
|---|---|
| Income needs | Max and Eleanor have adequate cash flow from Max's pension income alone. The investment portfolio is not required for any additional annual income needs, and this is not anticipated to change. |
| Liquidity needs | Occasionally, Max and Eleanor require capital for gifts, loans, and purchases for themselves and their family (four children). Any funding for these purposes will be taken from the fixed income portion of the portfolio. |
| Tax brackets | Max is in the top marginal Canadian tax bracket. Eleanor has only a small income each year. |
| | The taxable investment portfolio is owned through ABC Investment Enterprises Inc. and is subject to taxation within the corporation and then personally when removed from the company. ABC is owned by Max and Eleanor equally. |
| | All attempts will be made to minimize taxes on the investment portfolio through a minimization of investment turnover, by investing for tax-preferred income, and by splitting income between company and family. |
| Applicable accounts | This SIP&G applies to the following accounts: |
| | Max's RRSP at XYZ Financial Ltd.; |
| | ABC Investment Enterprises Inc. accounts at local bank. |
| Investment constraints | Overdraft positions are not to be intentionally created. |
| | All investment activities must be conducted in accordance with the applicable securities commissions and the CFA and IMCA code of ethics. |
| | Max has a preference to invest first in the U.S., second in Western Europe, and third in Canada. Max has a significant bias towards equities and against fixed income. |
| Risk profile | Max and Eleanor can tolerate above-average amounts of risk. Since they have no need for income or significant ongoing liquidity from their portfolio, they prefer a permanent large equity weighting. |
| | Max considers himself to have a moderate level of investment knowledge. Eleanor has a basic level of understanding of investing and capital markets. We have explained to them the risk associated with stock market investing and how volatility can be managed through diversification. Max and Eleanor have identified capital preservation and long-term growth as their primary investment goals. |
| Asset mix | Based on the above characteristics, the recommended SIP&G for Max and Eleanor consists of 10% Cdn. fixed income, 10% Cdn. equities, 55% U.S. equities, and 25% international equities. |
| | Equity investments are subject to volatility, but we have demonstrated to Max and Eleanor that historically equities have generated some of the highest returns with tolerable volatility over the long term. Historical returns should not be interpreted as a measure of future returns, however. Volatility will be managed through the construction of a well-diversified portfolio, by industry group, country, and asset class. Max and Eleanor understand the risk associated with equity investments and they are comfortable with up to 100% of their investable wealth in equities. |

# Long-Term SIP&G

| Asset Class | Policy | Range Allowed | Index/Other Comparative |
|---|---|---|---|
| **Money market instruments** | 0% | 0% | T-bills |
| Cdn. cash and near cash | 0% | 0% | |
| U.S. cash and near cash | | | |
| **Fixed income** | 10% | 0% to 25% | Scotia Capital Markets Bond Universe |
| Cdn. bonds | 10% | 0% to 25% | |
| U.S. bonds | | | |
| Global bonds | | | |
| **Cdn. equities** | 10% | 0% to 10% | TSE 300 |
| Large-cap growth | 5% | 0% to 10% | |
| Indexed TSE 60 | 5% | 0% to 10% | |
| Small cap | | | |
| **U.S. equities** | 50% | 25% to 75% | S&P 500 (Cdn$) |
| Large-cap growth | 25% | 15% to 40% | |
| Large-cap value | 25% | 15% to 40% | |
| **International equities** | 25% | 10% to 30% | Morgan Stanley World Index |
| International Value | 25% | 10% to 30% | |
| **Sector** | 5% | 0% to 10% | Nasdaq 100 Index |
| Technology | 5% | 0% to 10% | |
| Telecommunications | — | — | |
| Healthcare | — | — | |
| Financial services | — | — | |
| Resources | — | — | |
| Emerging markets | — | — | |
| **Specialty** | 0% | 0% | |
| Hedge fund | | | |
| Foreign currencies | | | |
| Real estate | | | |
| **Total** | 100% | | |

Accepted by:     Max Wadled: _____     Eleanor Wadled: _____

Kurt Rosentreter: _____

# 9

## When should I change my Statement of Investment Policy and Guidelines?

Since your SIP&G is based on an assessment of your personal situation and needs, the policy should only change when there is a change to your personal situation. It is important to pay attention to the characteristics of each asset class—specifically risk, cost, volatility, cash flow, liquidity, and other factors—and how they fit together to match your needs at a particular time. Following are several examples of when your SIP&G and asset mix would need revision:

**WIN A LOTTERY OR RECEIVE A BIG INHERITANCE.** If you win or inherit a lot of money, such that your financial future is now set, it would be time to re-evaluate your SIP&G and asset mix. You may find that you want to quit your job and live on the invested money, meaning the portfolio needs to be structured to provide an income stream. Or you may find that your risk tolerance goes up since there is now far more money in your hands and losing some on short-term stock market volatility is less alarming.

**LOSE YOUR JOB.** If you lose your job you may face a period when you will need to draw on your savings to live on until you find new work. Your portfolio may require restructuring to provide a short-term income focus. You may find that your risk tolerance goes down in this circumstance, where every dollar of savings becomes very valuable in the short term and losses cannot be afforded.

**RETIRE.** When you finally hang up your hat, you go from a wealth-building phase of your life into a wealth utilization phase in many cases. This can require adjustments to your asset mix in order to account for the new realities of your lifestyle: for example, monthly income needs and perhaps a lower tax bracket.

## What happens to my SIP&G when the markets rise and fall?

Strategic capital allocation and the creation of an SIP&G are used to set a semi-permanent asset mix for you regardless of market conditions. Your recommended asset mix should not be changed materially based on changes in market conditions. SCA defines your personal investor characteristics and has nothing to do with market fluctuations. If you are uncomfortable with market volatility at some point, it likely means that your original asset mix and SIP&G were not accurately set in the first place.

# 10

**I hear a lot about risk associated with my finances. What is risk and what can I do about it?**

Throughout this book I have made several references to investment risk. When I say risk, I am referring to volatility of returns. Specifically, different investments have different amounts of volatility associated with the rate of return they produce. This volatility can also vary according to the time period of ownership.

For example, the volatility of cash is different from that of a bond mutual fund, a Canadian equity mutual fund, a single stock, a piece of real estate, and so on. Cash may generate a fairly consistent rate of return, based on the interest rate year to year. A bond fund, however, generates two kinds of return: the interest rate on the bonds, and the potential for capital gains or losses, depending on changes in market interest rates. In any given year, depending on what happens with interest rate movements in the market places, a bond fund can generate a double-digit return or it can generate a negative return. Many people are surprised to learn that in the short term they can actually lose money with a bond fund. Equities have their own ranges of volatility, depending on their type. A Canadian equity mutual fund, depending on the category, could generate 30% or more in a particular year, or it could be down 30%.

When you extend the time horizon of ownership on investments, the volatility smooths out for most asset classes. This means that when you evaluate investments over several years, the average of good and bad returns is more important than the return of a specific year. And generally there are more good years than bad, producing a reasonable average rate of return. It is this smoothing effect that causes financial advisors to encourage investors to own more volatile investments if they have a longer investment time horizon.

Risk as measured by volatility is important for individual investors to monitor, and it is one of several factors that need to be considered when creating your SIP&G and investment program. Inability or ability to stomach volatility must be considered when choosing investments. If your preferences for volatility remain unexplored, you could sell in panic during market downtimes. Someone who has fully explored personal tolerance for market volatility has an investment program that reflects those tolerances, leaving the investor far more comfortable and understanding of market crashes and their short-term impact.

The following is a list of investment categories ranked from least volatile to most volatile, according to possible one-year returns. Note that this information is of limited use and must be examined in conjunction with your investing time horizon, your need for greater rate of return, and other factors that define your investment profile.

# Least one-year volatility

Cash and money market investments

GICs and bonds held to maturity

Short-term bond mutual funds

Bond mutual funds (Government of Canada bonds are less volatile than corporate bonds)

International bond mutual funds

U.S. Equity mutual funds (blue chip equity funds are less volatile than small cap or sector equity funds)

Western European equity mutual funds (stocks from developed nations are less volatile than those of less-developed countries)

Canadian equity mutual funds

International equity mutual funds (stocks from developed nations are less volatile than those of less-developed countries)

Sector investments (technology, telecommunications, natural resources, etc.)

*increasing volatility*

# Most one-year volatility

Beyond these core asset classes and investment product types, many more types of investments can be added. The following investments (in no particular order) can be more volatile over one year than those above:

- Labour-sponsored mutual funds
- Royalty trusts
- Private company investments
- Owning a single stock or only a few stocks
- Real estate investments
- Tax shelters

Note that many investments that are more volatile offer a higher return on average over the long term.

Overall, evaluate your investments according to risk and return together. Risk and return go hand in hand, and both need to be customized according to your investor profile.

# 11

## What is a risk-managed approach to investing, and why should I use it?

A risk-managed approach to investing means being aware of how much investment risk you need to tolerate to earn your target investment return. Unfortunately, this concept is often lost on Canadian investors because they underestimate their ability to stomach short-term losses, or worse, ignore risk completely as they shoot for the high double-digit returns that they want but don't really know if they need.

To better understand what a risk-managed approach to investing is, here's an example of ignoring risk. I recently sat down with a retired couple in their 70s who had managed to accumulate a savings nest egg of $3 million. Despite the fact that they lived a simple lifestyle that required only $40,000 a year of after-tax money to live on, their portfolio had been invested 100% in penny stocks on the Vancouver Stock Exchange for the last three years. This had been handled by the couple's broker, and they didn't even know about this situation. Here are a couple of ways they could have reduced their risk and still earned what they needed to live on:

- They could have generated their income needs with a simple rate of return from a bond of less than 5% per year. Instead, they were invested in high-risk stocks that offered the potential for 20% a year. They didn't need this high return rate or the risk that came with it. Yet no one examined their true needs to establish a target return and build a portfolio around it.
- They could have invested in more conservative blue-chip stocks. Instead, they were in risky small-cap resource stocks. This was far too risky for their tastes and their needs.

Today they have a portfolio that includes 85% safe fixed-income investments and 15% blue-chip equities. Their SIP&G is in line with their needs, and they can sleep at night knowing they will always be financially comfortable according to their standards. Their cash flows are a blend of annual interest, dividends, and capital gains, and they have a low-hassle, low-risk portfolio. (Unfortunately, they also have a $1 million loss carryforward for tax purposes, which was the cost to get out of the penny stock portfolio.)

Building a risk-managed investment portfolio simply means assessing your risk tolerance (how much money you can stand to lose should the markets tumble over the short term), creating an SIP&G, and setting a target annual investment return based on cash flow forecasting. Your portfolio should be put together based on expected return and risk in proportions that match your needs and tolerances.

Below are some other risk-managed investing techniques:

- Educate yourself to understand all aspects of your investment program.
- Proactively communicate with your financial advisor and your financial institution about the activity in your portfolio; when things get bad, the communication should increase.
- Diversify by asset class, geography, capitalization, currency, and by using other investments that will mitigate the volatility associated with investing in only one of these categories.
- Regularly measure and monitor your portfolio for continued effectiveness of your investments and for new opportunities.
- Regularly analyze your investment program to measure progress towards your goals.
- Analyze the tax attributes of your investments to ensure ongoing investment tax minimization.
- On an ongoing basis, assess the impact of inflation on your portfolio and revise your plan accordingly.

Risk management can add sophistication to your finances and investment planning while providing a comfort level over your finances. There are many variations of risk-managed investing techniques, and you can choose the ones that are right for you.

# 12

## I want to earn 15% a year on my investments, but the volatility is keeping me awake at nights. What can I do?

Risk and return usually go hand in hand. Normally, the greater the return potential, the greater the risk (defined as volatility of short-term returns) associated with getting these higher returns. Shooting for 15% or more a year is very aggressive—you will need to buy more volatile investments that may go down as much as they could go up in the short term. If you are not prepared to stomach short-term losses or if you have a short-term investment time horizon overall, you will have to revise your return expectations to something more in line with your risk tolerance.

If, however, you are not prepared to back off on your 15% return expectations, then you should consider a few things about your goal:

- When you look back at the history of the world's stock markets, long-term equity market returns in general have ranged from 8% to 14% or so. This is on average, so yes, there were many years where the markets exceeded 15%. But this rarely happens consistently. So recognize that in picking 15% as your target, it won't be easy. And to do it year after year is almost impossible.
- Why are you selecting 15% as your goal? Your key question should be, "What return do I need annually to reach my financial goals?" What if you could reach your goals with 6% a year? It is nice to dream of a 15%-a-year return, but prudent investors know the minimum return they need to earn each year on average, and then set a target return somewhere between the minimum and the maximum of 15%. This is a risk-managed approach to investing—if you don't need all the risk associated with aggressive investing, then don't take it on.
- Putting all your savings in one stock or a few stocks on your own in the hope of striking it rich can offer tremendous gut-wrenching short-term volatility and sometimes outright losses if poor stocks are selected. Understand the risks of investing in one or only a few stocks. Consider spreading your money around several different kinds of investments to reduce the likelihood of a devastating loss in one area. And while you may be able to jump on a rising star of an investment now and then, in reality, unless you can do this every month of every year until you die, leave investing to the professionals who have a greater chance of consistently outperforming market averages.
- Some investments have evolved to the point where you can purchase an aggressive equity investment (a fund, for example) while having your original investment amount guaranteed against losses. This sounds like the best of both worlds. But while these guaranteed investment funds or segregated funds can offer some comfort

to timid investors still wanting big returns, they come with strings attached: higher fees, a ten-year lockup of your money, and less than 100% guarantees of your principal in some cases. Evaluate these products carefully, as there are many varieties, and seek a second opinion on their appropriateness for you.

Temper your desire for off-the-chart returns with your tolerance for risk and volatility by thinking about the necessary rate of return to reach your goals. Out of this mix should arise an investment portfolio more in line with your needs.

# 13

## I like the excitement of chasing hot markets and the chance to make a lot of money. So what's wrong with market timing?

*Market timing* (also called tactical asset allocation) is the opposite of strategic capital allocation. When investors market time, they move their money in and out of the market, and within different parts of the market, frequently as they try to "time" the area of the market that will be the next big winner. Market timing is exciting, because you are always chasing the next big payoff. The question is, do you ever catch it?

Here are a few reasons why you shouldn't try to market time:

- Research has proven that market timing is almost impossible to do successfully over the long term.
- If market timing was easy, all the world's brokers would be millionaires lying on a beach in Mexico with a fruity drink in their hand—they wouldn't need to manage your money!
- The more frequent buying and selling of securities in market timing increases investment fees and commissions on trades and triggers taxes from any capital gains you realize on sales.
- Market timing may cause you much aggravation as you try to make money but never seem to succeed.

Market timing doesn't work as a long-term investment solution. You may be able to successfully time a couple of big wins now and then, but it is almost impossible to do it consistently day after day, year after year. Here are a couple of more specific reasons why you should not take this road:

- You are one person trying to successfully decide the right time to buy and sell. You are competing against highly qualified professional money managers, with extensive global research capabilities. They watch every blip on every market around the world all day long. Unless you have a similar infrastructure, you will never beat them consistently by spending a few hours of time on the Internet on a Sunday night in your basement rec room.
- No one knows whether interest rates or the markets will go up or down daily, and for how long. That means you may rarely buy at the bottom and sell at the top. Many investors actually end up selling at the bottom and buying at the top, which is disastrous to your long-term financial success.

Sure, throwing your money around the markets trying to guess the next hot sector is fun and adventurous, but many notable investors recognize that it is not the route to significant wealth.

If you feel you must actively trade at least a little bit, then open a small investment account, contribute no more than 10% of your overall savings to this account, and have fun. With a small account, if you lose it all it won't bring your entire financial future crashing down, yet 10% is a big enough amount to let you get your kicks on Sunday evenings.

Simply put, recognize your limitations as your own money manager. It is not your full-time job.

## Beware of financial advisors and money managers who support market timing

As you read the financial press and shop around for a financial advisor or investment products, you will see many brokers who suggest that they have the technique that allows them to successfully time the market. Some are momentum investors, some are sector rotators, others are tactical asset allocation managers. Regardless of the type, all practise some form of market timing.

Finding a money manager with consistent long-term investing success is rare. Before you consider investing with market timing products, at a minimum follow these three suggestions:

1. Ask to see samples of historical client performance for five years or more comparing the money manager's returns to a common index like the TSE 300 (Toronto Stock Exchange) or S&P 500 (Standard & Poor's), or to a peer group of similar money managers.
2. Ask to see their most recent financial statements (not the prospectuses) and verify the level of commissions charged within their investment products. This information is usually found in the notes to the financial statements. Compare these fees to fees of non–market timing managers to see if there is a significant increase. Be sensitive to these fees as they are paid on top of any investment management fee you are paying.
3. Let me know why the manager thinks he or she can time the market more successfully than the millions of other professionals worldwide who try and fail; I'd love to know his or her secret.

# 14

**I like investing in Canada because I know what is going on here better than in other countries. Is this the right thing to do?**

There have been periods in the past (and will be in the future no doubt) in the global business cycles where Canada has outperformed the rest of the world as an economy and, thus, it has been a good place to invest. At other times, it has not done as well. Unfortunately, it is impossible to predict when these good and bad times will hit the Canadian economy. Overall, however, history has proven that Canada is not typically the best place in the world to invest.

Let's analyze the world's stock markets to assess good and bad places to invest.

In the past 30 years the stock markets of North America and Europe performed as follows:

- Best average annual returns: U.S.A.
- Second best average annual returns: Western Europe
- Somewhere down the list: Canada

To properly assess returns, however, we need to look at them on a risk-adjusted basis. This means looking at the risk (volatility) taken to generate the best returns, since higher returns are often generated with more risk. You may not want to invest in a particular market if many risky investments are made to get you those better returns. So let's check risk in the same markets.

In the last 30 years the risk levels of North American and European stock markets have been as follows, according to frequency of negative returns:

- Riskiest: Canada
- Less risk: Western Europe
- Least risk: U.S.A.

So there you have it. In the past, the best returns with the least amount of risk have been generated by the U.S. stock market. The next best place was Western Europe. Then Canada placed somewhere down the list.

Here's my message: Before you retire, you will own a Canadian home, maybe a Canadian cottage. You may get a Canadian pension and a Canadian inheritance. You will even get, I bet, Canada Pension Plan payments. So how many more Canadian-based investments do you want to have in a country that accounts for 2% of the world economy? You might notice that there are better places to invest than Canada, according to the past. Of course, I have to point out that past returns are not indicative of the future.

By the way, if you still think that your RRSP or RRIF has to be largely Canadian content, you've missed a tax change and some new mutual fund developments in the recent past. It is now easily possible to have a 100% foreign content RRSP using derivative-based foreign funds that qualify as Canadian content. There is more on this issue in the answer to question 24.

In summary, put a lot of your investable wealth outside of Canada. When you add it all up, Canada is riskier than average in the short term while offering a long-term lower return despite the greater volatility. You are better served by spreading your wealth around the world for investment purposes.

One cautionary note, however, about currency fluctuations. Remember that investing outside of Canada means investing in the currency of the local economy, and currencies fluctuate from day to day and country to country. Investors can generally treat currency exchange in one of two ways: (1) Let it happen and impact your investment returns positively or negatively depending on the change in rates. (2) Alternatively, the money manager can "hedge" away foreign currency risk. Hedging is a process whereby the manager uses derivatives to offset the currency fluctuation exposure, effectively removing the foreign currency risk from the investment. When purchasing a foreign investment, you definitely want to know whether or not there is foreign currency exposure.

Practically speaking, foreign currency risk is another form of diversification within your portfolio that can help to mitigate your portfolio volatility. Make sure that you understand the impact of any foreign currencies within your portfolio.

# 15

## Is diversifying my portfolio really a good idea? How do I do it?

Diversification is important as a strategy to assist investors to tolerate the high levels of short-term volatility associated with some types of investments. Diversification can, however, harm your ability to get the highest returns, so, again, you need to decide what you really want.

Diversifying your investment portfolio means spreading out your investment money among several different types of investments and investment classes at the same time. You do this to reduce your likelihood of a major loss from having too much money in one investment that goes bad. By spreading your money out like a blanket across many types of investments, you reduce the overall likelihood of a devastating loss, without compromising your potential for strong investment returns.

You can diversify your investment portfolios in several ways. First, add up all of your different investment accounts (and include those of your spouse or partner, if you have one) and treat them as one. Following are some methods of achieving diversification.

## Own different types of products

Consider owning some cash, some fixed-income investments, and some equity investments. Every Canadian's investment portfolio should contain these three basic types of investment classes depending on your SIP&G. Now let's look at how you can diversify within each asset class.

## Diversification for the fixed-income category

Many people don't realize that a fixed-income portfolio can be diversified much like an equity portfolio. Diversification of your fixed-income holdings makes sense because it can help to enhance yield, while also managing volatility better. Here are several ways to diversify your fixed-income portfolio:

- Own long-term bonds and short-term bonds together; do the same if you own bond funds.
- Own different types of fixed-income investments: bonds, bond mutual funds, GICs, etc.
- Own Government of Canada bonds, corporate bonds, municipal bonds.
- Own Canadian and non-Canadian bonds and bond funds.
- Own Canadian-dollar bonds and foreign-currency bonds.
- If you own bond funds, hire more than one money manager and more than one management style. Bond funds can be managed using different management styles (e.g., duration, grade, interest rate anticipation).
- Own both actively managed bond funds and indexed bond funds.

Each one of these types of fixed income investments offers different strengths and weaknesses that together build a diversified portfolio.

## Diversification for the equity category

The following are examples of different ways to diversify an equity portfolio:

- Own equity investments that are indexed and others that are actively managed.
- Own equity investments with an investment focus in Canada, others where it is the U.S., and others where it is non–North American.
- Own equity investments that buy only large companies; own others that buy only small companies; and own others that specialize in specific sectors (like high tech or health sciences).
- Own equity investments that are based in Canadian currency and others in foreign currencies.
- Hire more than one money manager of your equities to bring different styles of management to your portfolio.

## Excessive diversification

Diversification can also become excessive and can duplicate your investments needlessly. Owning the same stock through five different mutual funds is of questionable value. As well, owning several hundred stocks or bonds may leave you with an unfocused portfolio and no clear-cut plan. You should always understand what you own, and what specific role it plays in your accounts. The next question will discuss the benefits of a narrowly diversified portfolio. Ensure you work with a qualified financial advisor to take advantage of diversification to the extent that you desire.

# 16

**I want to maximize my portfolio value over the long term. Is there a way to do this without taking on significant risk?**

Some of the greatest investors in the world (for example, Warren Buffet) earn some of the highest returns year after year. To become this successful there are some basic investment principles that are fundamentally sound and have led to great amounts of wealth. Forget target returns for a moment. Forget asset allocation and broad diversification. These successful principles are listed below, and would apply to only the equity component of your portfolio and if your only goal is to maximize return:

**BUY QUALITY EQUITY INVESTMENTS ONLY.** Ensure that you know what you are buying and buy only the best equities. If you buy industry-leading companies, there is a greater likelihood that these companies will thrive over the long term.

**BUY ONLY A FEW COMPANIES.** There is a powerful argument against diversification that says you will be financially better off over the long term by purchasing the stock in only a few strong companies. If you concentrate your investment wealth in only a few investments and these investments rise, your wealth will rise faster. Broad diversification serves to dilute your invested wealth, lessening the impact of good investments and reducing your long-term wealth potential. You don't have to look far to see how well this philosophy works: Ken Thompson, Izzy Asper, the Reichmann family, and the Bronfmans all built huge empires in Canada and abroad by investing in the family company alone and sticking with it.

Unfortunately, average investors let emotion into their investing process, often preventing them from actually following this time-proven process. Specifically, putting all your eggs in one basket can be financially lucrative over the long term, but the short-term volatility of a concentrated portfolio can be emotionally stressful—more than many investors can take. Many prefer a more broadly diversified portfolio that is easier to stomach but that gives up the potential for greater wealth over the long term. Often, working with a good financial advisor can help an investor to avoid panic attacks, because the financial advisor is the voice of reason during turbulent times. A good financial advisor, in my mind, is part psychologist at times, and this discipline exerted on an investor can often result in greater long-term wealth.

**HOLD THE COMPANIES YOU BUY FOR A LONG TIME.** It usually takes time to build substantial wealth, often decades. Looking back at our famous Canadian entrepreneurs, Mr. Thompson and the others have all owned their businesses for generations. Sure, the value of businesses will fluctuate in the short term, but as long as you have a long-term investing horizon, this should be your focus.

Holding for the long term also has another strong benefit: reduced taxes. By not selling your investments regularly in your taxable savings account, the pre-tax value is preserved, taxes are deferred, and more money is left in your investment account working for you. And in Canada, where taxes can approach 50% of your investment dollar, avoiding taxes as long as possible is a very powerful wealth generator.

So it is possible to build significant wealth without significant long-term risk. Simply follow these steps:

- Invest in quality equity investments. Seek the assistance of a financial advisor to determine if they are quality. Ensure over time that they continue to be quality.
- Invest in a few rather than many investments, but be prepared to put your emotions on the shelf. It may be just too much to tolerate emotionally to buy only one or two stocks, but it can be more tolerable if you purchase five, ten, or 15, possibly through a mutual fund. This is still a fairly concentrated portfolio so your returns can be high, yet there is enough diversification to make the short-term volatility more manageable.
- Own these investments for decades, as long as they continue to be quality holdings, to defer taxation and enhance wealth building.

Following the principles in this chapter that lead to true wealth maximization takes guts. The hardest part will be riding through the downtimes, waiting for the good times to return. The logic is solid. It's the emotion associated with short-term volatility that is hard to take. Working with a financial advisor who can be your rock in times of turbulence can often help you to think rationally about your ultimate goals, preventing panic selling and disruption of your investment program.

# RULE 3

## Evaluate the correct types of products for your needs before you shop for specific brand names.

Once your Statement of Investment Policy and Guidelines is developed, it is time to explore investment products. Our product analysis will be produced from two different perspectives: macro product analysis and micro product analysis.

First we examine investments from a macro point of view. Macro investment selection consists of sorting out the types of investments that best suit you. For example, before diving in to pick one of 2,500 mutual funds to buy, think about whether you even belong in mutual funds in the first place. Investigate the variety of products out there before you conclude that mutual funds are right for you. This step of evaluating products is often completely overlooked by many investors today. Yet it is arguably more important than the specific product brand you buy in the end.

Macro investment analysis and selection adds an important level of due diligence to your investment program. By using some common variables identified in this section of the book, you can evaluate and compare virtually any kind of investment product types according to the same evaluation framework. This is important, since many investors find it difficult to compare, for example, a wrap program to a mutual fund, or a segregated fund to an index-linked GIC. Macro investment analysis brings into play a common logic framework, allowing you to compare various product types equally. This enhances the decision-making process.

Should you decide through the macro process that mutual funds *are* right for you, then a micro product analysis of the 2,500 brand name funds will be your next step. Micro investment selection will be covered in Rule 4.

# 17

## How do I know which is the right type of investment for me?

In the marketplace today there are so many investment products to choose from: load mutual funds, no-load funds, index funds, segregated funds, wrapped programs, stocks and bonds, segregated accounts, and the list goes on.

If you recognize all of the different types of investments mentioned, then you have taken the right first step to selecting investments by simply realizing that there are many options. A lot of people know about stocks and mutual funds, but many don't realize there are literally dozens of other products out there to choose from. The question is, with all these various types of products, which type is right for you?

Included in the landscape chart below are all the different types of investments available in Canada today. Regardless of who's selling them, they are displayed on this chart generically. Using this chart, you can follow a logical path to the type of product best suited to you.

Definitions for some of these products can be found in the glossary at the back of this book. I also encourage you to refer to my first book, *50 Tax-Smart Investing Strategies*, since many of the products are defined there.

Sorting out which investment products to invest in is your objective. The way to do this is to set your expectations up front, and then evaluate all types of products according to your criteria. Only by doing this can you see beyond the glitzy marketing brochures and sales pitches to evaluate the products for what they really are. Without a framework like this to evaluate product types, it is easy to get lost in the hundreds of choices available in Canada today. So, let's develop a framework that you can apply to all products, allowing you to filter through the information like an expert, stopping only on alternatives that meet your defined needs.

To find your path on the chart, first prioritize the following criteria according to your own personal preferences. Choose a number for each of the items below based on your requirements: Put number 1 beside the characteristic that is most important to you, number 2 beside the next most important, and so on, with number 6 beside the least important.

___3___ Minimize fear of losing some of your money due to short-term market volatility and investment risk

___1___ Minimize total annual cost of your investments

___2___ Minimize your tax bill on your investment returns

___4___ Simplicity of owning an investment solution that is easy to manage and follow

___5___ Direct access to money managers buying your investments

_____ Additional desirable traits, if any

# Understanding the Canadian Financial Landscape

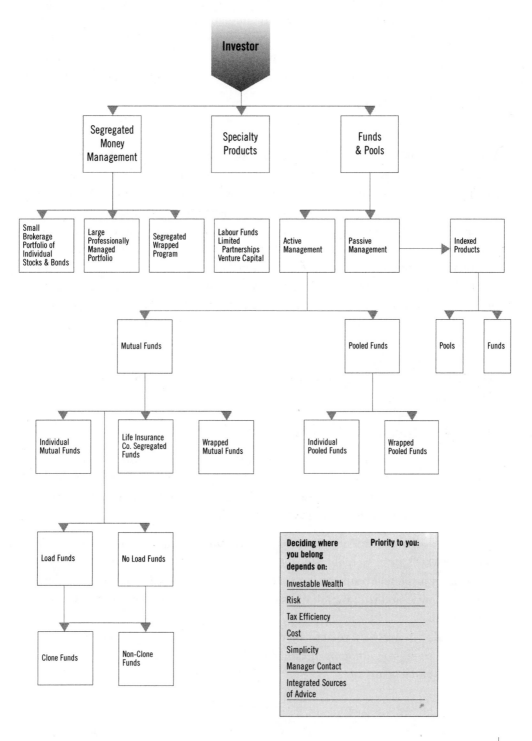

**Investor**

- **Segregated Money Management**
  - Small Brokerage Portfolio of Individual Stocks & Bonds
  - Large Professionally Managed Portfolio
  - Segregated Wrapped Program
- **Specialty Products**
  - Labour Funds Limited Partnerships Venture Capital
- **Funds & Pools**
  - Active Management
    - Mutual Funds
      - Individual Mutual Funds
      - Life Insurance Co. Segregated Funds
        - Load Funds
          - Clone Funds
        - No Load Funds
          - Non-Clone Funds
      - Wrapped Mutual Funds
    - Pooled Funds
      - Individual Pooled Funds
      - Wrapped Pooled Funds
  - Passive Management
    - Indexed Products
      - Pools
      - Funds

| Deciding where you belong depends on: | Priority to you: |
|---|---|
| Investable Wealth | |
| Risk | |
| Tax Efficiency | |
| Cost | |
| Simplicity | |
| Manager Contact | |
| Integrated Sources of Advice | |

Each type of investment on the chart offers different advantages and disadvantages that I have summarized in the form of these six criteria. A small stock portfolio, for example, is far more risky than the average equity mutual fund due to the limited number of investments. How you prioritize these six criteria will assist you to figure out what are the right types of investment products for your situation. In the answer to question 21, you'll see how each product type varies according to these criteria. Consult a professional advisor to review your analysis.

## How the landscape chart works

If you had $100,000 and you walked into your local bank branch and asked for help with your money, they might offer to assist you in-branch with their no-load mutual funds or refer you to their full service brokerage, their discount brokerage, their private investment counsel, their trust company investment management, their discretionary account managers, and so on. Many of Canada's banks provide all of these choices, and each referral leads you to different people, processes, products, fee schedules, and techniques to help you manage your money. It can be overwhelming!

The landscape chart helps you to apply five core questions to highlight the real differences between the services and products. One of the bank's service offerings may be too expensive. Another may have a minimum account size greater than your wealth level. Another service may not provide all the service and communication you want. The key is to analyze all the choices using the same variables—compare apples to apples, so to speak. Only by doing this can you evaluate across different product types and conclude which is right for you.

## The advantages of consolidating your accounts

When we invest, we often don't like one institution or financial advisor to know about all of our assets, so we give each institution a little piece of our investments and don't tell them about the rest that we have elsewhere. This is a big mistake! You are hurting yourself more than you are helping yourself, for several reasons:

- You can own many products from many institutions through a single account with one dealer. This can simplify your life.
- If you get just one investment statement with everything on it, you might finally be able to understand your overall financial position and evaluate progress towards your goals.
- Consolidation may help you enhance your RRSP or RRIF foreign-content levels if you own significant amounts of Canadian RRSP or RRIF assets in some of your accounts and less in others.

- Greater wealth levels generally get more advantages from investment institutions. This is probably no surprise to you, but let me clarify exactly how it works:
  - Many of the newer, more sophisticated investment products require a minimum access investment amount that ranges from about $75,000 to $5 million.
  - If you can purchase a greater number of stocks, bonds, mutual funds, specialty investments, etc., it helps to reduce risk by spreading your money among more investments. This lessens the likelihood of losing a lot of money if one investment fails.
  - If you can purchase larger quantities of each investment, you will have access to such benefits as the lower commission rates or purchase costs that can be associated with larger purchases.
  - There are tax advantages to purchasing large amounts of individual stocks on your own. Generally, pools and funds can also be very tax efficient, in some cases more so than owning individual stocks; however, when properly planned, and where wealth is great enough, an investor can put together the ultimate tax-smart portfolio of individual stocks. (This is discussed further in Rule 7.) However, most investors don't belong in a portfolio of stocks on their own unless they have several million dollars and the portfolio is built with a strong tax sensitivity.

So, rather than fragmenting your portfolio into pieces among several institutions, centralize your accounts (including all of your and your spouse's RRSP and non-RRSP accounts) at one institution with just one overall financial advisor. You will still be able to buy a variety of investment products, but you should be able to do it more cheaply and in a simpler way, potentially with better products that are more tax efficient and risk managed. The miracles of technology have made it possible to make purchases of several different products from one institution—take advantage of this simplicity!

# 18

## How many and what types of money managers do I need?

Never place all of your money with only one money manager (for example, one mutual fund). First, one money manager alone can never consistently outperform year to year, and this leaves you exposed to short-term losses. Second, a money manager may die or move to a competitor, so you would be exposed to these risks as well. The old adage of don't put all your eggs in one basket holds true with respect to investing.

Always invest with several money managers (several mutual funds, or several pooled funds, etc.) in order to benefit from different management styles, different expertise, different perspectives, different research capabilities, different mandates, and so on. By owning investments with more than one money manager, if one guesses wrong or has a bad year, you still have others to offset any negatives. Your upside isn't limited by having two or more money managers, but your downside is more protected!

The question then becomes, how many is enough? 25? 50? 2? What is the right answer? There is no right answer—other than to say that it should be more than one. The exact number of money managers you need depends on several factors, including how much money you have to invest and your personal financial objectives. Below is a summary of factors that have been discussed elsewhere in this book. Consider them when deciding how many money managers you need to hire.

- If one of your concerns is to minimize your investment risk, consider investing with several money managers that vary according to asset class mandates, geographic mandates, sector mandates, and so on. Having a little bit of your money invested with money managers who each take a slightly different perspective lays your money across the broad market, limiting your exposure to a significant short-term loss in any one area.

- In some cases, your wealth level affects your access to certain money managers. The number of money managers you are able to hire may be affected by how much money you have to invest, since many professional money managers require minimum investment levels before they will consider you as a client.

- If you own several money managers in one asset class (for example, Canadian equity), you need to be sensitive to excessive duplication within your portfolio. It may not be wise to own the same stock seven times within seven different mutual funds or investment accounts. This level of detail is not always explored by investors, but needs to be.

- Ensure each money manager or product in your portfolio plays a specific role. Know exactly why you own something—there should be a disciplined and professional reason for every product you own. If you don't have a reason, this could be the first indication that you lack a professional investment program. (Note that buying a specific product because a sector is "hot" is not a compelling reason to own something—market timing is always a losing strategy!)

- Put a financial advisor between you and your money managers. Someone needs to objectively evaluate your money manager solutions on a regular basis for the reason mentioned in the previous point. Having a financial advisor on your team representing you helps to keep your money management solutions consistent with your needs and expectations.

- Beware of money managers who say you only need one money manager to manage all your money. Remember, they have a big personal financial incentive to say this to you. Also keep in mind that if their financial house is burning down behind closed doors, they may not tell you this because they don't want you to leave. Having a financial advisor to help monitor your money manager products can add a level of objectivity to your investment program that is worthy of consideration.

The average investor in search of a volatility-managed portfolio would be well served by several different money managers, each hired for a specific role within a portfolio. Each of these managers should manage a piece of your wealth, in a different asset class, different geographic sector, different industry sector, etc.

# 19

## What are basic strategies that Canadians should follow to build a tax-smart investment portfolio?

Tax-smart investing is the process of building a taxable investment portfolio designed to maximize after-tax returns, not the pre-tax returns you see in the newspaper. After all, it's what you keep, not what you earn, that matters. Unfortunately, there is next to no information available on after-tax investing, and many advisors and institutions do not make it a priority. Yet the tax impact on investing, in a country where you can be taxed as much as 50% of your dollar, is one of the most important criteria in deciding how to invest and what to buy.

In Rule 7, I discuss tax-reduction strategies in more depth. For now, below are a few suggestions about tax-smart investing.

- Pay attention to investment portfolio turnover. Turnover is the rate at which you buy and sell investments or the frequency at which the mutual fund manager buys and sells inside the fund. A lot of buying and selling of stocks and bonds in a year can result in a greater level of annual taxation on any capital gains you realize. This is not tax-smart investing. In a taxable investment portfolio, select investments that you can hold for many years, or select mutual fund managers who buy investments to hold in their funds for many years at a time. Less annual turnover and more deferred growth mean greater after-tax net worth for you over the long term through less frequent annual taxation, since you only incur tax in years when investments are sold.

- Treat T3 and T5 slips you get in February or March as a red flag. Financial institutions are required by the government to send you a summary of your investment earnings each year. Mutual fund distributions are summarized on T3 slips, while interest earnings may be summarized on T5 slips. Rather than just filing these slips away when they arrive in your mailbox, question what you did to deserve them. If you are getting large distributions or large income amounts, and you don't need this income to live on, why do you own investments or mutual funds that are generating so much annual income and taxation? Move these investments into your RRSP or RRIF, or get rid of them all together, replacing them with investments that result in few annual distributions, thereby reducing your tax bill.

- Pay attention to tax characteristics and place your money in the appropriate tax-smart products. Fixed income investments such as GICs, bonds, and treasury bills generate interest income that is the highest taxed kind of investment income in Canada today. Other investments like equities and equity mutual funds can offer much lower forms of taxed income and capital gains. With such a difference in taxation results, it makes sense to organize the higher-taxed investments inside your RRSP or RRIF, while holding the lower-taxed investments in your taxable portfolio. As well, if one spouse is in a higher tax bracket than the other, organize the family investments to hold more tax-smart investments in the higher-taxed spouse's hands.

Research has shown that tax-smart investing can increase your after-tax investment returns by up to 5% annually. Take steps to implement as many tax-smart strategies as possible.

# 20

## Should I choose a discretionary or nondiscretionary investment account?

A *discretionary* account is one where the money manager has the authority to trade securities (buy and sell investments) on your behalf without your transactional authorization. Normally you will provide them with investing guidelines or they will assess your needs and tolerances and then build a portfolio and make changes to it on your behalf. Mutual funds and their money managers are really discretionary money managers, since you have no say about what they put in their portfolios.

A *nondiscretionary* account is one where money managers cannot trade anything without your understanding and approval. If they trade without your authorization you can sue them for this violation. Most brokerage accounts are nondiscretionary accounts, and that's why your advisor must consult you on all buys and sells of investments.

When deciding whether you want discretionary or nondiscretionary money management, consider your personal preferences. If you want greater control over your money management to the extent that the advisor needs to call you before every single transaction, so be it. But if you would rather not be involved to this extent, discretionary investment products may be more appropriate for you.

Many people settle in the middle somewhere, owning mutual funds that offer discretionary money management, but also hiring a financial advisor. A financial advisor will assist them in mutual fund selection according to their financial profile and will help monitor the funds.

In my opinion, most investors are well served by leaving the actual stock and bond selection and trading to money managers. Managing your finances is a big job, and money managers are professionals who work within an efficient process to help you with your specific investment needs. So let them do their work, but by all means monitor them for long-term effectiveness.

Consider hiring a financial advisor to help you manage your overall finances, including the selection and monitoring of your specific money managers. Managing your finances is a big job in which everyone benefits from the use of professional help. I'd rather see you on the golf course in your retirement than reviewing stock research reports.

# 21

## Can you explain some of the investment options available to me?

Following are some basic definitions of several different types of investment products:

## Load mutual funds (front or deferred loads)

Load mutual funds are the most common and talked-about types of investments in Canada today. For as little as $100 you can get instant diversification (risk-managed investing!) across a variety of asset classes (bonds, Canadian equities, U.S. equities, and so on), varying degrees of tax efficiency, but limited direct access to the money manager. Mutual fund fees vary from product to product, often exceeding 2% per year. For the average Canadian investor, this cost is well worth the access to some of the world's best money managers and a globally diversified portfolio of securities.

If you're in need of a financial advisor, service, and ongoing communication about investing and your finances, load mutual funds are a good choice since the funds provide compensation to the financial advisor directly in exchange for the advice and service provided to you.

## No-load mutual funds

No-load mutual funds are mutual funds with different fee options from load mutual funds. In many cases there are no differences in the total cost (or other variables) between load and no-load mutual funds, but investors will need to examine a specific company's funds in each case. No-load funds are popular with do-it-yourself investors.

## Index funds

Index funds own investment portfolios that replicate many commonly recognized indices such as the TSE 300, or the S&P 500 in the U.S. These passive funds don't use money managers to actively trade the portfolio. Instead, they simply maintain the same portfolio as the index they track. This strategy can offer tax advantages and cost savings in some cases, but can also be rather boring to some investors. As well, not all index investments are created equal, and poorer index funds provide less tax efficiency and higher costs. Make sure you shop around carefully if you are in the market for index funds.

## Mutual funds in general

Mutual funds are suitable for most Canadians. Generally, anyone with less than $1 million to spend is wise to purchase mutual funds of one kind or another because they cannot adequately create their own personal collection of stocks or bonds to match the risk management, cost effectiveness, and professional expertise of a mutual fund. In fact, for most Canadians, the most sensible choice is mutual funds for most or all of their investment needs.

## Pooled funds

I bet you didn't know that many of your mutual fund companies also offer pooled funds. These are fund investments that look exactly like mutual funds, and even often hold the identical investments, but there are two big differences: (1) The minimum investment amount per fund is often $85,000 or more; and (2) the fees of pooled funds are often half of retail mutual fund fees. Generally, I don't recommend pooled funds unless you have more than $1 million to invest so that you can purchase several pooled funds to cover each of the major asset classes. You are better off paying the higher fees of a mutual fund, which will build a more diversified portfolio that includes a variety of products from several money managers. That way, if one money manager crumbles, you are less exposed to a severe loss. The high minimum investment amount on pooled funds makes them of limited use for the average Canadian investor. Give careful consideration to all factors before buying a pooled fund.

## Segregated funds

"Seg funds" are mutual funds with training wheels. These new-fangled funds offer a guarantee of your original investment subject to certain terms—that's right: You can never lose your original money, assuming you follow some rules. Although it sounds like a wonderful deal, all is not as it appears. These products are being sold to the masses, but they are not a mass-market product and have advantages suitable only to certain investors. Read the answer to question 30 to learn more about segregated funds and their appropriateness for your portfolio. I also addressed them in my previous book, *50 Tax-Smart Investing Strategies*.

## Mutual fund wrap programs

These programs are a selection of mutual funds put together in predetermined amounts as a portfolio to make the investing process even easier. Simply pick the portfolio that matches your needs—the fund selection is already complete. Often you get fancier quarterly reporting and sometimes the fees are more tax-effective. These programs are suitable for investors with small amounts of money (less than $50,000) to invest and who want an investment on autopilot; that is, a simple investment to maintain. But be careful: Some of these wraps charge a wrap fee on top of the fund fees. You may be better off selecting some good mutual funds with a financial advisor.

## Pooled and individually managed account wrap programs

With higher net worth wrap programs, investors select from a stable of professional money managers handpicked to manage portions of an account. Fees are charged annually based on overall assets within the program. Advanced reporting is provided to investors and generally a professional consulting process is built around the product line. These programs can be pricey because of all the bells and whistles. A bigger issue with these programs, however, is portability: Many of these programs don't permit investors to move their accounts to another institution easily. Conversely, common mutual funds can be transferred to most institutions in Canada.

## Small portfolio of stocks

If you have less than $5 million to invest, in my opinion you should not build your own stock portfolio. Below this wealth level, you are better off in pooled and mutual funds or wrap programs because it is hard to achieve the same cost efficiencies, purchasing power clout, and risk management levels. In simple terms, it will likely cost you more and it will be more risky. I have seen people who hold their entire life savings in three Canadian stocks. When I asked about the success of their stocks, they bragged about how much money they made with these stocks over 25 years. Then I asked if these are the only stocks they have ever held. They said, no, they used to own 15 stocks but these are the only ones that survived!

## Big portfolio of stocks

Once you have several million dollars, you may be in a position to go out and hire a professional money manager to custom create an investment portfolio for you. You will need a few million dollars in order to purchase enough stocks and bonds to create an adequately diversified portfolio and to benefit from the cost savings of larger purchases. You also may want to hire more than one manager with different management mandates, so you'll need larger amounts of money to provide each manager with a fair-sized portfolio.

Hiring a money manager to create your own portfolio may offer tax advantages since you can have some control over the capital gains you incur by dictating when investments are sold (this depends on the nature of the relationship you have with the money manager). However, this tax advantage can be lost completely if the manager has high portfolio turnover—meaning they buy and sell stocks frequently—generating many unnecessary taxable capital gains.

It is hard in a few pages of text to educate readers about the pros and cons of various types of investments. Consider consulting a financial advisor to further explain the characteristics of various investment types, and use the landscape chart as a guide to help you find out which products suit you best. The important things to realize are how much product choice there is in the marketplace today and the need to first sort through product types suitable to you before you look at specific investments.

# 22

**Are there situations where purchasing individual stocks and bonds may be considered a good approach?**

The average investor should not build his or her own stock and bond portfolio because there are several variables that make this a disadvantageous approach. Below are two such variables:

1. **Fees.** A single investor with a small pool of cash to invest may pay higher trading commissions and get poorer investment choice than a huge institution investing billions of dollars of people's money together, as is the case with mutual funds.
2. **Risk.** A single investor may only have enough money to buy a few stock positions. Should one or a few of these positions blow up, a large portion of the small investor's finances will be lost. Small investors are better suited to funds where their money is combined with that of other investors to allow all investors to buy several stock and bond positions, reducing the likelihood of significant loss if one stock falters. Mutual funds offer this protection.

There are only a few situations where Canadians should be buying individual stocks versus funds and pools. I discuss some of those situations below.

## Start with a lot of money

If an investor has $5 million or more, there is enough money to purchase adequate amounts of stocks and bonds in several asset classes, using more than one money manager. Purchasing several stocks in each category ensures adequate diversification to balance short-term volatility. Having adequate cash to buy larger quantities of each stock ensures a more reasonable commission price on trades. And using several different money managers offers varying management styles, which will minimize the risk of loss from any one manager.

## Play money

It's okay to tinker with a few stocks as part of a "play money" account if the account total is a small portion of your overall portfolio—say less than 10%. Some people want to have a little fun in the markets: Trading is sexy. Many investors maintain a separate account to invest and to "go crazy" with. Buy all the technology stocks you want, but limit the account size to a low enough level so that a complete loss of these funds would not be a financial setback that you can't recover from.

## Stock options

Lucky executives and employees of some companies can purchase or are given shares or stock options. This can be a very lucrative road to wealth if the shares shoot up in value or the company goes public in a very successful way. That is what the employees wish for, but it may not always end up that way. One of the drawbacks of holding your company's stock is that you may end up with a lot of money tied up in that one stock—all your eggs in one basket, as they say. Often an employee is faced with juggling priorities with their excessive amounts of company stock: There is the high investment risk with one stock; the political risk of not following management's expectations that you hold the stock; and the tax implications of selling. There is no magic answer about the best route to follow—it depends on the employee. I have two comments, however: (1) Selling a little bit of the company stock each year and reinvesting in a diversified portfolio is a conservative strategy that you might want to take; and (2) never let the value of the company stock exceed 35% of the total value of your savings. If it does, sell the excess and reinvest in a diversified portfolio.

## Add stocks to a diversified portfolio

Finally, it is okay to hold a selection of stocks if they are mixed with a more broadly diversified portfolio of mutual or pooled funds and/or exchange-traded funds. Just ensure that the stocks are suitable according to your SIP&G.

# 23

## Some days I wish I had just a simple solution for my investments. Is that an impossible request?

No, it is not. However, simplicity is just another factor to consider when shopping for investment solutions. And since simplicity is a variable, you need to prioritize it among all the other investment variables that are important to you such as cost, risk, and tax efficiency. If the other variables end up being compromised too much in your quest for simplicity, give up the quest. When it comes down to it, a cost-effective, tax-smart, risk-managed investment program is more important than a simple solution.

So beware, don't let simplicity hurt you more than it helps you. Here are a few examples of simple investment solutions that I would discourage:

- Putting all your money in one or two stocks that are poorly selected can be very dangerous. Sure, if one of these stocks takes off it could make you a millionaire, but chances of this are slim, and if the same stock drops like a rock, it could put you in the poorhouse.
- Hiring only one money manager to manage all of your money can be dangerous as well. If you have one money manager focused on only one area of investing, you will feel a larger impact if they have some bad years of performance or lose key staff. Having more than one manager can lessen the negative impact of these factors because your money will be spread out. For example, hire one money manager to manage Canadian equities and another one to manage your U.S. equities.
- I would not recommend buying traditional investments such as GICs as a simple solution. Many Canadians still fear new investments like equity mutual funds despite their many advantages. Research and development in the investment industry worldwide is helping Canadians to have better investment choice, to get better value for their money, and to have more money overall. Don't fight change, take advantage of it! Get educated about new investment opportunities, and if you're still uncomfortable, consider investing a small amount to get used to it.

As you search for a simple investment solution, ensure that you consider the following aspects for every solution:

- Comparison shop to understand what is a reasonable cost of management of your investments. Remember that a service package that includes advice, handholding, and regular communication will naturally cost more, so decide what you want.
- Money management by several different managers who can each bring their own unique mandate to investing to your money can reduce volatility of returns without compromising potential return.

- The average return expectations from all your money managers should match or exceed the return you need to get from your finances annually in order to reach your goals.
- Evaluate each money manager carefully for their strengths and weaknesses according to criteria identified in other parts of this book.

## One easy way to simplify your investments

Use one platform or account to hold all of your assets from different money managers (different funds, for example) together. This is a form of simplicity that is desirable, because when all of your investments are held in one account, it is easier to measure and view them. From one platform you get ease of reporting, without restricting your access to a variety of products and investment companies in many cases.

While everyone would prefer to follow a simple investment program, simplicity is not a factor that should be given much importance or priority overall. It is much more important to have a high-quality investment program that is better able to meet all of your financial goals.

# 24

## Which fixed-income investments are better: bonds or bond mutual funds?

A lot of people buy bond mutual funds thinking they can't lose money because they are buying bonds. However, on a short-term basis, you can lose money on bond funds, depending on market interest rate fluctuations. Bond funds generally consist of a collection of market-traded government and/or corporate bonds, and they generate two kinds of return for an investor. The coupon rate is the interest rate on each bond, and it is this type of return that Canadians usually think of with fixed-income investments. In addition to this, active buying and selling of bonds by the fund manager can also generate capital gains and capital losses, depending on interest rate movements and other factors. It is this active trading that can lead to big returns. Generally, you should own both bonds and bond funds, but this will depend on your situation.

A bond fund should be held by investors who have a greater than five-year time horizon. This is a long enough time that smooth returns should result over the entire period, on average. Since bond funds are actively traded and bring an element of risk to investing, holding them for several years should protect against the odd negative return or less than expected return.

Consider owning individual bonds—and hold them to maturity—for a less than five-year time horizon. When you hold bonds to maturity, you eliminate the market risk associated with active trading. In other words, you know exactly how much money you will get on maturity and with each interest payment. Consider a series of bonds, each maturing one after the other annually, and use these for your short-term cash flow needs or for reinvestment.

Here are a few sample scenarios:

- If you are middle age and retirement is 25 years away and your SIP&G calls for some fixed income, go with bond funds instead of bonds for long-term enhanced returns.
- If you are 65 and retired—and therefore five years away from drawing from your RRIF—take the fixed-income portion of your portfolio and hold half of it in diversified bond funds and half in bonds directly. Have several bonds maturing each year to fund any liquidity or larger cash flow needs for the next five years.
- If you are 32 and saving for a home purchase in two years, invest all of your home deposit savings in a single bond maturing around the time that you plan to purchase the home.

## The cost of bonds and bond funds

When you buy market-traded bonds, you typically purchase them with a commission attached. This commission may be a percentage of the yield. For example, if you purchase a bond that is quoted at a 5.25% yield, a commission of 0.25% or more may be charged by the financial advisor. This is a one-time fee.

When you purchase a bond mutual fund, you incur an annual fee (MER) ranging from approximately 0.5% to close to 2% each year. This ongoing fee pays for the active management of the bond portfolio.

The nature and extent of fees you pay on your fixed-income portfolio should be dictated by the value you receive from the product and your advisory relationship. For example, an actively traded bond fund offers the potential for enhanced returns over time, compared with owning a single bond to maturity. This can justify the higher fee. However, it always comes back to your specific needs to ensure that you get value from your products and services.

# 25

## Are index-linked GICs a good way to start investing in the stock market?

The short answer is No. Index-linked GICs are a type of product that emerged in the 1990s to fill a specific need. Many older Canadians have relied for their income on the interest generated from GICs. But something happened in the 1990s that changed investor attitude towards GICs. GIC returns fell to as little as 4% per year while the stock market returns soared to more than 30% for a few years in a row. Traditional GIC owners wanted some of this stock market action. And a 4% return just wasn't enough to live on anymore.

But at the same time these investors didn't want to lose money by investing in the stock market. They had no stomach for (or experience with) investing volatility. So along came index-linked GICs as the answer.

Index-linked GICs offer the security of a GIC by providing a guarantee of your original investment amount. In other words, you can never lose your original purchase amount. They also offer a return that is linked to a particular stock market in the world. For example, you can purchase an index-linked GIC that pays an annual return dependent on the return of the TSE 300. So whatever the stock market does over a year, you would earn some or all of the same return but without the risk of losing your original investment.

But there are several reasons why this investment is not as good as it initially sounds:

- Index-linked GICs are not tax effective. Remember, you are earning a return that is linked to the stock market, but you are not actually investing in the stock market. This means you don't get any tax effective dividends or capital gains associated with stock investments. Instead, the return of the index-linked GIC is taxed as regular income, like interest, which is the most highly taxed type of investment income you can earn in Canada today.
- When you survey all the institutions that offer index-linked GICs in Canada, you will find that many of the companies limit your upside return potential on their product. This means they don't actually pay you the entire return earned by a stock-market-linked GIC in a year; instead, they only pay you up to a fixed amount. So if you have an index-linked GIC that tracks the U.S. Dow Index, and the Dow rises 20% this year, you may find yourself earning only 15% or less. The difference is effectively a fee that you pay—and a big one!
- Index-linked GICs are being sold frequently to seniors who may need to live on the cash flow from their investments. Yet index-linked GICs pay no annual income, and this could leave a senior in a potential cash flow crunch.

Index-linked GICs may be appropriate for some investors, but definitely not for most investors. If you are a risk-averse investor, you are better off building a real investment portfolio with a lot of safe bond investments and a few equity investments in the stock market. You will have a manageable investment volatility (suited to your tolerance level), but you will also get all of the upside return of the stock market investment and any tax breaks associated with stock market investing. You will also have easier access to your money when you need it since investments are not locked in the way index-linked GICs are. This seems to be a more commonsense approach.

If you would still like to own index-linked GICs, shop around for the best deals, since these products are offered with varying characteristics by many institutions.

# 26

## Is it wise to hire my own portfolio manager instead of buying mutual funds?

Many financial service organizations and money managers are setting up departments today where for an annual fee of around 1% you can have a personal money manager who will build and manage a portfolio of stocks and bonds for you in an individually managed account (IMA). Is this better than owning mutual funds? Here are some things to think about in concluding what is best for you.

## Fees

The annual fee may seem lower, but it may not include trading commissions or custody costs incurred inside the account. Commissions in particular are incurred by trading. If there is a lot of trading occurring in your account, your 1% fee may only be part of a much higher annual cost that is hidden inside the portfolio in the form of commission costs from purchases and sales. In the end, this may be a more expensive solution than other investments.

Not all mutual funds are expensive. For the cost-sensitive investor, there are many mutual funds that are very inexpensive to own. But buyer beware: lower cost may not be a better solution if quality is compromised for the sake of cost savings!

Many products (both funds and IMAs) now offer tiered pricing where investors who invest more money in one account pay lower fees for greater investment amounts. Often, combining your savings into fewer accounts can give you access to this tiered pricing if you are investing larger amounts.

## Tax efficiency

Owning stocks individually may be more tax smart than funds and pools but not always! Although owning stocks individually avoids the potential problem of buying a fund where there are significant gains built up inside the fund—gains that you didn't earn but may pay tax on prematurely—tax efficiency has more to do with portfolio turnover. Any account, of any type, with a high portfolio turnover rate each year (a lot of buying and selling of stocks versus a buy-and-hold approach), can result in a lot of capital gains that investors must pay tax on. This is unnecessary if the investor doesn't need annual income from their taxable portfolio. So your portfolio of stocks may actually be more tax inefficient than a mutual fund, depending on the trading strategy being used by the money manager. (See Rule 8 for more on tax efficiency.)

## Quality of your financial advisor

Is your portfolio manager also the person picking stocks to put in your portfolio? If so, this may not be an effective money management approach. Stock research and stock selection must be a full-time job to have any chance of providing decent returns to investors over the long term. I don't think that a financial advisor can effectively provide client services to you while trying to watch every move on the markets on your behalf. Especially when your financial advisor probably has another 300 relationships to manage!

A preferred approach is to separate stock-picking roles from customer service, so that your financial advisor is responsible for service to you, but that's it. Separate money managers (such as mutual fund managers) are responsible for making you money and trading your account. Just be cautious about the quality of the money managers and evaluate both the qualitative and quantitative factors that have been discussed earlier in this book. (See also Rule 5.)

## Risk

It is riskier to allow only one money manager to build you a portfolio using a single approach to money management. You need at least two competing money managers bringing two distinct investment mandates to money management to enhance your returns, smooth short-term volatility, and reduce the likelihood of a major loss. This logic is recommended whether you invest in funds or in individually managed accounts. Most money manager companies offer several money managers with different mandates to make this basic diversification easy.

Selecting the money managers to manage your savings is serious business. You are putting your financial future in their hands. Take the time to research options carefully, analyzing all choices according to consistent variables that matter to you.

# 27

## Growing up in Canada, I was always told that GICs were a good investment. Was buying GICs a mistake?

You are being penalized if you buy a GIC (Guaranteed Investment Certificate). This has always been the case. Canadians have purchased GICs for many years because of the attraction of a guarantee. Through the Canadian Deposit Insurance Corporation (CDIC), the government guarantees up to $60,000 of your GIC investment. But that coverage is actually a penalty because you are investing with a financial institution instead of directly with the Canadian government. If you invest with the government directly—by buying a Government of Canada bond, for example—you will be insured for your entire investment amount, whatever it is; there is no $60,000 limit. So why would anyone ever buy a GIC that only offers a partial guarantee?

There are other reasons to buy bonds or bond funds instead of GICs:

- Market-traded bonds offer one-year maturities to 30-year maturities; GICs offer only one- to five-year maturities. Bonds offer much more flexibility in planning your finances.
- I suggest that you consider buying market-traded bonds, not Canada Savings Bonds. Market-traded bonds fluctuate in value every day based on market interest rates, and they come in all varieties: federal government, provincial government, corporate, international, etc. Since these bonds are market traded, should interest rates fall in comparison to the bond you own, there is the potential to enhance your return with an additional capital gain on top of the interest income. Many of the bond mutual funds obtained double-digit returns in the 1990s through a mix of interest income and capital gains.
- An investor can purchase bonds from around the world, in all shapes and varieties, and bond portfolios should be diversified just like equity portfolios. But this same kind of diversification is not possible with GICs. GICs offer only one plain type that can only be diversified by maturity date.

The only advantage of GICs over bonds is that GICs are available over the counter at the local bank, while bonds require a brokerage account. This small inconvenience, however, is well worth it.

The table on the following page summarizes the differences between bonds and GICs.

# Characteristics of Bonds and GICs

| Characteristics | Bonds | GICs |
| --- | --- | --- |
| Returns | Bonds pay a fixed rate of interest for a specific period, but can also generate additional return in the form of capital gains/losses | GICs pay a fixed rate of interest for a specific period |
| Fees | A fee is paid in the form of a commission when you buy or sell the bond | A fee is paid in the form of lost return if GIC rates are lower than bond rates of return |
| Range of maturities | Bonds offer 1 day to 30 years of maturities | GICs typically offer 30-day to 5-year maturities |
| Ability to sell without penalty | Bonds can be sold at any time without loss of interest. However, a bond may be sold at a capital loss. | GICs can rarely be cashed in early. If they are, you typically lose your interest. |
| Tax treatment | Bonds generate interest and also may offer capital gains or losses. Gains and losses are taxed at a lower rate than interest. | GICs generate interest income, which is the highest-taxed investment income in Canada today |
| Simplicity | Bonds are easy to buy, but not as easy as GICs | GICs are very simple to buy |
| Varieties | Government of Canada bonds, provincial bonds, municipal bonds, U.S. bonds, international bonds, and more | One basic kind of GIC |
| Guarantee | The Government of Canada guarantees their bonds without limits | Canada Deposit Insurance Corp. (CDIC) guarantees GICs up to $60,000 only |

# 28

## What is indexed investing? Is it right for me?

If you ever watch the news on TV, you may hear the broadcaster mention that the TSE 300 rose today or that the Dow Jones in the U.S. went down. Both indexes represent a collection of the biggest companies in Canada and the U.S.A., collectively tracked and used as a measure of the progress of an economy. The TSE 300 is an index of the 300 biggest companies in Canada, representing most of the major industries. All of these companies trade daily on Canada's stock exchanges and their values change every day.

Some mutual funds purchase the same investments as found in the indexes, so they are called index funds. Importantly, these index funds rarely trade the companies they own because they must match the index, and the index only changes when a company in Canada's big 300 goes bankrupt or merges with another, or if a smaller company grows big enough to make it into the 300. This is called passive or indexed management because of the low turnover style and lack of active trading making by the money managers of the funds. On the other hand, non-index funds have active money managers and researchers, and they change their investments as they pick stocks to try to outperform the market or indexes. Should you own indexed products or funds with active managers?

I think that every Canadian should consider a combination of active and passive products, whether they are mutual funds or other. Here are some of the reasons why you should consider buying some indexed products for your portfolio:

- Indexed products can sometimes be purchased at a fraction of the cost of the average actively managed product. In some cases a fee reduction of 2% per year is possible! It should be noted, however, that many actively managed products also offer low fee alternatives and that not all index products are cheaper.
- With the low annual portfolio turnover of many index products, your annual tax bill decreases and after-tax return increases compared with some actively managed products. However, only certain indexes have had this lower turnover in the past. Shop around before you buy. Also, actively managed products can sometimes replicate these higher after-tax returns by practicing a low-turnover philosophy.
- The cost reduction, coupled with lower taxation, means index products generate after-tax returns that over the long term can be superior to many actively managed products. There are some actively managed products, however, that still outperform the indexes over the long term, so a case-by-case analysis is required.
- Since index funds are broadly invested across all major industries of a country (oils, forestry, consumer products, high tech, industrials, etc.) they offer a blanket exposure across a country's economy. This extensive diversification protects your downside should only one part of an economy take a beating for a short period. Actively

managed funds can also protect investors during down times by holding larger amounts of cash than an index fund will hold. This cash serves to cushion investors while markets fall, lessening the impact of losses.

Canadians seeking a well-rounded investment approach should consider including some index funds in their portfolio alongside their actively managed investments. By combining both active and passive investment products, you will create an overall investment portfolio that is risk managed, cost effective, and tax efficient. And the performance will likely never be worse than the broad market while still giving you the ability to outperform the market.

# 29

## Are balanced mutual funds a good idea?

I call balanced mutual funds the lazy person's investment solution. In a balanced mutual fund, the money manager takes complete control over which asset classes are invested in, based on market timing, and no consideration is given to your personal situation, which I think is wrong. When you first invest, the money manager may own 20% cash, 60% Canadian bonds, and 20% U.S. stocks, but these percentages may change, and one day you might wake up and find that the balance is 60% Canadian stocks and 40% Canadian bonds. This is a very different risk level that you may not have wanted.

Rather than purchasing a balanced mutual fund, properly determine—according to your personal situation—what proportions you should invest in the different asset classes, and purchase investments that specialize in those asset classes alone. In other words, take back control, and build a plan unique to you!

There are several reasons why I would discourage anyone from purchasing a balanced fund:

- A money manager may be an expert stock picker or an expert bond manager, but rarely both. Yet in a balanced fund, you may be asking one money manager to manage two different investments. Instead of buying balanced funds, why not buy equity funds and bond funds separately and hire specialists of both categories? Let me put it another way: If you needed heart surgery would you rather be operated on by a cardiac specialist or a general practitioner? Treat your investments the same way—find the specialists to manage each type of your investments.
- The cost of purchasing balanced funds can be 2% per year or more. This is too much to pay to own bonds where the return may only be 6% a year or less. Owning bonds separately allows you to bring the cost down on the bond component and will leave you with more money in your pocket.
- You hire a balanced money manager to successfully time the market for you by making judgement calls between bonds and stocks. But research has shown time and time again that it is almost impossible to successfully beat the market over the long term, so this rarely proves to be a winning strategy.
- Because a balanced fund combines stocks and bonds together, you can do little in terms of tax planning because you cannot separate the two components. Stocks have much different tax consequences than bonds, and purchasing the two components separately permits much more effective tax planning.
- The main reason why I don't recommend balanced funds is that a balanced fund pays absolutely no attention to your personal investment characteristics—the blueprint called an SIP&G that defines you as an investor. The proportion of stocks,

bonds, cash, and foreign investments that you own should match your risk profile, tax position, and other personal investor traits as outlined in your SIP&G. But owning a balanced fund means that the proportion of each asset can change at any time and that the money manager sets this mix without any consideration of your specific needs. You may be left with a level of equity exposure way beyond your comfort level.

In my opinion, rarely is there a situation where you should consider purchasing balanced funds. If you own any today, re-evaluate whether they are really suitable for your investing needs.

# 30

## Segregated funds with guaranteed principal are all the rage. Should I purchase some?

Seg funds are not for everyone. And even when they are suitable for you, you still have to sort out what amount/proportion to buy based on your financial big picture, as discussed in earlier questions.

Segregrated mutual funds appear to be like regular mutual funds, except they are offered with a life insurance wrapper, giving them special characteristics over regular mutual funds. Here is a summary of some of the most desirable characteristics of seg funds:

- Seg funds provide a guarantee that you will not lose your original principal over ten years. If you hold seg funds for a minimum of ten years, or if you die within that period, the original investment amount is guaranteed up to 100% in some cases. This can be attractive for investors truly in fear of losing money in the stock markets over the long term.
- Seg funds are a life insurance product. You can designate a beneficiary and avoid probate fees on your estate when you die. Mutual funds don't contain this feature. Your estate may have to pay as much as 1% in probate fees, depending on the laws in your province of residence.
- Seg funds can be purchased for creditor protection. Should you go bankrupt, the trustees selling off your assets to pay your creditors may not be able to liquidate your seg funds.

As attractive as many of the above benefits are, it is also necessary to examine the disadvantages of seg funds. Following are some of the common disadvantages:

- The cost of the fund, measured as the management expense ratio (MER), may be significantly higher on seg funds.
- The guarantee to not lose your original principal applies only if you don't cash in the funds for ten years, or if you die within that time. You can't receive distributions during the ten years. (A distribution is money allocated to you through a fund as a result of investing activity within the fund.) If you sell any amount of the funds within ten years, the amount sold will not be guaranteed. So is this guarantee worth the extra cost? Interestingly enough, when you look back into the history of the stock markets, you will not find many ten-year periods where an investor lost money! So, you may be paying extra fees for a guarantee that is worthless, assuming the market circumstances continue in the future.

- The probate fee advantage is not what it appears: You purchase a seg fund to avoid a one-time probate fee of 1%, yet the cost of the product will be several percent *each year*. This doesn't make good business sense. (See question 71 for a further discussion of seg funds and probate fees.)
- The creditor-proofing aspect of seg funds is not guaranteed. You might qualify, depending on your personal situation. Also, only a small percentage of Canadians, typically those in high-risk professions, go bankrupt. Buying seg funds for bankruptcy protection is, for most Canadians, something we don't really need.

If your gut feeling tells you to buy seg funds instead of regular mutual funds, do it if it will let you sleep at night! There is no doubt that seg funds offer a long-term safety net on your stock market investments and, ultimately, you must do what suits you best.

With the MERs (fees) of some seg funds approaching 4% a year, however, if you must purchase seg funds, at least purchase those that offer the possibility of returns significant enough to justify the high fees. Consider global equity funds, U.S. equity funds, and specialty funds such as high-tech funds. Don't buy seg bond funds or seg money market funds—it is almost impossible to lose money on these kinds of funds over the long term, and high MERs will eat up an already relatively low return.

Seg funds are good for certain types of people. Get a second opinion to find out whether you are one of these people.

# 31

## What is a wrap program?

Wrap programs are sophisticated investment programs offered primarily through full-service brokerages to certain clients. Wrap programs offer a disciplined investment process, a stable of handpicked money managers from around the world, better-than-average quarterly reporting information on your results, and one all-inclusive fee based on the assets invested in the program. There are two different types of wrap programs in Canada today: mutual fund wrap programs and individually managed account wrap programs. The specific characteristics of any wrap program will vary.

The following table highlights the differences between buying a collection of mutual funds individually and investing with several money managers in a wrap program.

Whether you belong in mutual funds or a wrap program depends on your personal characteristics and preferences. A thorough evaluation of these characteristics as they apply to specific investment programs is necessary before investors can conclude what is most appropriate for them.

# Individual Mutual Funds Versus Wrap Mutual Fund Programs

| Characteristics | Mutual Funds | Wrap Program |
|---|---|---|
| Selection of the particular manager to manage your money | Thousands of funds and managers to select from in Canada today | Program offers a select choice of 20 or more pre-screened managers who have usually been selected according to quality control criteria |
| Minimum starting investment amount | $100 | Around $50,000, depending on the type of program |
| Fee amounts | A wide range of fees with some reductions for larger investment amounts | Wide fee ranges with fee reductions for larger investments |
| Fee collection | Fees are netted against fund performance inside the fund | Fees may be collected on the outside of the program and can offer greater tax deductibility in some cases. Some fees may also be collected within the program. |
| Tax-effective investing | Tax disadvantages if investors buy into funds with high portfolio turnover. Tax-smart low-turnover funds also exist. | All wrap programs offer the same attributes of individual mutual funds. Tax effectiveness of products must be evaluated on a product-by-product basis. |
| Reporting of performance | Standard statements, which rarely show portfolio rate of return. | Advanced reporting that shows quarterly portfolio returns, usually with comparisons against benchmarks. |
| Objectivity on selection of products for your portfolio | You or your advisor is responsible for selection of products. Advisor may be biased to recommend funds that pay larger commissions. | Wrap money managers are often selected by external consulting firms with objectivity. Advisor earns same fees regardless of managers used, which removes the bias. Some wrap programs, however, include product options that are not objectively selected, so a careful evaluation is necessary. |
| How you pick money managers | Mutual fund money managers can be selected based on a disciplined review of your financial profile and risk tolerance. I recommend the preparation of an SIPG to create a blueprint for selection. | A disciplined and organized review of your financial profile and risk tolerance leading to a formal SIPG that is used as a blueprint for selection of money managers for your program. |
| Which option is better? | Savvy & educated investors can find great value in many instances with mutual funds. Custom building a portfolio using any funds you want offers greater flexibility and portability than any wrap program. | The quality of wrap programs can vary greatly according to the product. The only real advantage I see for wrap programs is advanced client reporting, some potential tax advantages, and lower minimum investment amounts for some money managers within the platform that you couldn't otherwise access. However, in some cases this better reporting also has a higher fee attached. The biggest disadvantage of many wrap programs is that they cannot be transferred to different institutions, leaving you unable to take your money out easily. |

# 32

## What kinds of wrap programs are available?

When you break it all down, a wrap is a different approach to buying traditional products. There are several types of wrap programs available: mutual fund wraps that carry regular mutual funds as the investment options; pooled fund wraps that also usually carry mutual funds as the product options; and individually managed wrap programs that utilize money managers to provide individual stock and bond portfolios for clients (not funds or pools).

In this strategy, I would like to explain wrap programs from a different angle.

## The affluent client wrap program

Many of the wrap programs emerging in Canada not only offer a new way to buy an old product, but they also bring with them a new investment management culture. This culture is a new way of conducting business for financial advisors, and a new investment experience for investors. Some would say it is just a new marketing spin, but that's unfair. It's much more than that in some cases.

For financial advisors, adding a wrap program to their product line-up can bring an element of sophistication to their product offerings. To a client, any old wrap program may provide this sophisticated look. However, to the knowing shopper, not all wrap programs are created equal.

Generally the affluent client wrap program offers product solutions that are truly different from (and better than?) other products widely available. In this category I generally include some individually managed account wrap programs. These individually managed account wrap programs (a.k.a. segregated accounts) bring the tax advantages of individual security ownership to a client with lower net worth (e.g., $100,000 or more) when otherwise this type of account would not be available without $1,000,000 or more. Add to this advanced client reporting features, tiered tax-deductible investment counsel fees, and the ability to access many above-average money managers through one platform, and you have the making of a high-class wrap program.

Affluent client wrap programs are not widely available to financial advisors in Canada, so they preserve an air that only special advisors can provide these products for their best clients. Beyond these investment products that appear to be novel when compared with mutual funds, investment dealers are also giving a complete makeover to their advisors and the way they give advice. After all, if you are going to offer a high-end product, you had better match it up with a high-end advisor.

This "repackaging" is enhanced when advisors change their title from financial advisor or broker to consultant or specialist, for example. Further, some institutions are giving their financial advisors detailed training in investment consulting so that they can learn what a "Statement of Investment Policy and Guidelines" is and how to consult on a money manager search and selection instead of "picking a fund." Essentially, financial advisors are converted from product pushers into professional consultants focused on giving advice. The process that financial advisors are taught is essentially the process highlighted in the first half of this book: a logical and disciplined approach to investing.

## The blue-collar wrap program

Many wrap programs now widely available in Canada aren't considered affluent client wrap programs, but instead serve the lower end of the market.

These programs repackage regular mutual funds or seg funds into bundles of funds that reflect the investor's needs. They offer the same mutual funds you can buy without a wrap in many cases, at often the same or higher fees. In the previous question I evaluated these mutual fund wrap programs against normal mutual funds. The largest advantage of a mutual fund wrap program is simply that it brings instant discipline and diversification to your investment portfolio. Such a program can be tremendously useful if your have no time to build your own portfolio properly, or if your financial advisor is reluctant to spend much time custom building your portfolio.

From the beginning, many of these mutual fund wrap programs have been positioned for clients with minimum investment amounts of $25,000 or more. But many institutions have this backwards—these products are more suitable for investors with *less* than $25,000. Financial advisors can seldom justify spending tremendous amounts of planning time on these small accounts. It is these small accounts that can benefit from the instantly organized solution of a mutual fund wrap program. Financial advisors earn their keep when they custom build mutual fund portfolios for the larger accounts. Using a mutual fund wrap program on larger accounts puts financial advisors in a precarious position of not offering much added value for their fee.

Mutual fund wrap programs are available from any licensed financial advisor and rarely require special advanced training or special credentials. This is different from the high-class wrap program for which not just any old advisor will do.

## The future of wraps

It seems that wrap programs are here to stay. In fact, they are now the fastest growing financial product in Canada. Some programs offer great money managers at great value. It's important to remember that not all programs offer these things. Carefully scrutinize what you are being sold and whether it is right for you.

# 33

## Can I have 100% foreign content in my RRSP or RRIF?

Technically, the foreign content limit on RRSPs and RRIFs is still limited to 30% (based on the original cost of the investments in the account), according to the Income Tax Act. However, several new mutual funds have been developed in the last few years—called *clone funds*—that qualify as Canadian content for your RRSP or RRIF (and do not contravene the foreign content rules), while the return generated by the fund is linked to a foreign investment that gives you foreign returns.

These clone funds use derivatives, such as forward contracts, to replicate foreign returns while not actually investing in foreign investments. With these derivatives, some of your money is invested in these contracts, while most of the money in the fund is held as cash (or near-cash securities) as collateral for the contract. In this way, the fund is technically never over the 30% foreign-content limit, yet your return is completely foreign based since it is generated from the forward contract. So you are provided with foreign diversification using a Canadian-based asset.

Many clone funds are available today for your RRSP or RRIF. A simple way to find them is to examine the title or name of a fund company's mutual funds. If the fund has "RSP" in the title, it usually means it is a foreign fund that is 100% RRSP eligible. Use these funds to maximize your RRSP foreign content far beyond 30%. Most Canadian fund companies now offer these clone funds.

Two words of caution, however: First, these funds often charge a higher MER as the price for greater foreign content. Select these foreign clone funds wisely to justify the increased cost. Generally limit your use of clone funds to international equity funds and foreign sector funds such as technology, health care, financial services, and telecommunications. These types of funds have high return potential, so they make a higher annual fee easier to swallow.

Second, the return on these clone funds is taxed as regular income and does not receive the tax benefits that a similar non-cloned foreign fund would offer if it generated capital gains. So use the clone funds only for RRSPs and RRIFs where all tax is sheltered, and use the similar real foreign funds for any taxable portfolio so that you can access any preferential tax aspects.

Would you like to get exceptional investment performance? If this is one of your main goals, owning equities or equity mutual funds that hold only a few stocks may generate big returns if you select the right investments.

Do you want to have a short-term volatility-dampened portfolio that is less stressful? Then build a diversified portfolio with exposure to every major asset class (cash, bonds, stocks); invest around the world and in Canada; invest in big companies and little ones together; hire several different money managers to manage different portfolio pieces, each money manager following a different investment mandate. Spreading your money around in this disciplined manner reduces your volatility and chances of a major loss.

Your SIP&G should integrate your specific financial needs with the characteristics of various asset classes (cash, bonds, stocks).

## Evaluate funds that fill these needs

Mutual funds are almost always categorized according to categories such as Canadian fixed income, Canadian equity, U.S. equity, small-cap equity, and so on. As an investor, you need to screen them all using fair criteria, and buy products or hire money managers with specific categories in proportion to fit your needs.

It doesn't matter which fund you look at, the criteria never change. That way you can easily compare both qualitative and quantitative factors:

## Qualitative criteria

The factors that create the money management organizational infrastructure and the company culture are far more important than performance, for it is these factors that, if put together appropriately, generate the long-term consistent performance we all want. These qualitative factors often require that you visit the manager's premises and "kick their tires" to complete the evaluation.

1. Capabilities of the money manager. Teams of highly qualified researchers and a large research budget are important to maintain the quality of investment selection.
2. Profitability of the money manager company. A well-financed money manager means enough money for research and equipment and happily paid employees.
3. Ownership structure of the money manager's company. Money management companies that offer share ownership in the company to money managers are preferred since the money manager is then more closely linked to the success of the company.
4. Rate of turnover of employees. A lot of employee turnover is a bad sign, especially if money managers and researchers are leaving.
5. Money manager's style and philosophy about investing. It is important to understand the manager's approach to investing—is it logical in your mind?

## Quantitative criteria

1. Five-year or ten-year historical performance. Any shorter time period may not be a fair evaluation of a manager's ability over business cycles.
2. Risk-adjusted return. It is necessary to analyze a manager's historical returns according to the amount of risk incurred. Risk can be measured by a variety of statistical methods available in Canada today.
3. Number of years that the money manager has managed the fund. If a fund has a great track record, is the current manager the one responsible for it?
4. Annual cost. Management expense ratios or MERs. Add load fees to this to see what you pay in total and then judge value.
5. Portfolio turnover. In your taxable portfolio, it makes sense to have a low turnover of 20% a year or less to maximize after-tax returns. Check out what your fund turnover is—the rate at which the manager buys and sells inside the fund each year (for example, turnover for a fund of 100% a year means the entire fund is changed in a year).

The choice for products in Canada is overwhelming today. Following a disciplined evaluation process, aided by a qualified financial advisor, can help to take the stress out of the evaluation process. Ensure that you are consistently following a quality due-diligence process to evaluate anything you buy or sell within your portfolio.

# RULE 5

## Carefully plan portfolio transitioning and who helps you to do it.

This section is all about trust and transition.

Trust: Now that you have an investment program and know what products to buy, what kind of financial advisor do you need? Which type of institution should you approach? Should you just do it all yourself? The landscape in Canada for purchasing investment products is becoming a collection of financial supermarkets—you can buy everyone's products everywhere, and the differences between institutions seem minimal. Sorting out which store you should deal with is a matter of prioritizing what is important to you. Is it service? If so, which services do you need? Is it price? Is it friendliness? The same goes for picking a financial advisor. There are many different types, and it falls on your shoulders to take the time to understand the differences.

Transition: If your current investment portfolio looks nothing like the new professional investment program highlighted on your Statement of Investment Policy and Guidelines, transitioning from the old to the new may not be simple. There are a variety of issues to think through, such as fees, taxes, and maturity dates on some investments. At a minimum, your transition plan should be well documented, showing your portfolio today, the changes needed, and what your portfolio will look like structurally in the future. Changes should be justified by fee evaluations, tax considerations, and all other constraints and characteristics of your portfolio. In the end, transition should not be rushed. It may take up to a few years before you have your new investment program fully implemented.

# 35

## Before I can implement a new investment program, what do I need to do with my existing portfolio?

Depending on what your new program involves, your existing investments may all fit, or some may fit, or none at all. Make sure due diligence is followed before deciding to blow out your entire portfolio. Transitioning an old portfolio into a new one can take years, depending on all the variables listed here. Even something as easy as a GIC may have a maturity date three years from now that prevents you from getting rid of it today. Other key variables are exit fees (particularly deferred sales charges to exit mutual funds) and taxes that may be triggered by dispositions. Closely evaluate these factors before you make a move.

You need to assess the quality and fit of your existing portfolios and their investment holdings within the new investment program. This involves an analysis of your existing holdings using a variety of criteria that are suitable for your situation.

**PAST PERFORMANCE.** It is important to review at least five years of past performance to get a feeling for how a money manager performs over time. In a shorter time period, anyone can get lucky or have a bad stretch.

- Have each of your portfolio investments performed better than a similar passively managed index during the same period? For example, have your blue-chip Canadian equity mutual funds consistently outperformed the TSE 300?
- Have each of your portfolio investments performed consistently better than a collection of peers in the same category over the same time horizon?
- Has the current money manager (for example, mutual fund manager) been responsible for the entire period of good performance? It is important to attribute performance to the managers that delivered it!

**FUTURE PERFORMANCE.** Qualitative factors of the money manager organization are more important than quantitative factors since the corporate infrastructure sets the tone for potential good future performance. Therefore, does the same infrastructure remain in place (same money managers, investment process, key management, strong market research, etc.) that resulted in the good past performance, so that the conditions are right to repeat prior successes? This information is hard to track down, and may require an interview of management at head office to get the answers.

**COST.** Are the annual fees and other costs of the product reasonable? For mutual funds these costs are stated in the fund prospectus. For other products there may be a fee schedule or it may be easier to ask your financial advisor.

**FEES TO DISPOSE.** Can you exit or sell the current products without incurring a whack of fees? If fees are high, it may warrant holding the investment longer until fees decline. A cost/benefit analysis would be required to decide on the appropriate timing for selling.

**TAX EFFICIENCY.** There are two parts to this criterion: First, is a sale of the product going to trigger a large tax liability that could be deferred if you didn't sell today? Second, is the investment tax smart to own on an ongoing basis in your taxable portfolio? (For example, if there are few distributions annually, this won't increase your tax bill.) Both of these factors could affect the timing of a sale depending on the magnitude of the tax implications.

**RISK.** Are your current investments too volatile or, conversely, not aggressive enough, based on your current financial profile defined in the Statement of Investment Policy and Guidelines? The answer requires an understanding of the return potential of the investment evaluated against the risk/volatility of the product. This risk/return evaluation integrated with your target investment return expectations is the start to assessing the level of aggressiveness you need in your investment products.

**DUPLICATION.** Get rid of unwanted duplication. If you own six Canadian equity mutual funds, for example, you may own shares of the XYZ Bank six times. This is potentially costly duplication that needs to be minimized.

Before you make wholesale changes to your plan, always get a second opinion on exactly what needs to be replaced in your portfolio. Such a dramatic shift in strategy may trigger taxes and/or fees, and warrants a second look before execution.

# 36

## After I build my investment program, should I invest all at once? That makes me nervous.

There are generally two schools of thought when it comes to investing and when to buy:

1. Wait until it feels right. Maybe markets are too high today and you plan to invest right after the next crash.
2. Invest immediately regardless of market conditions.

I support the second philosophy in most cases for long-term investors. Trying to guess which markets will be hot—and when—is next to impossible to do on a long-term consistent basis. Research has shown that in the past, you would have made far more money by just putting your money in the markets and leaving it there, ignoring the short-term ups and downs along the way. If your time horizon for investing is long enough it really doesn't matter what the markets are like today or tomorrow. Although the past is not indicative of the future, we have to use some method to judge strategy!

What makes this "invest now" philosophy difficult to swallow is that investors left on their own let their emotions get involved. Working with a financial advisor will ensure that logic and reason are not clouded by sudden emotion. The facts clearly show that historically over the long-term, there is no need to worry about what happens today or tomorrow if you are going to be invested for quite a while. No one knows when the markets will go up or down, but most experts believe that markets will generally go up over the long term. If you believe this, it is prudent simply to buy in and stay in!

## The trouble with an active market timer

The only real reason you might try to market time is the thrill of it—the chance for the big win. And sadly, over the long term, this thrill can result in less money, not more. There is no disputing that active market trading and trying to time the markets is sexy: You shift chunks of your savings around regularly as you try to avoid what is cold and chase what is hot. Investors follow the short-term movement of interest rates and other economic measures as they try to predict the next hot market. This approach is tax inefficient (when there is a lot of trading it is tax inefficient since it triggers realization of gains in taxable portfolios), expensive (trading commissions), and follows a herd mentality (when a market is hot, many investors may jump on the bandwagon to get some for themselves). These are not sound business principles to base an investment program on.

Ultimately, market timing and active trading means investing without discipline, logic, and an organized plan. Over time, this is not a recipe for success.

## A compromise

If you really would prefer not to invest all your cash right now because of your discomfort with market levels, but you also admit that you don't know what will happen with the markets tomorrow, you can choose to take a middle of the road strategy: Invest 20% of your money each month for the next five months. Or 10% of the total over ten months—whatever makes you comfortable. In this way you can ease into the markets by working towards your Statement of Investment Policy and Guidelines gradually.

# 37

**Does it make sense to spread my money around different institutions because I don't want any one financial advisor to know about everything I have?**

Yes and no.

It makes sense to have several different money managers each managing some of your wealth so that you can benefit from diversification—spreading your money around to mitigate the risk of a substantial loss. By investing with several managers (even within the same institution) there is less likelihood that you will suffer a substantial loss on all of your wealth since your money is spread out among several investments or managers. This is a good thing.

But it doesn't make sense to hold your different investments separately on different platforms. This means you should seek out a platform that can allow you to hold all of your investments together, even if they are from several different money managers. There are now many companies that permit you to hold all of your different investments in one account, or several accounts, through one institution. Think of these organizations like investment supermarkets where you can buy anything, from anyone, and that one organization holds it all for you.

Owning all of your investments on one platform has many benefits:

- It may be the first time you can view and manage all of your investments on one page. This leads to better overall portfolio management and helps to integrate all the pieces together.
- It will reduce the amount of paperwork you receive from all the investments. If you receive a lot of investment statements each month or quarter, from all your investments everywhere, it is difficult to know how well you are doing on an overall basis. Do you know your overall portfolio rate of return from last year? It is doubtful, if you have different investments from different financial advisors and companies.
- Combining your different investments onto one platform may result in fee breaks from having larger amounts of your wealth held in one spot. Many institutions give price reductions for larger investment accounts.

Consolidating your investments onto one platform has many merits. Technology today makes it possible to manage all of your investments as one, while continuing to invest with many money managers.

# 38

## How do I determine who are the right people to assist me with my personal finances?

Financial planner. Investment specialist. Private wealth consultant. Financial advisor. Insurance advisor. Registered financial planner. Certified investment manager. Private client advisor. Investment and insurance consultant. Certified financial planner. Personal financial advisor. Registered investment consultant. Broker. Insurance agent. Personal wealth manager. And then there are the designations: CA, RFP, CIM, FCSI, LLB, BA, CGA, CFA, CIMA, PFP, CFP, CHFC, etc. You may see any of these titles and designations on your financial advisor's business card today, and I could go on and on; the choice is overwhelming!

In Canada today there is little government regulation over who can call themselves a financial advisor. You can literally have been a geologist or a teacher last month, and be a financial planner managing people's life savings today. Without the regulations to ensure that any financial advisor is qualified, it's a scary world out there! Let's examine how you can find a qualified financial advisor, using a few simple screening criteria:

**ACADEMIC BACKGROUND.** Ask potential advisors about their schooling. Give more weight to a four-year university degree in finance or economics than to someone who is taking three months of night courses on the world of investing. Apply the same kinds of educational expectations to your financial advisor as you do to your doctor.

**WORK EXPERIENCE.** Ask potential advisors to outline their experience dealing with clients just like you. For example, if you are a senior executive with stock options, or a doctor, or a woman, or disabled, ask the financial advisor how many other clients they have in exactly the same situation. In addition, you want to choose an advisor with at least five years of relevant business experience. Watch out for any advisor who refers you to their junior assistant who isn't properly supervised. Find someone who wants your business and will take proper steps to help you.

**CREDENTIALS.** Research their credentials. All those fancy designations on a business card have been issued by an association somewhere. Call the association to find out if your proposed financial advisor is registered in good standing. And ask them what the designation is all about.

**PROFESSIONAL DEVELOPMENT.** Anyone with a professional designation today (doctors, accountants, financial planners) is required to constantly update their education as it relates to their profession. They must continue to take courses, read new materials, and attend seminars on new developments in their areas of expertise. Financial advisors are required to do this until they retire, and they have to report what they do each year to their professional association. Question your potential financial advisor about the associations they belong to, and what courses they took this year to maintain their credentials. If they have done nothing, or don't belong to a professional association, lose them.

**CLIENT REFERRALS.** Ask for 20 client referrals and choose some of them to investigate. If you only ask for three referrals, there is a greater chance that the financial advisor is referring you to best clients who would never say anything bad. By selecting three yourself, you have a greater chance of getting objective testimonials.

**FEES.** Financial advisors can earn a living from commissions generated by products or from charging you some form of advisory fee. Being paid through product commissions can make a financial advisor appear biased towards selling more product in order to generate those commissions. An advisory fee is more objective since the fee is charged for advice, not on products. Many financial advisors charge both types of fees for different services. Shop around to understand fee choices but be prepared to pay reasonable fees for good value.

**NUMBER OF CLIENTS.** Financial advisors with many clients aren't necessarily good financial advisors; they may just be good salespersons. With only 365 days in a year, and only 240 or so work days, a financial advisor with more than 500 clients is stretching thin the time commitment and service available to you.

**FAMILY/FRIEND REFERRALS.** Don't hire a financial advisor based only on a friend or relative referral. If your neighbour or your brother doesn't know how to properly research financial advisors, that won't help you. Don't rely on others to find your financial advisors—everyone's preferences are different, so do your own hunting.

The boom of the mutual fund industry in the 1990s saw many people change careers to become financial advisors. Without a strong regulatory quality standard around financial advisors (which doesn't exist currently), Canadians are exposed to poorly trained and inexperienced financial advisors who have questionable credibility to manage your money. So don't trust too easily. Ask questions and shop around.

# 39

## What types of financial advisors are there?

Earlier in this book I discussed integrating all aspects of your personal finances into one big picture. This integration of all your professional financial advisors and products can occur in two different ways:

1. You can work with a financial advisor who acts as a manager of managers, meeting with all of your financial advisors and integrating advice between your accountant, lawyer, and all other financial advisors involved with your finances. This advisor can also integrate your investments from all the various institutions you choose to invest with.
2. You can work with a financial advisor who can offer you a variety of financial services directly, saving you time and the cost of dealing with a variety of people.

Ultimately either of these approaches can work fine, and the one that is better for you depends on your preferences. However, I have a few words of warning.

### Your advisor as a manager of managers

This is a popular approach today. Many people are hiring an overall financial manager to manage all their affairs together. This approach is consistent with the integration concept of looking at all of your finances as one. An overall financial advisor of your affairs is in a position to know about all your issues, and can integrate solutions using the external advisors required (lawyer, accountant, money managers, etc.) and communicate results and plans with you. This generalist advisor overseeing a team of specialists can be an effective method of managing all of your affairs.

### Your advisor as a jack-of-all-trades

Beware of a financial advisor who is positioned as a jack-of-all-trades (that is, someone who alone can give you advice on investing, tax, estate, insurance, and other financial topics) without having the credentials and experience to back this up. It is almost impossible for one person to manage all of your personal finances effectively. It is important that all financial advisors recognize their professional limits and know when it is appropriate to engage specialist advisors for specific areas of your finances.

### The specialists

I recommend that you seek out specialists in each area of your finances, or an individual who is a specialist in some areas of your finances together. Add a general financial advisor overall to quarterback all of your affairs, including the coordination of all the professional financial advisors you might have occasion to use over time.

Why do I believe in specialists? Let me go back to my example from Rule 3. Suppose you had a heart attack and suddenly needed a transplant. Would you want a general practitioner, who is kind of good at a lot of different medical situations, to perform the operation? Or would you want a cardiac surgeon, who is a specialist in heart transplants and thoroughly understands all cardiac issues and complications because that is all he or she works in? Of course, you want the specialist. Treat your personal finances and investments the same way.

Here are some examples of specialists you could enlist for help with your finances:

**CHIEF FINANCIAL MANAGER.** Hire a generalist financial advisor who can bring all your specialist advisors together to provide integrated and coordinated advice.

**INVESTING.** Your financial advisor should assist in selection and monitoring of money managers you hire and fire. Hire professional money managers you find based on criteria listed earlier in this book. These money managers should work full time managing pieces of your money within a master plan, as defined by your Statement of Investment Policy and Guidelines.

**TAX PLANNING.** Do your own tax return, and have it reviewed by a tax accountant or a tax lawyer who knows income tax very well and deals with personal tax issues regularly. Alternatively, get a qualified tax professional to complete your tax return for you.

**ESTATE PLANNING.** Utilize a tax lawyer or a lawyer and a tax accountant to build a tax-effective will.

**INSURANCE.** Use a full-time insurance agent who thoroughly understands the entire marketplace of choice for insurance products and has many years of professional insurance experience.

**BASIC FINANCIAL PLANNING.** Utilize a financial planner who has practical experience preparing professional financial plans for many clients just like you.

In all cases, shop around, use the criteria explained above to screen, and always get a second opinion on your situation.

# 40

## I don't trust financial advisors with my investments. Can I do it myself instead?

After the dozens of articles in the last few years that sing the praises of being a do-it-yourself investor and the discount brokerage approach to investing, it is time to remind investors about the advantages of full-service financial advisors and the peace of mind they can bring to you regarding your personal finances.

Recently, a Canadian discount brokerage company asked me to speak to a room full of their account holders at an evening seminar on investing and taxation. By the end of the night two facts came to light that left me shaking my head and concerned about the volumes of Canadians who have recently become do-it-yourself investors:

First, when I looked out across the large audience, I was surprised at the large number of older Canadians in the audience. I was encouraged by the fact that all the attendees wanted to learn more about their finances, but I was also wondering if all these seniors had dreamed their entire lives about living out their retirement watching CNBC and stressed about their investments all day long—instead of enjoying a round of golf or playing with their grandchildren.

Second, I was worried about the lack of sophistication many of the investors demonstrated, based on the many questions I was asked. Clearly a large number of attendees were novice investors and new account holders out to learn more about investing. Yet these same people had their accounts open already and were actively investing their life savings on their own. It made me shudder to think of the great investment risks they were taking with so little knowledge—and at that moment I knew it was time to write about this topic.

## The sexiness of do-it-yourself investing

You just have to read the newspapers to see that discount brokerages are booming these days as Canadians flock to invest on their own. There are several reasons why investors are doing this:

- The rapid upward climb of the markets in recent years has made it appear that anyone can make money on the markets. The old saying, "when the tide rises, everyone's boat floats" was true of investing recently. The ease with which so many people made money in the markets lured many more to believe that it would always be easy to earn 20% per year. Long-time investors know better. New investors have found out the hard way that this is not always the case.
- The marketing makes it look easy. Several of the discount brokerages are spending millions on flashy ad campaigns designed to convince investors that do-it-yourself

investing is the only way to go. Canadians, hungry for new investment alternatives, are biting hard on these marketing campaigns, rushing to open new accounts.

- Word-of-mouth endorsements from those we trust (a neighbour, a friend, or a relative) often sway people to do things they may otherwise not do. Think twice before you follow advice from anyone other than a professional.

- Internet trading and Internet investing tools have made do-it-yourself investing as easy as point and click. This same simplicity also means that you can sit in your basement and lose your life savings. Thirty years of savings potentially lost in one click of a mouse.

- You've had at least one bad experience with a broker and think you can do better on your own. Horror stories in the papers about rogue brokers, your own bad experiences with financial advisors, and your search for the value you deserve may lead you to believe that you are your own best financial advisor. Despite this, the best question to ask yourself is, how did you end up with that financial advisor in the first place?

## The realities of do-it-yourself investing

Nothing is more important than your own accumulated savings, for without it you may end up spending your retirement in poverty. Your lifelong savings deserve full-time professional attention if you want to increase your likelihood of avoiding a lower standard of living in your senior years. It is naive to think that you can be your own savior by spending a few hours trading your account from your basement each week.

Here are more realities of do-it-yourself investing:

- Your competitors for the best products are formidable. When you buy and sell stocks and bonds you are competing against Canada's largest fund managers, pension managers, and other professional money managers, all backed by teams of university-trained researchers working around the clock to get the best prices and the best stocks on billions of dollars of assets—ahead of you. It may be very difficult for you on your own, in your basement, with your small account, to come out on top over the long term ahead of the pros. Sure, you might save some fees over the years from your do-it-yourself approach, but have you compromised more in lost returns and lost personal life?

- Professional money managers buying millions of dollars of stocks and bonds at once will be entitled to deep fee discounts on their purchases and sales. These fee discounts will often be far greater than individual investors could obtain on their own. These reduced costs can add to an investor's overall return. Enhancements such as this aren't always easily visible to the investor.

- Unless you have a few million dollars to invest in many different stock and bond investments, you cannot adequately diversify your portfolio by buying stocks and bonds on your own.
- It is unlikely that you thoroughly understand Canadian tax law or death taxation or can assess the legal risks and creditor risks as they may affect your investments. A professional financial advisor could assist in greater preservation of your investments by advising you on the many perils (taxes, legal threats, hidden fees) of wealth and how to avoid or minimize them.
- Without regular financial planning of your portfolio and your personal finances by a qualified financial advisor, it is questionable whether you will know if you are progressing towards your financial goals in the most efficient manner possible.
- As a do-it-yourself investor, you may pay excess taxation on your investments each year. Tax laws constantly change in Canada and unless you are on top of recent developments you may miss tax-planning opportunities as they relate to your investments. Further, it takes an understanding of how tax laws impact investment turnover, investment income, and capital gains and how different people and investments are taxed, to truly be able to minimize investment taxes and enhance after-tax net worth over the long term.
- The possibility of error is far greater when you invest on your own. If you have fired a previous financial advisor because of bad results or poor decisions, that was likely because you were monitoring their actions. As a do-it-yourself investor, who is monitoring you? Since you may have little training or no professional training on investing, the likelihood of errors is greater. And you may not know they are errors until it is too late! Find some way to get a second opinion on what you do even if you have to pay for it. You likely cannot afford to live through even one large error.
- Golf, vacationing, gardening, playing with grandchildren, and sailing are all things most people would rather be doing in their spare time or in their retirement. Yet, as a discount investor, you choose to deal with the stress of researching stocks and funds, executing trades, and spending countless hours on the computer or phone managing your investments each week. And your spouse may be forced to accommodate this lifestyle as well. Wouldn't it be more enjoyable for all if you pay a few bucks to let a competent professional worry about your investments and you go live your life the way you had always dreamed?
- Emotion is one of the reasons you are now investing on your own. At some point your emotions told you to fire an old financial advisor and do your planning yourself. Instead of finding another, more competent financial advisor, you chose the discount brokerage route. Yet the discount brokerage only cares about maximizing trades in your account: They don't care about your family or if you make or lose money; they won't hold your hand during market turmoil or call to see if everything

is alright; they don't even know what your name is, the way that a full-service financial advisor can get to know you personally. It doesn't get more cold and impersonal than this. In a world where service is sometimes the only differentiator among choices, it is foolish to choose a discount brokerage option.

- It is almost impossible to be objective in your own investing, and this could hurt you. On your own, you will be far more sensitive to trading your life savings. Your heart will race with every market downtick. You may end up watching the markets constantly and fretting. You may even worry about who will manage the money after you pass away and your spouse is left alone. Having a full-service financial advisor at your side as a voice of reason, an objective outsider focused on analytical and logical investing strategies, can serve as a lighthouse in a raging storm of up-and-down markets. Financial advisors are far more likely to invest with discipline over the long term. Their guidance is invaluable.

- Accessibility to your money matters. The next time the markets come crashing down, and you know it will happen sometime, how easy will it be to get at your money when you use a discount brokerage account? You and a million others may try to access the discount brokerage Internet site and not be able to get through for hours. Phone lines may be busy or leave you on hold forever. Telephone financial advisors may lack judgement or professional expertise, and worst of all, they just don't know you. You go through all of this while the markets tick lower, costing you more money. Your full-service financial advisor will always be a better safety net—someone who is accessible from wherever you are in the world, someone who will champion your needs and get things done. That comfort level is hard to replace.

- A discount brokerage approach may lack a "big picture" focus to your investment strategy. Too many Canadians fail to integrate their investment planning with their tax planning, estate planning, employment situation, cash flow needs, and other aspects of their personal finances. Long before investment products are even discussed, investors need to get to a higher level first and evaluate their big-picture financial needs. Investment products are one solution, but they aren't the process. The risks of not planning are many: buying the wrong products, missing your financial goals, taking on more risk than you can tolerate, incurring avoidable losses, and other problems. Most discount brokerages do not typically offer these value-added planning techniques—they simply help you research and trade products.

- With markets now returning to normal, it should be easier to differentiate the pros from the amateurs. How will you fare? Long-term historical stock market returns have averaged around 10% globally, not the 30%+ many investors now expect annually. A lot of discount investors continue to have unrealistic expectations of return, setting themselves up for disappointment and the possibility of not reaching their financial goals. Many professional financial advisors demonstrate their value in their ability not to lose money in bad times in addition to their ability to make money in the good times. They can also revisit your plans on an ongoing basis and make adjustments with you to stay on track towards your goals. For amateur investors, this safety net feature is a powerful incentive and offers you peace of mind.

- Never swear off an entire company because you encounter one bad financial advisor. The onus is on you to find a good financial advisor. How much due diligence did you do on the bad financial advisor before you hired him? Did you verify professional credentials and relevant work experience? Did you talk to at least five of his existing clients? Did you research his investment approach, his access to research, and validated past performance statistics? Did you look into the company? Did you agree to a package of services and a fee level that matched your preferences before you hired the advisor? Most importantly, did you evaluate the pros and cons of several financial advisors together? And always get a second opinion on your thoughts given the magnitude of your decision!

## The results of using a discount brokerage for your investing needs

For many of you, it may be too early to make conclusions about your long-term success in using a discount brokerage and being a do-it-yourself investor. The discount environment has really exploded in only the last ten years, and that's not enough time to determine if you will make it on your own. But research has shown that chances are slim that you will be able to keep up double-digit compounded returns over the long term the way the pros do. And even if you do, at what sacrifice to your personal life?

Having a discount brokerage account and being a do-it-yourself investor can be fun. Being a do-it-yourself investor will also enhance your investment education and knowledge, and make you a better investor overall. This is something to encourage.

If you truly treat discount investing as a hobby, have a small account with only a small portion of your overall wealth, limit your time involvement, pay attention to tax implications, build your portfolio into your overall financial plan with a big-picture focus, and let your full-service financial advisor give you second opinions and monitor your performance, then enjoy being a do-it-yourself investor! Everyone who enjoys the thrill of playing the markets should find a small way to do so, as long as it is controlled.

However, every Canadian investor can benefit from having a full-service financial advisor. The key is finding a credible, professional financial advisor who provides value and peace of mind in your personal finances. Take the time to evaluate professional financial advisors according to the hard criteria mentioned above and think twice before moving all your assets to a discount broker—it may be the most important financial decision you ever make.

# 41

## Some investors ignore investment fees, while others do everything it takes to minimize fees. Which is the right approach?

The right approach to fees depends on the type of investor you are. But generally everyone should be fee sensitive and care about value. There are two different kinds of investor, and you need to decide which you are:

1.  Do-it-yourself investors. These are people who are prepared to do their own investment research on what to buy and sell; they may chat on the Internet with other investors for opinions on stocks and funds; they may attend evening seminars, where they hear the perspectives of analysts and fund managers. Do-it-yourself investors rely on themselves for their investing needs and deserve fee breaks to reflect the do-it-yourself approach. A do-it-yourself approach may or may not also include doing your own tax planning, estate planning, insurance needs analysis, retirement forecasting, etc.

2.  Investors who use financial advisors. If you don't want to be completely responsible for your investments and your personal finances, then you are going to need to develop a relationship with a financial advisor of one kind or another. The type and extent of the relationship will depend on your needs, and the greater your needs, the higher the cost. Here are some questions you will need to ask yourself when searching for the kind of financial advisor suitable to you:

    *   How often do I want to talk to/see my financial advisor?
    *   Do I want them to provide investment research and buy/sell advice, and build a portfolio for me, or only some of this?
    *   Do I also want my financial advisor to provide financial planning advice on my retirement, estate, insurance, and other areas of my personal finances?
    *   Do I want my financial advisor to consult me on tax planning and do my tax return?
    *   Do I want to meet my financial advisor at my home or at his or her office?
    *   Do I want to give my financial advisor all of my investment money or only a small piece?

These are a few of the questions that will lead you to focus on the type of advisory relationship you want and need from a financial advisor. There are hundreds of advisory services available in Canada today, each offering a slight variation on service, and at many different prices.

More than once I have heard clients say, "I'm not paying $500 for that advice when I can download it off the Internet for free." This very much exemplifies the state of the investment industry in Canada today, where more and more services are being offered for free or at low prices, making it harder for full-service advisors to get paid fairly. Good advisors can add a lot of value to the average investor/consumer and deserve compensation for this role.

It all comes back to my opening statement that clients need to define what kind of investor they are, and then price it accordingly. If you need a financial advisor for advice or simply to hold your hand during ups and downs, then you should be willing to pay something for this financial advisor's time and expertise.

# 42

**There is a lot of pressure for investment fees to come down in Canada today. What do you have to say about fees?**

Paying high fees for personal advice is okay, provided you receive good value for your money. Is value being provided for the cost? Most Canadians do not fully explore what value they get for whatever fees they pay.

Seeking the lowest cost provider can be very dangerous. Would you purchase the cheapest prescription drug if it does not heal you, or would you prefer to purchase the drug that will be the most effective? The same thing goes for your financial advisor. Put the time in to define what you want from a financial advisor and comparison shop to determine whom to hire.

I think Canadians in general are somewhat in the dark about the total cost of their financial services provider. We often refuse to ask fee questions when it comes to investing with a financial advisor. Yet it is impossible to judge the value of your financial advisor or products without knowing the costs!

## The new fee-based culture

The trend in Canadian financial services today is to replace transactional mutual fund load fees and stock commissions with one all-inclusive fee that is charged annually as a percentage of the assets invested. The fee is calculated on the total market value of the assets in your investment account. This fee-based account billing approach can be more objective because there is no incentive for a financial advisor to trade your portfolio more frequently than necessary to generate commissions. Now the fee a financial advisor collects is based on the growth of your assets overall so that you and your financial advisor make money together. This fee approach aligns your goals more effectively with financial advisor motivation and compensation.

Another trend happening in Canada is a general fee reduction due to the commoditization of advice. Not so many years ago, full-service advisors would charge 3% of the market value of a trade to buy stocks for clients. Today, you can buy stocks yourself on the Internet for as low as $9.99, a fraction of the previous cost. This reduction in fees has benefited the investor, but in some cases has made it difficult for the full-service advisor to survive. And fee-sensitive investors are taking their low fee expectations to full-service providers demanding fee reductions. Full-service providers are dropping their fees just to keep their clients. This is unfair if the full-service advisor is providing good value.

Many financial advisors and institutions are including more and more services bundled along with their investment services and products. For example, you can have all your investment needs taken care of, as well as your insurance needs and estate planning in some cases, under one roof for one fee. This leads many investors to expect many types of financial planning for free in the marketplace, and makes it hard for some financial advisors to charge for preparation of a financial plan. Just remember that when you get something for free, you get what you paid for! The quality of the work may be questionable. Cutting corners on your personal finance issues can be dangerous and costly.

On the tax efficiency of fees, it is generally preferable to have no fees charged at all on any investments within an RRSP in order to preserve the value of your RRSP. Specifically, it is not desirable to use tax-sheltered money to pay any kind of fee. If you do not take fees from investment products inside your RRSP or RRIF, it preserves the capital in the plan, thereby maximizing your tax-deferred growth. If possible, write a cheque from your regular savings to pay RRSP investment fees.

In a taxable account, whether the annual fees are charged inside a mutual fund (the MER, which is netted against fund performance) or outside of the investment product (such as investment counsel fees, which are deducted on your personal tax return), the fees are tax deductible and result in a similar benefit. The only real difference is the location of the fee. Although some financial advisors preach the greater tax deductibility of externally charged fees, it is important to recognize that the external fee may not be an advantage at all. It depends on the situation.

Much has been made in the last few years about the high costs of investing and investment products. While in some cases there are abuses and fees are simply too high, I believe it is more about value than cost. If tremendous value is being provided for a high fee, and you are pleased with this, I think this is acceptable.

The financial press will often praise the merits of finding the cheapest products and the cheapest way to buy and sell products. Unfortunately, it is causing some Canadians who are well served by the abilities of a professional advisor to run away from them. Bottom line, value from your financial advisor matters most.

# 43

## Is it true that I need a full-blown financial review at least once a year? This seems too often.

That's not too often. Actually, you would probably benefit from a review more frequently.

There are many reasons why you need to review your investments, and all other parts of your personal finances, on a proactive basis at least once a year. I am talking about a comprehensive review of your entire financial picture (compared with a review of your investments, discussed in the answer to question 45). Financial goals, taxes, savings, cash flow, and so on should be re-examined to ensure your plans continue to reflect your changing life. The following are some reasons to complete a broad financial review regularly:

- Changes to the Income Tax Act that can occur any business day of the year and may impact the level of taxes you pay, highlight new tax planning strategies for your situation, or affect the tax you incur on your investments. A once-a-year review of your tax situation can result in substantial savings.
- In a short period of time, your money manager or your investments can erode. What were solid investment picks one day can break down over time, or overnight.
- An annual review may be the time to examine investment considerations for new money added to your portfolio. And even if there is no new money, new developments in investments require a constant re-evaluation of whether some of the new products are better suited to your needs than current holdings.
- As you age, your financial profile may change, warranting adjustment to your portfolio holdings. For example, when you retire, often your portfolio changes from being growth oriented to income oriented, since in retirement you will need to draw an income. Such a change in profile usually requires a significant revision to your SIP&G.
- Market conditions will make parts of your portfolio rise and fall, moving your original asset class allocations away from your SIP&G benchmarks. Regular rebalancing of your portfolio may be desirable to move the portfolio back to your benchmarks.
- On a regular basis, it is necessary for you to evaluate progress towards your financial goals or your retirement. This is accomplished for your retirement by annually forecasting your savings growth into the future using assumed rates of return and inflation to predict the amount of money needed to meet your goals. This exercise can be accomplished at your annual review.
- Other changes to your financial profile may warrant changes to your portfolio or other financial planning work. For example, you may change jobs, get married, have a baby, move to another province, or get divorced. Each of these personal events would require changes to your personal finances and maybe your investment

# RULE 6

**Regular checkups and changes to your financial strategies and products are a must to ensure that y are on track.**

Regular monitoring of your investment portfolio is not something to be taken lot can go wrong with your portfolio, as early as the day after you put it ir Financial advisors should understand that it is their role to watch over your fi ensure that you are up to date and on track, and that strategies and products co reflect your situation.

Measurement and monitoring of your financial situation and investment p a science. Clear standards must be set that you can use to evaluate your product Frequency of evaluation is also important: The time period must be long eno able to evaluate changes, but not so long that opportunities are missed. Evaluatio investment products should consist of both qualitative and quantitative presented regularly by your financial advisor.

## Monitoring your investments means monitoring more than investments

Since your investment portfolio is affected by all the other areas of your fin important to track changes to those other areas for their impact on your portfo ment, taxes, cash flow, etc.) In today's busy world, it is easy to invest and forget being proactive throughout every year is critical to ensuring your finances investments remain up to date.

portfolio. However, when these major life changes occur, don't wait for your annual review to deal with them: Deal with them immediately.

- Financial performance of your investments should be reviewed more often than once a year, but perhaps at your annual meeting with your financial advisor a more thorough evaluation of your investments can be conducted.
- Investment fees on products you own can change over time. Take steps regularly to understand what fees you are paying and why.
- New court cases and changes to provincial and federal laws can affect everything from your will to home ownership. It is downright dangerous not to update your will on a regular basis, especially when an error can result in hardship for your heirs.
- Whether you have a smooth annual income source or volatile incoming cash flow year to year, regular rethinking about the amount of money you get, and how you get it, is critical.

If your meetings with your financial advisor include only a review of investment performance, then it's time to expand the advice to include all of these other things that are also important.

# 44

## I invested in a great money management solution. Should I revisit this plan anytime soon?

Any great money manager can fall apart over time for a variety of reasons. Don't be fooled into believing that today's great money managers will be superstars forever, year after year. Tomorrow, you could read in the newspaper that the entire management team of your favourite mutual fund is leaving the company to start up their own company with new mutual funds, and that the fund you are in will now be managed by someone just out of university. It can happen. No money manager is a guaranteed safe investment. So you need to take care of your investments and revisit your investment program regularly!

You need to proactively monitor and evaluate all investment solutions on an ongoing basis for various reasons:

- Good investments can go bad.
- New investments may evolve and be more suitable for you.
- Investment rules and government regulations may change.
- Your investment profile may change (for example, you become more/less risk tolerant, or your portfolio cash flow needs may change).
- Good or bad market conditions may warrant rebalancing in your portfolio to move the mix of investments back towards your desired Statement of Investment Policy and Guidelines.
- Other aspects of your personal finances may change requiring adjustment to your investment program and SIP&G. For example, new tax rules may affect the tax-effectiveness of your investment strategy.

These are just a sample of reasons why your investment portfolio and your broader personal finances require constant, regular, and proactive attention. I suggest that your entire financial picture should be reviewed thoroughly once a year (for new opportunities and to check on the status of current plans), and your investment portfolio should be reviewed three times a year.

## Dangers of excessive monitoring

There are many investors who track their investments daily and panic whenever they see the market move downward. While monitoring investment performance is important, don't overreact to short-term performance volatility because of market conditions. The need for ongoing measurement and monitoring of investment solutions is critical and best done by a professional financial advisor on your behalf. A watchdog service over your finances by a professional provides valuable peace of mind. And life is too short for you to be spending time on this type of activity. Do yourself a favour—turn off CNBC and stop reading the mutual fund reports each day.

## Dangers of undermonitoring

There is an equal danger of not paying enough attention to your investment portfolio and your overall finances. Many investors have hired financial advisors who visit their clients once every two years or less. If an advisor is too busy or doesn't treat your account as a priority, this may lead to dangerous neglect of your accounts. Constant and serious monitoring of your money must occur behind the scenes all year long, every year. Ensure that someone is doing this effectively on your behalf.

# 45

## If a money manager has three years of bad performance, should I sell?

It is not wise to sell on poor short-term performance, which I define as three years or less. Sale of a product or firing of a money manager should be completed based on far more than poor short-term performance alone. As discussed in other questions, the success of a money manager is judged by a collection of qualitative and quantitative factors, of which performance is only one variable.

Selling based on bad short-term performance is a form of market timing since it is a gut reaction based more on emotion than logic. And it has been proven that market timing doesn't work over the long term because of the impossibility of predicting where the markets will go. Trading your investments based on emotion leaves you without any kind of logic within your investment program. If you are selling today based on a guess, how long will it be before once again you are doing the same thing? Build a program, hire money managers for specific needs, and stick with them unless there are valid reasons to sell.

Your Statement of Investment Policy and Guidelines serves to formalize your investment needs, setting parameters around the overall program. As much as possible you should try to stick to this program, as it is constructed with your goals in mind. Circumventing the program by yanking your cash out during volatile times voids the program's usefulness.

Importantly, short-term and long-term performance is a function of a money manager's management style interacting with market conditions at a particular time in a business cycle. If you hired a small-cap growth manager, and small cap growth companies underperformed based on current market conditions, you may have had a poor three-year performance. But you hired a small-cap growth manager alongside all your other money managers using different management styles and focusing on different industries because you knew that when some of your money managers would be up, some of them would be down—yet your portfolio would end up with a smoother overall performance. Never sell an underperforming money manager or product that is fundamentally sound and is investing exactly the way you wanted!

If a new and inexperienced money manager takes charge of your existing mutual fund, that may be a good reason to sell if the manager has an unproven track record. If the fund changes its investment style, that may also be a reason to sell. And if the money manager organization is losing staff to competitors that may be a reason to sell. But short-term underperformance is not a reason to sell if a quality money manager is structurally intact, following the original investment mandate, and simply suffering through a period where the management style is not working well with the business conditions of the day. Hire and fire managers based on qualitative factors, not on numbers alone.

## Overweighting sectors based on timing can be very dangerous

Generally, be very cautious about selling one investment that is playing a specific role in part of your portfolio to chase performance by overweighting another part of your portfolio. Leaving holes in your portfolio and overweighting other categories can dangerously increase your risk exposure beyond your tolerance threshold, and it can hurt your long-term investment returns if fortunes reverse. Build a professional investment program with a SIP&G and stick to it.

In the late 1990s, many investors slowly accumulated more money in technology investments than in most other categories. Any SIP&G in place was ignored and money crept into the technology investments at amounts far beyond the risk tolerance levels and the target investment return requirements needed by the investor. We all know how this story ended, with tech stocks falling back to earth and many people left with losses.

## Reasons to sell

Below are examples of reasons to sell an investment product or fire a money manager. Note that each of these factors alone may not be enough to cause a sale, but two or more of these factors combined increase the likelihood that a sale is necessary.

- Money manager is underperforming a peer group of similar money managers for an extended period, generally three years or more;
- Money manager organization is in financial trouble;
- Money manager organization is undergoing internal troubles, such as key employees departing, disagreements on how to run the company, lack of consensus on the future direction of the company, or unhappiness over cost-cutting measures or compensation;
- Budget cutting within the money manager organization leads to underfunding of money manager research;
- The money manager constantly changes investment style when you had hired the manager to maintain a specific investment style. For example, if you had purchased a mutual fund where the fund buys large Canadian stocks using a growth style, and the fund starts to buy small, riskier Canadian stocks, this may not be desirable.

## Two more acceptable reasons to sell a product or fire a money manager

There are at least two acceptable times when a product should be sold based on poor *short-term* performance:

1. Sometimes you need to sell a product when your financial circumstances have changed such that your SIP&G must be revised to reflect your new realities. For example, if you retire, you may require more income from your portfolio than ever before. If you have only equity money managers/products within your portfolio, you may need to replace some of the growth products with income-generating products or money managers.

2. In some cases, it may be advantageous to sell a product in a loss position in order to trigger realization of the loss. Capital losses can be applied against capital gains that are also realized, and only the net is taxable in the hands of the investor. This tax strategy can be very valuable to minimize investment taxation, but should only be considered in the context of overall portfolio objectives. Additionally, any product sold should be sold because it is a poor investment overall, not just for tax reasons.

The sale of a product or firing of a money manager should not be taken lightly. Ensure that removal of a product from your portfolio is done for structural and logical reasons, not on emotion.

# 46

## Some institutions and investment programs offer regular and/or automated portfolio rebalancing regularly. What is this, and why is it needed?

In earlier questions, I talked about how every investor should have a written Statement of Investment Policy and Guidelines that matches their personal financial situation. So, for example, someone might have a blueprint for all of their and their spouse's investments that looks like this:

| Asset Class | SIP&G Recommended Allocation | Permitted Range |
| --- | --- | --- |
| Cash | 5% | 0–10% |
| Fixed income | 45% | 40–60% |
| Canadian equity | 10% | 5–10% |
| U.S. equity | 30% | 30–40% |
| International equity | 10% | 5–20% |
| Total | 100% | |

The permitted range outlines the acceptable levels that each asset class can rise and fall before rebalancing could occur to bring weightings back to the SIP&G recommendations. These ranges keep allocations within the desired ranges according to your profile. They have little or nothing to do with market timing guesses and bets.

Let's say that six months later, due to rises and falls in the markets, your asset mix looks like this for all investment accounts on a consolidated basis:

| | |
| --- | --- |
| Cash | 4% |
| Fixed income | 38% |
| Canadian equity | 12% |
| U.S. equity | 42% |
| International equity | 4% |
| Total | 100% |

Let's say you originally put 30% of your total wealth in U.S. equities and the market rose high enough that your percentage of U.S. equities according to market value became 42% of your total portfolios. Your SIP&G would suggest that you rebalance back to the recommended percentages of your original SIP&G because this level is outside the permitted range of what defines you as an investor.

## Two views about rebalancing the portfolio back to within the policy range

### Yes to rebalancing...

Rebalancing the portfolio back towards your SIP&G could be appropriate for several reasons. For example,

- Since your SIP&G is set to match your specific needs from the asset classes based on your investor profile, moving too far from the SIP&G could mean too much equity for your comfort level.
- Rebalancing typically forces an investor to sell high and buy low. This is counter to what many emotional investors tend to do, when they lose money by selling at market lows.

To rebalance in this scenario, you would sell 12% of your weighting in U.S. equities and purchase other asset classes as follows:

| | | |
|---|---|---|
| U.S. equity | −12% | (sell 12% of value) |
| Cash | +1% | (purchase 1% of value) |
| Fixed income | +7% | |
| Canadian equity | −2% | |
| International equity | +6% | |

Many institutions today offer a rebalancing service for your portfolio that can be manually done, or can be automatically done by computer. These can both be convenient services; however, be wary of the extra fees charged for the process.

### No to rebalancing...

There is also a good argument for never rebalancing your portfolio, and instead letting your successes grow forever. This could mean significant holdings of whatever you buy and potentially large amounts of equities or equity funds that could lead to significant accumulated wealth—after all, why sell a successful investment?

Rebalancing may trigger capital gains taxes if you are selling an asset with an appreciated value in a taxable account. This loss of wealth due to taxes incurred each time you rebalance will reduce the amount of wealth you have in the long term.

### The conclusion about rebalancing

Whether you rebalance your portfolio back to your SIP&G is a personal choice. On one hand, there may be taxes incurred that reduce long-term wealth overall. On the other hand is the discomfort of short-term volatility associated with owning significant equity holdings over time. Investors must reconcile their preferences and tolerances and do what is right for them.

# 47

## How can I get greater control over my personal finances?

Everyone should spend time each year focusing on personal finances. Some issues, like tax planning and investing, must be dealt with more frequently; while other issues, like estate planning and analysis of insurance needs, require less frequent attention.

The following is a general schedule that outlines the frequency with which you should turn your attention to your finances:

- Investing. Review investment performance up to three times a year at most. Note that this is a monitoring review only, not necessarily a need to change your investments.
- Taxes. Focus specifically on tax planning once a year to examine for new opportunities. Note that this tax planning review is not the same as preparing your tax return.
- Insurance. Life and disability insurance is generally an issue at specific times during your life, rather than during a calendar year. For example, having a baby may warrant new life insurance. Review your insurance levels every few years. Otherwise, limit analysis to specific life events.
- Cash-flow maintenance. Your need for an income can warrant almost weekly review of the structure of your cash flows, their tax effect, and their timing.
- Estate. Update your will every few years, or when life events change your personal circumstances. For example, divorce usually necessitates a change to your will.
- Retirement. In your pre-retirement years, annually gauge your progress towards your retirement financial goals and your need to tweak your strategies.
- Your financial big picture. Once a year, get above it all. Look down on your entire financial gameplan and assess its effectiveness in an integrated and comprehensive fashion. This may be the most important aspect of planning you can do, yet it is often overlooked. Note that having regular checkups is a good start, but that urgent matters should not wait for scheduled reviews. If you have a sudden life event that affects your finances, or if an investment falls apart, make time immediately to deal with the issues.

What does gaining control over your personal finances entail?

- Communicating effectively. Regular, proactive communication with your financial advisors is essential in order for you to know what is going on and what new opportunities lie ahead.
- Understanding options and recommendations. If you take time for financial education, ask why you are buying a product, and encourage your family to get financially "with it," you will become more comfortable with—and knowledgeable about—

financial strategies that you implement. When markets fall, you will be more tolerant if you are more informed.

- Trusting cautiously. Financial advisors should earn your trust and respect. Not every bank teller is an experienced financial expert who can advise you in your affairs. Practise due diligence, establish expectations, measure them, shop around, and re-evaluate your advisors regularly.
- Learning about finances on your own. The Internet, financial magazines, seminars, and other media offer ample opportunities to learn about money. It doesn't take long to learn enough basic personal finance to be a more informed consumer.
- Understanding what is happening financially. Many financial advisors are more than happy to embrace your desire to learn. If they are not prepared to explain strategies and products thoroughly, question why you hired them.

The financial world is very complicated today. It is easy to tune out and leave the issues to your financial advisor or to ignore them completely, but you cannot afford to do that. Money is the centre of your financial future, and your stewardship of it matters. Become informed. Ask questions. You are the best guardian of your finances.

# RULE 7

## Be proactive about tax reduction in every aspect of your finances every year.

Many people hate taxes more than they love investing. This effectively makes tax planning the most popular and valuable area of personal financial planning. In deciding my own career path, I knew early on that providing tax advice was a valuable service to offer and decided to become a Tax Specialist Chartered Accountant.

Canadians have some of the highest income tax rates in the world. Worse, taxes reach into every corner of our lives. Income tax alone touches all aspects of our personal finances. You need a tax specialist who can ensure you stay on top of tax planning opportunities as your life changes and as the tax rules change.

Here are some examples of how taxes affect your life:

- Your salary or wages are reduced by income tax.
- Your investment savings have a variety of possible tax consequences.
- Effectively saving for your children's futures is complicated by tax implications.
- There are many estate tax issues when you die.
- Marriage and birth create more tax issues.
- Different life and disability insurance policies have different tax implications.
- Leaving a province or leaving the country opens up more tax issues and strategies.
- In retirement you should be focusing on maximizing after-tax cash flow.
- RRSP contributions and deductions should be carefully planned to minimize tax.

As you can see, it is almost impossible to avoid tax issues within your personal finances at any point in your life. Tax is everywhere, and good tax advice is fundamentally critical to your everyday life. In a country where the top marginal tax rate is almost 50% in some provinces, finding even one small tax break can add up to big savings.

Tax planning is about more than preparing a tax return. Far more, as you will see in this section. I have provided a sample of key tax-planning strategies—only a small fraction of the planning opportunities out there. It is important to note that tax planning is not something you do once and forget about. The tax rules change constantly, requiring regular tax planning reviews for new opportunities.

# 48

## I pay a lot of income tax each year. Is there something I can do about it?

Income taxes may be the single largest expenditure average Canadians make during their lifetime, and income tax planning is the most important form of financial planning among them all—at least as important as investing. Yet people spend far more time on their investments than on their taxes. In my opinion, every Canadian should regularly seek out and take advantage of tax planning. You cannot afford not to.

Tax planning entails examining the rules of the Income Tax Act and looking for strategies that benefit your personal situation. However, tax strategies that reduce your tax bill do not fall into your lap; you must hunt them out. Finding lucrative tax strategies involves two steps, to be taken at least once a year:

1. Hire a tax specialist to review your situation—a professional financial advisor well experienced with the Income Tax Act.
2. Review the financial aspects of your life for tax-planning opportunities.

Tax planning has nothing to do with preparing your tax return. You will find no tax strategies just by preparing your tax return alone. You need to do more. You need a regular tax planning checkup.

## The importance of tax planning

Taxes permeate almost every aspect of our personal finances. When most people think about taxes, they think only about the income taxes taken off their paycheque. But that is only the start of taxes. What follows is a list of areas of your personal finances that are affected by the tax collector:

**DEATH.** Death is one of the biggest tax events of your life. Your executor will be faced with filing multiple tax returns on your death. Different tax rules apply in the year of dying, and different tax strategies apply upon death. Often an individual's tax bill rises significantly in the year of death. Death tax planning and pre-death tax planning are some of the most important tax planning you can do.

**ESTATE.** Preparing your estate and will for your death should involve tax planning as much as it should involve how to divide your estate. Different assets of your net worth face different tax rules upon death. Passing assets to your heirs upon death involves the taxes of your heirs as well, warranting greater tax planning. Proper tax planning in your estate can often greatly enhance inheritances. A tax specialist is just as important as a lawyer in planning your estate.

**INVESTMENT.** Far too many investors focus solely on maximizing total return, which is generally the return you see published in the newspapers. For a taxable investor, far greater attention should be paid to after-tax returns, because that is what matters most. Tax planning should be one of the most important aspects of your investing. Tax planning should be a key criterion when considering purchase or sale of investments. Tax planning should be considered when deciding how to structure income streams from your portfolio. There are dozens of ways that tax planning should be built into your investments that can enhance your after-tax returns. See my previous book, *50 Tax Smart Investing Strategies.*

**CASH FLOW.** The amount of cash flow you earn each year and the type of cash flow you earn are affected by taxes. Tax planning for your income streams can help to increase the after-tax cash flow you receive. Whether maximizing your RRIF flows or preserving government benefits, much can be done in tax planning to increase your bank account.

**CHILDREN AND GRANDCHILDREN.** Having children can greatly affect your tax situation and provide wonderful tax breaks. Just don't go so far as to have children just for the tax breaks! From tuition tax credits to income-splitting opportunities among family members, there are many different tax strategies that can be utilized with children.

**INSURANCE.** All of us have some need for some life or disability insurance during our lives. Tax again plays a role. Different insurance policies have different tax implications, making it necessary to evaluate the tax consequences of all insurance products you consider.

**EMPLOYMENT.** A lot of tax is deducted from your paycheque during each pay period. Employees, professionals, and business owners have numerous tax planning opportunities that can result in reduced employment taxation. A tax specialist can help anyone understand how employment affairs can be structured to reduce taxes.

As you can see, taxes touch every element of our financial lives. Tax planning, and regular use of a tax specialist can be one of the smartest financial strategies you ever undertake. Take steps today to get tax planning help—more than getting your tax return prepared!

# 49

**April 30 is the key tax date in my mind each year. Why do you think I should think about tax more often than that?**

April 30 is the filing deadline for your personal tax return each year. If anything, this is the least important tax date of the year.

Taxes touch our financial lives almost every day of the year. Proactive tax planning is imperative for all Canadians.

Here is a list of tax dates that you should follow to increase your chances of paying less tax:

**JANUARY 1.** Taxation of people in Canada is based on a calendar year. This means that the first of the year brings a whole new year of tax planning to consider. Everyone should be prepared to implement a new strategy for the entire year—the sooner the better—so that the strategy applies for the entire year on your tax return. For this reason, it is important to have your tax planning affairs in line by January 1.

Here's one example of tax planning that should be considered by January 1: Keeping a log book in your car for business usage of your vehicle. Parking expenses and mileage will be tax deductible each calendar year, if it is related to business. To help determine the tax-deductible portion, take an odometer reading on your vehicle for January 1 and December 31 of the same year, while tracking business kilometres throughout the year, in order to calculate business travel.

**FEBRUARY 28.** This is the date that investment companies must file their T5 and T3 slips with CCRA. T3 and T5 slips are federally required tax forms that declare how much investment income you earned in the given year. Regular mutual funds issue T3 slips to unit-holders who receive distributions from mutual funds held in taxable accounts. T5 slips are most often seen summarizing interest income on a bank account or a bond. Since companies must file these forms by the end of February, they likely arrive in your mailbox between January and late March. Don't complete your tax return until late March, just to ensure that you have received all slips you should receive.

**FEBRUARY.** In the month of February we have come to expect a federal budget from the Minister of Finance. Often these budgets announce new tax breaks that may be suitable to you. It is generally a good idea to get a budget debriefing from your financial advisor each year, and to explore new tax planning strategies.

**MARCH 15.** This the date that your first income tax instalment is due. If you do not have enough tax withheld at source on your income, CCRA will inform you that you need to make income tax instalments quarterly. The dates of these other instalments are June 15, September 15, and December 15. Often seniors make instalments of tax to CCRA if they receive large amounts of investment income each year. Simply send a cheque with your SIN on it to CCRA. You can even pay your tax instalments at the bank today. What is important to note about tax instalments is that many people are surprised to hear that there are actually three different formulas for calculating tax instalment amounts. Often CCRA tells you what instalment you should pay, but note that you don't have to follow their recommendation. They automatically use one of three methods to calculate the tax owing, but if one of the other two methods is a better fit for you, you are permitted to use it. Generally such an approach is desirable if another method results in lower tax instalments. Talk to a tax specialist if you want to explore alternative methods of paying tax instalments.

**APRIL 15.** Deadline for U.S. citizens to file their personal tax returns. If you spend a lot of time visiting the U.S. each year you may actually qualify as a U.S. citizen.

**APRIL 30.** Deadline for filing your tax return unless it falls on a weekend, in which case it usually is the next business day. Note that this is a deadline only if you owe taxes. If you are expecting a refund, there is no rush to file, except that you are losing the benefit of getting money back in your hands. Most people want it as soon as possible.

**JUNE 15.** Deadline for filing your tax return if you are a professional or are self-employed. Note that any tax owing is still due by April 30.

**NOVEMBER.** It is important to understand that announcements made in the February federal budget are only proposed at that time. Usually later in the year there are amendments, enhancements, or outright cancellation of proposals made in the budget. Finally, the new rules occasionally do not become law until years later. November is a time for you and your financial advisor to check the status of the year's tax legislation.

**EARLY DECEMBER.** Since the calendar year is a single tax filing year, December 31 is the last date you can implement tax planning strategies for effect in the current tax year. It is important to have a tax planning review before the end of the year to ensure that you maximize tax strategies before the year end—that way you can benefit from them on your tax return. Examples of items relevant to a year-end tax review include: ensuring tax-deductible investment counsel fees are paid; making charitable contributions and incurring medical costs that are tax credits; and making RESP contributions on behalf of children's savings and triggering losses in your investment accounts to offset gains realized in the same year. December is the most important tax planning month. Everyone should be thinking tax and be reviewing opportunities before December 15 each year.

Tax dates that you should know about go beyond those listed here. Take time to schedule key dates and make appointments with your financial advisors to discuss all aspects of your finances. Committing to meetings and actions long in advance is a good way to ensure they happen.

# 50
## What is the best way to deal with taxes and investing?

Some investors let tax hatred dictate their investing strategies, while others completely ignore taxes. This is a good example of extremes in the personality of investors.

I meet a lot of Canadians who are totally driven to minimize taxes on their investments. I mean, that's all they care about. A good example of these types of investors are people who buy labour-sponsored funds every year. A labour fund is a specialty investment fund that offers significant tax credits to the investor in exchange for investment in small, private companies across Canada. I have seen several Canadians whose RRSPs consist of nothing but labour funds because the investor has been lured each year by the tax break that can be achieved with a last-minute purchase of labour funds.

Some people are too focused on taxation, to the point where the quality of the investment portfolio may be sacrificed. Labour-sponsored funds are specialty investments and can play a role in your investment portfolio, but they need to be recognized for what they are—one of the riskiest forms of investment that you can buy. In some labour funds you are literally buying your favourite restaurant down the street—hardly blue chip!

In recent years, the performance of many Canadian labour investment funds has been so weak compared to regular equity investment funds that any tax breaks achieved on the purchase of the funds years ago may have long been surpassed by lost investment returns. If you buy labour funds, limit your purchase to less than 10% of your overall portfolio, and don't get hung up on tax breaks alone. Fundamentally, the investment must stand on its own for investment reasons alone.

The other extreme investor is one who ignores the taxation impact of investing completely. Yet it is unwise to ignore the taxation impact of investing. In some cases, you may be taxed 50% of your investment earnings.

The mutual fund performance data you see in the newspapers is effectively the wrong information to make an investment purchase decision on if you are investing in a taxable portfolio where tax matters. These published return numbers are pre-tax returns, not after-tax returns, and it is after-tax returns that matter most to a taxable investor. It is what you keep, not what you earn, that matters most. Yet some investors continue to use incorrect or incomplete information to base investment decisions on when investing in a taxable (non-RRSP/RRIF) account.

Some financial advisors who charge commission fees are actually biased against tax-smart investing by the nature of their fees. If they make more commissions each time you sell, they may desire investment turnover in their approach with you. With equity investments particularly, this buying and selling can trigger capital gains and high taxation. A buy-and-hold approach leaves more money in your pockets, and ultimately leads to a greater long-term wealth level. Yet I see few investors following this tax minimization approach in their taxable investment portfolio.

Few investors challenge why they pay so much tax on their investments. Few take the time to ask about portfolio turnover in a mutual fund, and yet turnover of investments is by far the largest cause of taxation within a portfolio (through creation of taxable capital gains). Not many investors question why they get mutual fund distributions. A distribution is an income flow received from a mutual fund. These distributions can be controlled by a mutual fund company, and receiving them should not be desirable by investors since distributions are generally taxable. So question why you get a T3 slip each year, because this may be needless investment taxation that can be avoided.

Many investors fail to question the composition of the types of investment income they can earn. For example, in Canada today, interest income is taxed at almost double the tax rate of realized capital gains, and at a much higher rate than dividend income. Foreign cash flows are taxed at different rates again. Paying attention to investment taxation allows investors to maximize their after-tax returns, yet I see few investors taking advantage of this.

The right answer to mixing tax and investing is that you want to combine the two in the right proportions. Totally focusing on tax (and ignoring investment factors) is dangerous. And yet you can't afford to ignore taxation. Taxation should be a key evaluation factor when purchasing new investments, and it should be an important criterion to examine when contemplating the sale of investments.

# 51

## When I have my taxes done each year, why do I never find tax-planning strategies that can help me reduce my tax bill?

It is important to know the difference between tax-planning services and tax-compliance services. One can be extremely valuable, the other usually is not.

*Tax-compliance service* is preparation of a personal tax return that is required by the government and that summarizes your income and expenses. In plain English, it is taking all the slips you get in February each year and sticking them on your return (or hiring an accountant to do this for you). This task requires little understanding of the Income Tax Act and can usually be easily completed using tax software that is available on the market today.

There is no value in tax compliance services. It is truly only worth the $65 or so that you pay to have it prepared down the street. There is little likelihood that tax-planning opportunities will be identified during this process. The fee may not include identifying tax-planning strategies for you.

*Tax-planning services* are completely different, and far more valuable. You sit down with a tax-planning specialist—someone who knows the Income Tax Act thoroughly. The tax specialist will ask you many questions about how you (and your family, if applicable) live your life day to day. With this knowledge the tax specialist will relate your situation to the rules of the Income Tax Act to see if there are tax saving or planning opportunities that can apply to your personal situation. This personal tax planning can be tremendously helpful.

Of course, this type of service will cost a lot more than the tax return preparation service, but it is well worth the money. Within minutes, the tax-planning specialist may find a tax opportunity or strategy that could save you hundreds or even thousands of dollars. Sometimes this information can also be applied retroactively to previous tax returns for even more savings.

I spent almost a decade working in public practice at one of the world's leading chartered accounting firms in Winnipeg and later in Toronto. Over that time I completed hundreds of personal tax returns for a wide variety of Canadians. No matter how simple the return was, I typically charged $1,000 or more each time. My personal billing rate was well over $300 an hour. These costs may seem really high to someone paying $65 to have their return prepared. But I'll argue it's quite a deal. Here's why.

For the last 20 years you may have prepared your own tax return, or had the local tax service do it. I doubt that you uncovered many memorable tax breaks during that period because that approach focuses on just tax compliance, not tax planning.

But let's say this year you did your return, and then sat down with a qualified tax specialist for an hour to (a) let them review your return for accuracy; and (b) chat with you about tax planning opportunities for your situation. I've done this recently where in ten minutes I found a tax break worth hundreds (potentially thousands) of dollars to the client. Just from listening to how they live their life.

If I find a big tax break that you can claim this year, and if you can go back and refile to claim for the last three years, and if you can claim well into the future on your tax returns as well, that could amount to thousands and thousands of dollars of savings. If that is the case, does my $300 an hour rate or $1,000 for a tax return seem so expensive? Not likely. The secret is in the tax planning!

And even if the tax specialist doesn't find any tax breaks in your return, it is still worth the money for the validation that you are not missing out on opportunities. Since the Income Tax Act can change daily and at any time during the year (not just during budget season, as many people think), consider getting a tax planning review on a regular basis.

You need to sit down with a tax specialist one on one in order to find the strategies that will work in your particular situation. Getting a newsletter with tax tips in it, or listening to a tax speaker in a convention hall, is not the same as receiving personal tax-planning services.

Here's a tip for helping you find a good tax specialist: The tax specialist you want to hire will have a well-broken-in version of the Income Tax Act in his or her office and a working knowledge of the Act. When you sit down with a tax specialist, ask to see the office copy of the Income Tax Act. If the specialist doesn't have one, or if it looks like it has never been used, find someone else!

# 52

## Should I consider filing a tax return for my teenager even though there is no tax to pay on the earned income?

You may want to file a tax return for your child even if the income earned is not enough to pay tax on (if it is less than the basic tax credit of approximately $7,400). If the teenager has any employment income at all it qualifies for the purposes of determining RRSP contribution room. This means that the child's RRSP contribution room starts to accumulate. You just have to file a return with this income on it so that the Canada Customs and Revenue Agency (formerly Revenue Canada) can start tracking the child's RRSP room.

Here's an example. Let's say your ten-year-old child delivers newspapers for three years and earns $1,000 a year. When your child is 13, a part-time job earns $3,500 for the next three years. At 16, more part-time hours and full-time work over the summer earns $5,500 a year for two years, until age 18. The following contribution room has been created:

| | |
|---|---|
| Total earned income: | $24,500 |
| RRSP contribution room factor: | 18% |
| RRSP contribution room: | $4,410 |

The parents or grandparents could open an RRSP for this child, and contribute the full $4,410 on the child's behalf. This would be a smart move financially in many circumstances. If this amount earned 8% a year until age 69 (51-year compounding period), the child would have an RRSP worth $223,000 at retirement. As you can see, it can be very lucrative to file a return even for a small amount of qualifying income.

## Other reasons to file returns for minors

There are at least two other reasons to consider filing a tax return for a child who has no taxable income.

First, it is possible that tax was withheld from your child's paycheque even if they didn't earn enough money on which to be taxed. The only way to recover any withheld tax is to file a tax return for the child. Filing the tax return should result in full recovery of this money.

Second, if your children are over 18 years old, still in school (university), and continue to have only minor income, they can claim provincial and GST tax credits (if applicable) if they file a tax return. Tuition tax credits can be carried forward and claimed in future taxable years. Spending some time with a tax professional who can review these and other opportunities is a good idea.

# 53

## Is there a way to help my adult children plan for their retirement while reducing my taxes today?

There are many options you can take with respect to your adult children—some strategies are so simple, they may surprise you. Following are two examples (one in this question and one in the next) of how you can improve your and your family's net worth.

Contribute to your adult children's RRSPs. Children in their late 20s and early 30s are usually still buried under student debt and car loans, or may even have a mortgage. At the same time, they are working full time and accumulating significant RRSP contribution room—they just don't have the money to contribute to their plans! A parent or grandparent can contribute money to an adult child's RRSP to improve the overall family wealth position.

Here's why: If you are the parent and you are paying tax at up to 50% on your earnings from your investments currently, you can essentially tax shelter all of these earnings if you contribute the cash into your child's RRSP. This is a tax deferral of up to 50 cents of every dollar earned every year as long as the money stays tax sheltered within the child's RRSP. Additionally, the child will get a tax refund from the RRSP deduction that can be used to start to pay down the child's debt.

Sharing money among family members can enhance overall family wealth if some of the family members are net savers and others are net debtors. This is often the case with parents and children.

One word of caution, however: Once you place money into someone else's RRSP, you give up control over that money. If your child goes bankrupt or has a marriage breakup, that money may be at risk. So remember to weigh these factors—along with your need for the money—before you make any contributions. There are ways to structure gifts to family members to protect against the risk of future loss. Talk to a professional financial advisor about these strategies.

## Starting early matters most

Basic math shows that starting to save for retirement early in your life can have a dramatic impact on the total wealth accumulated. Since money can double every five to ten years (depending on the rate of return), it is important to grow your savings early and quickly to build a base for future growth. This means that 20-somethings must be convinced to focus on retirement savings at a time when they may not have the desire or the money to do so. Yet starting a savings plan in your 20s or early 30s can make a significant difference to your amount of retirement capital. It may mean the difference between a comfortable retirement and a poor one. So sit your kids down and get them to focus on savings, even if it means you have to help them out financially.

# 54

## Can I help my debt-ridden adult children while reducing my income taxes at the same time?

Consider paying down your adult children's mortgages or other debts. Think about maximizing family wealth instead of just your own. Consider the following example that shows the impact of paying down your children's or grandchildren's debts:

A child has a $30,000 loan and pays 8% a year—$2,400—on it. This interest expense is paid from the after-tax cash flow of your child. At the same time, the parent has a $30,000 GIC that earns 8% a year—$2,400—interest and also pays 50% tax on this interest ($1,200), which leaves a net return of only $1,200 of after-tax interest income. As a family, the total return for a year is as follows: $2,400 cost of debt offset by a $1,200 after-tax return equals a total loss to the family of $1,200.

Now let's look at the difference to the bottom line when using a strategy that moves assets around within the family unit and improves the family wealth significantly.

The parent pays off the $30,000 debt of the child using the $30,000 GIC. No interest expense is incurred since the child no longer carries the debt. Interest income is not produced (or taxed) since the parent no longer owns the GIC. As a family, the total return is now zero compared with the previous loss of $1,200.

This results in a saving of $1,200 per year, for as long as the debt would have existed in the child's hands.

## Think about debt economics before making the payoff

If your child has a variety of types of debt (mortgage, car loan, student debt, credit card debt, etc.) and you, as the parent, have a variety of savings (GICs, cash, bonds, stocks, funds, etc.), you need to determine which investments should be used to pay down which of the child's debts. To do this evaluation properly requires a comparison of the after-tax interest cost against the after-tax return. Generally the after-tax interest cost will be the same as the interest rate. And the after-tax return of the investments will vary according to the type of investment and the parent's tax bracket. In some cases it may not be wise to use certain assets to pay off the child's debt. For example, in the above example it would likely be foolish for the parent to sell an equity mutual fund and use the proceeds to pay off the child's debt because the sale of the mutual fund may trigger realization of a huge capital gain resulting in a large tax bill. Be sure to examine all of the pros and cons of assets being considered for movement within the family. There are many variables to consider!

Once again a word of caution: gifting money to children may not be appropriate if you will need the money yourself, or if there is a concern about your children's marriage or credit situation. Take precautionary steps to structure any gift appropriately to guard against unexpected risks. Talk to a professional financial advisor.

# 55

## Do I have to tell the Canada Customs and Revenue Agency about my non-Canadian investments even if I don't receive income from them?

Recent federal budget changes, designed to reduce offshore investing that avoids Canadian taxation, have resulted in some new tax rules for Canadians.

Now your income tax return includes questions about the total assets you own outside of Canada if the costs add up to Cdn$100,000 or more. The CCRA wants details of these assets submitted with your annual tax return on the new form T1135 to ensure that you are paying your fair share of taxes on any income earned from these assets.

Here are the basic details you need to know about these new rules:

- The cost threshold is Cdn$100,000. That means your US$70,000 stock portfolio must be reported because, when converted to Canadian dollars, the cost of the portfolio is worth more than $100,000.
- If you go over the threshold at any time during the year, even for a day, you have to report the amount on your tax return at the end of the year because the threshold is not based on your holdings at a specific date (such December 31).
- Generally speaking, foreign stocks and foreign rental properties qualify and must be reported. Some exceptions include foreign investments held in your RRSPs, RRIFs, and personal-use real estate.
- Non-compliance with these new rules brings some of the nastiest penalties in the Income Tax Act—up to 5% of the unreported amount. So don't even think about it!
- The form must be filed annually with your income tax return.
- The form must be filed regardless of whether you earn income from these foreign investments. You must report the fact that you own them.

Since these are new rules and there are exceptions to filing the form, consider getting some advice from a tax accountant about what you have to report. They will steer you right this year, and you can take it from there in future years.

## Previous foreign assets that have not been reported

It is a little more complicated for some Canadians who are already invested outside of Canada and have not reported any income on these investments before. For example, seniors who vacation in the U.S. each winter (snowbirds) and operate local U.S. bank accounts for their spending money may have accumulated sizeable U.S. investments that were not declared on their Canadian returns. If you are one of these investors, consult a qualified tax accountant as soon as possible to understand what your options are. This is a good idea since the CCRA and the IRS in the United States are sharing information about investors like never before.

So remember, wherever you own assets in the world—from the house in England to the bank account in Hong Kong—you may have to report them under these new foreign reporting rules.

# 56

## I paid a lot of tax on my investment income last year. Is there something I can do to change this situation?

Here are a few strategies to help you minimize the tax bill associated with investing.

## Get rid of unnecessary income

Many Canadians get regular distributions from mutual funds, and earn interest and dividend income from their taxable investments. But unless you need the money to live on, why are you getting this income stream and paying tax on it? There are ways to restructure your taxable portfolio so that your rate of return is comprised more of deferred growth, which is not taxable annually; and you get rid of the annual taxation associated with other forms of earnings (interest and dividends).

Specifically, there are three ways to earn taxable investment income:

1. Own fixed income investments such as GICs or bonds that generate highly taxed interest all year long;
2. Own high-dividend-yielding companies. These will be taxed at lower rates if the dividends are paid from Canadian companies;
3. Realize a lot of capital gains from active trading (high portfolio turnover) in equities all year long. Capital gains are taxed at lower rates, generally, than GICs or bonds.

There are simple ways of reducing your amounts of taxable investment income:

1. Move highly taxed fixed income investments into RRSPs or RRIFs where interest is tax deferred; put lower-taxed investments such as low-turnover equity investments or buy-and-hold stocks in your taxable portfolio where taxation is only incurred when capital gains are realized—and capital gains won't be realized very often if the general strategy is to buy and hold. This will effectively transfer high-tax items into your tax-sheltered accounts and low-tax items into your taxable accounts.
2. Stay out of annual-dividend-yielding stocks all together, and focus instead on growth stock investments where return is earned annually in the form of capital growth from a rising stock price; no tax is due on the appreciated stock growth until the ultimate sale—this is tax smart. If you don't need the income to live on, consider investments that generate a deferred return.

Remember, these strategies assume that you don't need an annual income from these investments. If you do need income and just want to minimize taxes on it, there are many other tax-smart strategies available for you to implement.

## Minimize the selling of equity investments

Each sale of an investment in equities potentially triggers a taxable capital, causing you to pay taxes the following tax season. Purchasing equity investments you can own for the long term and then minimizing the trading you do will defer taxes until the investment is sold. This deferral leaves more money in your pocket longer, building greater long-term wealth. In your taxable savings account, this portfolio turnover—or frequency of buying and selling—matters and should be minimized in order to preserve your wealth and accelerate its growth.

## Pay attention to your tax bracket

Pay attention to the tax bracket you and your family are in. If there are several people in your family unit, and/or you also have a company or trust, there are potentially many entities, all in different tax brackets. Having members of your family at different tax brackets presents a tax-planning opportunity among your family members where it may be possible to optimize after-tax wealth by focusing on an entire family unit and moving taxable income to the lowest-taxed family member.

## Understand specialty investments

The investment landscape is full of many kinds of specialty investments. These are products that have unusual (good or bad) tax attributes as part of their structure. Examples of specialty products include tax shelters, real estate investments, limited partnerships, and income trusts. Each of these products should be thoroughly understood, not only from an investment point of view, but also from a tax point of view. I find that in some cases the tax characteristics can often be glossed over inappropriately on complicated investment and insurance products. Take time to find out all the rules of what you buy, particularly for investments that are less common and not well known.

The following specialty investments warrant special tax and investment consideration and understanding:

- Tax shelter (e.g., film, software)
- Any real estate investment
- Limited partnerships
- Unit income trusts (royalty trusts)
- Labour-sponsored investment funds
- Any offshore investment
- Any private equity investment
- Any venture capital investment
- Oil and gas investments
- All forms of wrap products and programs

- Segregated funds
- Universal life insurance policies

There are many different elements of tax-smart investing that warrant a basic understanding of the tax rules, tax-smart strategies, and tax-smart products. Understanding all these variables together will leave you better positioned to build an investment portfolio focused on maximizing after-tax wealth. And since what we keep matters more than what we earn, take steps to become a more tax-smart investor.

# 57

## Can I boost my after-tax income by buying dividend-yielding investments that attract lower taxation?

There are two issues here that need to be addressed. First, you *can* boost your after-tax cash flow by buying dividend-yielding stocks and dividend mutual funds. Second, dividends from Canadian companies provide a much more favourable tax situation than dividends from U.S. or other foreign companies.

Stocks owned directly or through mutual funds often can offer attractively high dividends. This, coupled with the lower taxation of Canadian-sourced dividends, can render a cash flow that exceeds what you may have earned on an interest-bearing investment such as a GIC or a bond. Let me show you an example:

Assume Mom owns a $100,000 GIC that earns 4%, and she is in the top marginal tax bracket in Ontario (estimated 50% tax bracket). This leaves her with an after-tax cash flow from the GIC of $100,000 times 4%—$4,000—less 50% tax on the income—$2,000—for a final cash flow of $2,000.

Now assume Dad owns a $100,000 equity investment that earns 4% in Canadian dividends annually, and he is also in the top tax bracket in Ontario. His after-tax cash flow is as follows: $100,000 times 4%—$4,000—taxed at 31%—$1,240—leaves after-tax cash of $2,760.

Dad has more to spend due to lower taxes attached to Canadian dividend income. This is generally the case in every province. One point to note on buying high-dividend-yielding equity investments: High fees may wipe out dividend payouts. Ensure you are sensitive to this factor.

Dad's higher after-tax return is due to the fact that dividends from Canadian companies—not U.S. or other foreign companies—are subject to much more favourable taxation. Typically, Canadian-sourced dividends are taxed at rates up to approximately 35%. Foreign dividends, such as those received from your foreign company investments, will be taxed at rates up to approximately 50%. To benefit from more favourable taxation, consider owning high-dividend-yielding stocks from Canadian companies or Canadian dividend mutual funds rather than foreign equities.

This strategy can be applied to senior citizens who boost their cash flow by owning a collection of high-dividend-yielding stocks or dividend mutual funds. These seniors need to ensure that they own Canadian companies (whether directly or through mutual funds).

This strategy can work well in some cases. However, I generally do not advocate owning only a small collection of dividend-yielding stocks. Examine your entire financial profile to properly assess it and build the investment portfolio you need according to your own Statement of Investment Policy and Guidelines.

## Beware high-yield substitutes

There are many investments available today in Canada that are sold as "high yield." This means they are supposed to provide high levels of regular income. In some cases the investments are also marketed as offering "tax-effective high yield." While a discussion of these investments is beyond the scope of this book, it is worthwhile to note that many of these high-yield products are aggressive investments, involving above-average risk levels. Ensure that you understand all of the factors, including the risk and tax consequences before you buy. Rarely should these high yield investments be the sole source for retirement income for a senior. Neither should they be compared to a fixed income investment like a GIC or bond.

# 58

## Can I split incomes with my spouse to pay less tax?

Income splitting for tax savings is big business in the tax world. There are income-splitting strategies for spouses, parents and children, business and personal, and different countries, for example.

Some tax professionals make entire careers out of income-splitting strategies for family members. This is because there are many rules surrounding income splitting among family members and because often one spouse pays a lot more or less tax than the other.

Here I provide one lesser-known strategy. If it can work for you, you will save a lot of money every year for the rest of your life.

Here's an example to illustrate:

Spouse 1 earns $100,000 a year, has a $300,000 taxable investment portfolio of GICs that earns 8% a year, and is paying 50% tax on the full 8% each year. This amounts to an annual tax bill of $12,000 on the investment income.

Spouse 2 earns nothing while working at home raising the children, has no investments, but has recently inherited a cottage that is worth $300,000.

Here's the strategy: Spouse 1 should buy the cottage from Spouse 2 for fair market value ($300,000). In substance, nothing in the family changes. Formally, however, this will be a legal transfer of assets between spouses, which permits legitimate tax planning and future income splitting. (This transfer should be formally written up through a lawyer.)

Spouse 2 can now invest the $300,000 cash and pay a very low tax rate. This strategy could amount to a $12,000 tax savings every year.

This strategy is not limited to a cottage property: Art, jewelry, or other valuable assets—even the family home—may be transferred for tax savings, given the right situation. Talk to a qualified tax accountant or lawyer about all the issues related to your personal situation to see if you are in a position to take advantage of this income-splitting and tax-minimization strategy.

# 59

## Can I avoid paying taxes through offshore investing?

Few offshore tax-planning opportunities remain for Canadians, but there are exceptions.

For example, if you have a relative in Germany who will leave you an inheritance someday, you may be able to benefit from setting up an offshore trust to minimize taxes. Or, if you are planning to emigrate from Canada sometime soon, talk to a tax professional about appropriate tax planning before you do so. If you have any offshore connections at all, seek out a qualified international tax accountant or lawyer to see if your circumstance fits into one of the exceptions that will allow you to legitimately gain tax breaks from offshore investing.

In the majority of cases, though, there is nothing you can do to legitimately avoid taxes if you are a typical Canadian. You see, Canadians are taxed on their worldwide income, no matter what country or the currency. Each year you are required to convert all your foreign income into the Canadian equivalent and list it on your tax return. (So, if you have not been declaring the interest income in your Hong Kong bank account or the rental income from your house in France, you are likely breaking the law in Canada.)

However, although few offshore tax-planning opportunities remain for the Canadian investor, more and more people are using offshore structures for other, non-tax reasons.

- Creditor proofing. Individuals in professions that are in high risk of being sued can transfer their personal net worth to a foreign jurisdiction to protect their assets against loss from law suits. If you get sued in Canada, the plaintiff may be hard pressed to collect your foreign assets, depending on how your affairs are structured.
- Confidentiality. Everyone has heard of the famous Swiss bank account. High-profile people often search for confidentiality of their affairs. Holding your assets offshore may assist in this objective as many foreign jurisdictions won't reveal account information, even to the RCMP or other police.
- Diversification. The world is full of professional money managers who can assist with your investment management needs. While many of these professionals already sell their services to Canadian clients, many more do not. Affluent Canadians often can invest directly with these foreign money managers, adding a broader level of international diversification to their portfolio.

So if your next door neighbor has this neat RRSP strategy to get all the money out of the RRSP without paying any taxes, or if your Canadian brother-in-law has this new investment account in a foreign bank on the tiny island of TaxScam, don't fret that you are missing out. There is a good likelihood that if they aren't reporting investment income on their Canadian tax returns annually then their actions are illegal.

# 60

## Can I move some of my investments into my spouse's name in order to pay less tax on the annual income?

Some people think that they can simply take investments and change the legal name on the account to the name of the spouse who is in the lower tax bracket in order to pay less tax. They think that the lower-taxed spouse can start claiming the related investment income on their tax return each year. *But this is not true.*

Taxation of investment income is attached to the person responsible for the source of the investment. In other words, the person who contributed the money for the investment in the first place is the person who has to pay tax on the investment income, regardless of who legally owns the account. The original investor must pay tax on the income unless transfers of assets occur between spouses using legitimate income-splitting techniques from the Income Tax Act.

Let me give some examples:

- If spouses have a joint bank account but all the proceeds in the account come from one spouse's paycheques, that salaried spouse must claim all interest income generated by the account. They cannot split the interest to each claim half.
- If one spouse has accumulated a $25,000 equity mutual fund from paycheque savings and gives it to the other spouse as a birthday gift, the giver still must pay taxes on all distributions (interest, dividends, and capital gains) from the fund each year. However, the spouse who received the gift will pay tax on any earnings received from reinvestment of the distributions.
- If Spouse 1 loans Spouse 2 $10,000 and charges a market rate of interest, Spouse 2 can invest the proceeds and pay tax on the investment income. (This interest must be paid by January 30 after any year a loan balance remains outstanding.) Since the loan is also an investment loan, Spouse 2 can likely also deduct on his or her tax return the interest paid to Spouse 1. Spouse 1 must, of course, declare the interest earnings on the loan and pay tax on this. In this example, Spouse 2 can benefit if the investment earnings exceed the loan cost. Otherwise this is a losing scenario.

If you have inappropriately shifted taxation of income around between you and your spouse, or you and your kids, talk to a qualified tax accountant to see how the rules apply to you.

Note that the rules of sharing your investments with your children or grandchildren are (completely) different from the rules for sharing with your spouse. And the rules are different again between minor children and adult children (age 18 or over). There are significant opportunities to reduce overall family taxation by gifting assets to kids, but make sure you take protective measures if you are concerned about the loss of control over your money.

# RULE 8

## The importance of estate planning: Your death could tear your family's net worth apart.

Death is inevitable, so you might as well be prepared. Many people are hesitant to talk about dying, but a poorly planned estate could cause family hardship after you're gone. It is important to set an estate plan and to review and update it every few years. Your lifestyle may change, and legal and tax rules will definitely change, so you will need to keep up to date.

In this section, I explore a collection of specific estate planning issues, such as the importance of obtaining professional advice to help you sort through the complicated issues. Will planning includes a variety of strategies that can maximize estate values, preserve and protect assets within the estate, determine guardianship of children, and set rules of your estate for the lifetime of your heirs. I also look at the types of institutions that offer services in this area, and highlight the things to think about when choosing who should take on the huge responsibility of becoming your estate executor.

If there is an area of your personal finances where you don't want to cut corners, it is estate planning. That is because one small error in your will could mess up the finances for the entire next generation of your heirs. Use the information in the following section as a starting point to build a proper estate plan.

There are, however, a few basics that I'd like to mention now:

**DON'T PLAN YOUR OWN ESTATE.** No matter how simple your estate is, complications can arise. Further, you are likely not a lawyer or a tax specialist who knows about and can take advantage of legal and tax planning opportunities related to your estate. Preparing your will or planning your estate is a good time to pay the big fees to bring in professionals and obtain some worthwhile planning. Dying is the culmination of your life—don't underestimate the complications that can arise for your family. If you have any doubts, talk to someone who has had to deal with winding up an estate. They will tell you how complicated it can get.

**DON'T PREPARE YOUR OWN WILL.** Will planning is not just about deciding what to do with your current assets and liabilities. Get your lawyer and tax specialist to team up to prepare your will; that way it will be legally accurate and tax wise. Stay away from do-it-yourself will kits; they are oversimplified, and one omission of a planning strategy can lead to an entirely different estate result.

**INVOLVE YOUR FAMILY.** When it comes to picking an estate executor, think very carefully. It is a huge responsibility that you may want to share among all your children or none of them. If you are thinking about using your neighbour or your brother-in-law as the executor, make sure they are aware of the tremendous legal liability associated with such a role. Ensure they are paid fairly for their role. Get your heirs together and try to get them involved in your estate planning. They may not wish to talk about such a topic, but make it happen! You may be surprised to see what true "wishes" come out of such a meeting, and it may sway exactly how your estate plan is designed. Maybe your daughter doesn't want all your furniture!

**SHOP AROUND FOR ASSISTANCE IN DEALING WITH YOUR ESTATE MATTERS.** In the last ten years we have watched just about every financial institution start offering estate planning services to their menu of services. Just look at the banks: Most of them now call themselves "bank and trust." With so many providers now going after your business, it is easier than ever for Canadians in need of estate planning services to find help, but at what cost?

In dealing with estate matters, you will need an entire team of advisors: definitely a lawyer, and an accountant for the tax returns to be filed, an executor, a real estate agent to sell any property, and an insurance agent to collect any payouts due. These professional advisors will require clear directions and roles. Ensure your estate plan is set up to deal with them all appropriately, as it could be costly if they are not aligned from the day you die.

# 61
## What is estate planning?

Estate planning is the act of taking steps to properly plan for the financial implications of your death. This can involve legal issues, tax issues, cash flow issues, and other issues such as appointing guardians for children. There are all kinds of rules that need to be followed—rules from the Income Tax Act and provincial and federal laws, for example. Estate planning involves the implementation of planning strategies that take advantage of all the rules in order to save estate taxes, legal fees, accounting fees, probate fees, and time and hassle.

On a more specific basis, estate planning involves, for example, preparing a will and powers of attorney, establishing the use of trusts in your estate, appointing executors, appointing trustees for any trusts you create, setting guardians for your survivors if needed, setting charitable donation plans, and selecting other professional advisors for your estate.

Many people think that estate planning is about minimizing income taxes and probate fees as much as possible. It's not. Sure, income tax and probate fee minimization is important, but it is not the most important thing about estate planning. The most important aspect of estate planning is simplicity. Wherever the costs and benefits are clear, keep your estate after death reasonably simple.

If estate issues are not kept simple, the heirs end up having to deal with complex financial and legal affairs, sometimes when they are still in mourning. These matters might include dealing with testamentary trusts, life insurance proceeds, joint accounts, income tax returns, or trying to find all the bank accounts the deceased owned, and so on. If they are estate executors, they may not have the financial sophistication to do the job, or they may not have the time for or the interest in such work. If the estate planning is not simple and clear, it may also cause animosity among the heirs and result in high legal and accounting fees to sort out the issues. So, sometimes keeping your estate simple may result in a bit more cost up front, but it may save piles of aggravation and professional fees later.

Here are some examples of complications in your estate planning that can cause grief to your survivors when your estate is being wound up after your death:

- Leaving assets jointly owned among family members can add a level of complexity to your estate. Making assets jointly owned permits these assets to flow around an estate on death, going directly to the surviving joint owner. If you had intended to treat all of your heirs equally in your estate, joint ownership of assets may wreck those plans unless the jointly owned assets are properly planned for.
- Leaving your heirs as beneficiaries on your RRSP, RRIF, or life insurance can also result in estate complications if you had planned to equalize the value of your estate

among all your heirs. These assets pass directly to beneficiaries and need to be given special consideration when dividing up the remainder of the estate.

- Preparing your own will using a do-it-yourself kit can be disastrous. There are so many legal and tax rules to factor into your estate planning that you cannot be well served preparing your own will. If there is ever a time to spend some money on professional help, will planning is that time. Making a mistake in your will due to poor planning can destroy your family or cause them grief for the rest of their lives, possibly another 70 years or more after your death. To ensure that all of your estate planning wishes are carried out appropriately, consult a tax lawyer or a lawyer and a tax accountant to have a proper will prepared.

- Have your will prepared on a tax-effective basis. It may not be appropriate to divide up your estate based on market value of assets alone if some of your assets have large tax liabilities attached to them. Specifically, stock portfolios, real estate, equity mutual funds and RRSPs/RRIFs deserve special consideration during will planning. Failure to examine these types of assets on an after-tax basis can have disastrous consequences. Generally, before heirs get their share of your estate, all outstanding taxes previously deferred during your life will now be due. Failure to plan for the tax bill on death can leave heirs with unequal inheritances.

Estate planning is not easy to talk about since it involves death. But proper estate planning is critical to preserving the value of a lifetime of wealth accumulation. Ensure that you take the time to enlist qualified professionals to help you plan all aspects of your estate needs and wishes.

# 62

## Could my estate be liable for U.S. taxes on my death even though I am not an American citizen?

Yes. Even if you don't vacation in the U.S. and haven't ever visited the U.S., your estate may still have to pay U.S. estate taxes on your death.

U.S. estate taxes are a tax on certain U.S. assets, they are not a tax on people. This means if you own certain U.S. assets over a particular U.S. dollar threshold, your estate may be required to pay U.S. estate taxes. This tax has nothing to do with whether you spend time in the United States, as U.S. income tax does. And although U.S. income taxation is much lower than it is in Canada, U.S. estate taxes don't follow this pattern. They can be as high as 55% of the value of your qualifying estate!

**WHO QUALIFIES?** At this time, Canadians must pay U.S. estate taxes if they own qualifying U.S. assets. There are also thresholds of U.S. estate tax to consider, depending on the amount of U.S. assets you own, and your worldwide estate value in U.S. dollars at time of death.

**WHAT QUALIFIES?** There are several different kinds of assets that qualify, but the two key ones are U.S. stocks and U.S. real estate. For example, if you own a condo in Florida that is worth US$300,000 and you have a U.S. stock portfolio worth US$1,000,000 held in three different accounts here in Canada, you may have a U.S. estate tax problem.

**WHAT DOESN'T QUALIFY?** Conveniently enough, if you own your U.S. investments through Canadian mutual funds or Canadian corporations, these assets can be free from U.S. estate taxes.

**ARE THERE WAYS TO AVOID THIS TAX?** First, the threshold to qualify is rising so fewer Canadians will have to pay this tax. Second, there is a U.S. tax credit system that your estate may benefit from that reduces the U.S. estate tax payable. Third, even if your estate does end up paying some U.S. estate tax, this tax will generally qualify as a credit on your Canadian tax return, offsetting your Canadian tax liability on death. Fourth, there are planning strategies that you can implement to avoid U.S. estate taxes all together. For example, sell enough of your U.S. stock portfolio to move below the threshold. Or purchase ownership of the condo through a holding company you own, since U.S. estate laws do not apply to Canadian corporations.

Note that your estate will need to file a U.S. estate tax return if you own qualifying U.S. assets on death. The return will need to be filed regardless of tax due. Don't ignore your liability for qualifying investments—the IRS may go after your U.S. assets to collect what you owe!

The important thing is to be aware of U.S. estate taxes, and if your U.S. assets start to become significant, talk to a qualified tax accountant or lawyer to learn how to lessen the taxes or eliminate them altogether.

# 63

## Should I appoint one of my children as my estate executor?

An executor is the person (or persons) that you appoint in your will to be responsible for winding up your estate after you die. They will have responsibility over several things, including paying for funeral costs, finding the will and having it probated, taking care of assets within the estate until they are distributed to heirs, having the final tax returns prepared on a timely basis, paying bills, collecting income, selling assets, and completing any other tasks necessary to deal with your estate. Most people don't want to be an executor because it can be very time consuming, often with little or no pay from the estate. But more important than this, the executor is financially liable for any errors made in the estate. For example, if the executor distributes all the cash to heirs and then finds out that the estate owes CCRA $50,000, the executor is personally on the hook for that money. Think hard before agreeing to be an executor—it is a huge responsibility that should not be agreed to lightly.

Here is a sample scenario: In your will, you appoint one of your three children as the estate executor when you die. You selected your son, who in your opinion, is the most financially "with it." While he is living on the coast right now, you can't imagine that he will have a problem winding up your little estate.

As to the question of appointing a child as executor, I recommend that you either appoint all of your children equally or don't appoint any of them. It is important that all the children are put in the same position of control, even if one doesn't want to do it, or lives too far away, or isn't financial savvy. Each of the children should be required to sign cheques for distributions of money from the estate. If only one child is appointed as executor, the others may come back and blame that child for unfair treatment. Even if you completely trust your children to be fair after you are gone, if there is a lot of money on the table, anything can happen. And you won't be there to mediate.

If it is impossible to appoint all of your children as co-executors, consider having an outside party (friend, accountant, trust company) as co-executor with one or more of the children that you do appoint as executor. The outside professional can assure the other children that the estate will be dealt with fairly, because of the outsider's objectivity. Often the other children will be more comfortable knowing that a sibling cannot sign an estate cheque without a second signature.

Whomever you select as executors, you need to ask these people if they want the role. Many will be scared off by the legal liability and the amount of time necessary to commit to the estate proceedings, which in some cases can amount to years of part-time work. Make sure you also give consideration to the age of the executors—a family friend may die before you do!

Next, give consideration to proximity. If you select an executor who lives on the other side of the country or even across town, this may not be practical. If, for example, your home is listed for sale after your death, the executor may need to cut the grass, show the home, pay the bills, etc. Is there money available to pay for the airplane tickets to fly the executor to your area every time something needs to be done? Is this how you want to spend the money?

Finally, remember to set out instructions in your will to have the estate pay the executors for all their time and effort. The amount of payment can be determined in several different ways, but a general rule of thumb is to pay an hourly rate or to pay a percentage of the assets within the estate every year. A rate of 2% to 5% of the estate value is reasonable based on the work involved and the legal liability.

# 64

## Should my will be reviewed by a tax accountant even if it was prepared by a lawyer?

I recommend that someone with tax planning expertise should be involved with the preparation of your will. If your lawyer is not a tax lawyer, then a tax accountant should assist in will preparation.

If the lawyer alone prepares the will, consideration may not be given to the tax due on certain assets on your death. This can result in a wildly different result than intended, as you will see in the example below. You need to have your will prepared on an after-tax basis, so that distributions to your heirs are tax adjusted. A lawyer who simply makes plans to add up all your assets and divide by the number of your heirs could be setting your heirs up for trouble.

## An example of poor will planning

Mom and Dad, before they died, had only three assets in their net worth. They had $500,000 cash in an investment account, their house in the city worth $250,000, and a cottage worth $500,000. The city home was the parents' principal residence.

The cottage was owned jointly with Child 1 for the last ten years before the real estate boom that saw the price of the cottage rise from their cost of $100,000. They had originally made the cottage jointly owned with Child 1 because their other son was living in another province and no longer used the cottage at all. Child 1, who lived locally, wanted to inherit the cottage so they transferred the cottage to joint ownership in order to avoid probate fees on death. Mom and Dad intended to have Child 2, who lived elsewhere, get the other half of the estate—$500,000 cash—to keep everything fair. The city house would be sold on their death and the tax-free proceeds divided equally between the two children. For the rest of this example, we will ignore the money from the city house. The parents had their wills written to reflect the above.

When the first parent died, no tax was due since all assets were transferred to the surviving spouse at cost. When the second parent died, taxes became due on the assets.

Let's look first at the situation of the cottage. Since it was jointly held, it passed outside of the estate and was immediately turned over to the other surviving joint owner (Child 1). There were no holdups in the release of this asset. Child 1 received the keys upon presentation of the death certificate and was finished dealing with the estate.

Now let's deal with the free cash in the estate. The cash that was meant for Child 2 could not be released immediately, no matter how badly the child wanted or needed it. This cash ended up in the estate, which meant that it couldn't be distributed until all aspects of the estate had been considered. Bills needed to be paid, the executor needed to be paid, probate fees had to be paid, and, most importantly, the CCRA needed to be paid for outstanding tax liabilities.

## Tax liability

On the death of the surviving spouse, all assets owned by the spouse are "deemed disposed of." This means that any income or gains that had been accumulating on assets owned are now fully taxable on the final tax return. This would include RRSPs and RRIF values as taxable income in the deceased's final tax return. Several different tax returns may need to be filed in the year of someone's death.

In the example above, the final tax return of the parent had to account for the unrealized capital gain on the half of the cottage that was owned by the parents. The deceased's share of the gain on the cottage was ($500,000 minus $100,000) times 50%, which equals $200,000. Tax on the final return for this gain would be approximately $50,000. So $50,000 had to be paid to the CCRA from the estate proceeds. Once that was done and a Clearance Certificate on the deceased's tax situation was received, then the estate proceeds remaining could be distributed to Child 2.

But Child 1 received $500,000 and Child 2 only received $450,000. Child 2 sued Child 1 to sell the cottage and pay the rest of the money to equalize the estate the way that the parents had intended. From then on, the sons talked to each other only through lawyers.

## The moral of the story

In the above example, the parents had good intentions, but because the will wasn't set up tax effectively, the family was destroyed forever. On the death of the parents, the assets should have been divided up based on their after-tax values, not market values. Don't let this happen to you and your family. Get your will prepared tax effectively.

# 65

## Should I use the trust services and executor services of my local bank?

Over the last ten years, as the financial pillars have eroded in this country, many financial institutions have moved into estates and trusts services. These new services include almost every aspect of planning and services dealing with death. For example, you can engage these institutions to be your executor, advise your executor, probate your wills, file your last tax returns, set up trusts, maintain your trusts after death, distribute proceeds to your heirs, and so on.

The following are advantages of using these institutions to take care of your estate plans:

- The company is an ongoing entity that will never die; you can never outlive your executor if it is a company.
- Many of these companies are large enough that they have all kinds of professional resources to assist you with a variety of needs: They have lawyers, bankers, accountants, and investment managers on staff to deal with all aspects of your estate in one location.
- Using one of these companies as your executor is a completely objective way to seek advice. There are no family biases, and they won't play favourites.
- These companies are national, and in some cases international, so they can deal with the complexities of an estate spread out nationally and internationally.
- Hiring these service providers means you don't have to burden a family member or friend with the responsibility and legal liability of being an executor.

There are also some disadvantages of using a trust company for estate planning:

- Employees in these companies will come and go, and you or your heirs may not see the same person twice.
- Employees in these companies may lack the expertise and training to handle advanced aspects of your estate. No one wants a young, inexperienced "kid" managing the affairs.
- The biggest disadvantage of using these trust services is the cost. It is such an issue that the institutions offering theses services rarely give you a fee schedule up front, and even getting a fee schedule at all is difficult. They are reluctant to discuss the fees they will charge you because they are very high. Some companies charge you every time they lift a finger on your account. Also, sometimes items such as the final tax return or selling the family home cost extra on top of the high initial fees.

It is a personal choice whether you want to use a trust company for your estate service needs. Get an opinion about whether your estate will have sufficient complexities to warrant such a service. If you decide to hire one of these companies, shop around to compare services and ask a lot of questions—particularly about fees.

# 66

## What is a testamentary trust? Do I need one?

This has to be one of the most overlooked estate planning opportunities for Canadians. A *testamentary trust* is created on the death of an individual to take advantage of lower tax rates applicable to trust income than may be available to the beneficiaries of your estate. The advantage is that the trust is taxed as a person, benefiting from the graduated tax system that we all benefit from as individuals. But since the trust has no income except for estate investment income, the effective tax rate can be low.

If your estate is immediately distributed to your heirs, typically your children, and they are all in the top tax bracket already, they will pay a high tax rate on the income they earn if they invest their inheritance. On the other hand, if the money remains in the estate within a testamentary trust, then the tax is paid within the trust on investment income earned, and the after-tax proceeds are then flowed out to the beneficiaries, often resulting in less tax paid.

Let's say a person had a net worth of $600,000 cash. She had a simple will, everything was clear and correct, and within days the entire value of the estate was evenly divided between the two children, who are now adults. Each child received $300,000 and invested it in their own name. They earned 10% return—$30,000 interest—in the first year after their parent's death, which was added to their regular income. Since they were already in the top tax bracket, all of the interest in both cases was taxed at approximately 50%. They each lost $15,000 to tax and kept $15,000 of their total return. Each year combined they paid $30,000 of income tax on earnings and kept $30,000.

In the next scenario, the parent revised the will to have all estate proceeds flow into a testamentary trust that was created on death. Both children were beneficiaries of the trust and would ultimately receive all the assets. Before that time, the estate assets stayed within the trust, were invested there and were taxed there. After-tax proceeds were paid out annually to the beneficiaries. There was a big difference in the tax impact:

Using the same amounts as in the example above, this time all the investments were in the trust after death and the full $60,000 of annual income was taxed in the trust. The trust had no other income so the average tax rate for the trust was less than 27.1%. This means the trust paid less than $16,000 of tax on the full $60,000 of income earned in the first year. And this was repeated every year! So the beneficiaries each received half of the $44,000 ($60,000 minus $16,000) of after-tax proceeds from the trust, and had no further taxation to pay.

In summary, the second option provides after-tax cash flow to *each* beneficiary that is $7,000 more than the cash flow from the first scenario. And the same cash flow will be repeated every year until the trust is wound up. Talk to a qualified professional about the uses of a testamentary trust for your estate.

# 67

## What factors should I consider if I decide to leave a large inheritance to my 18-year-old granddaughter or give her the money now while I am alive?

Whether it is an inheritance or a gift, you may not want younger people to get their hands on the money too soon. And as the children get older, future events in their lives may affect the money you give them now. There may be concerns about possible marriage breakdowns, going bankrupt, and spendthrift tendencies that cause the giver of the money to want to take precautions to protect this money. Even if you trust your children or grandchildren completely, you cannot control what happens in their lives when they are exposed to risks of loss, so you should take precautions to prevent the money from being reduced or lost. (I am going to assume that we are not talking about saving for a child's future education. I will address that in Rule 10.)

For significant savings I encourage you to have a family trust put in place. Your family lawyer or accountant can assist you with the creation, planning, and paperwork. Once it is set up, you'll also need to file an annual tax return. The accountant can take care of this on your behalf. All in all, the cost of setting up the structure and maintaining it may be as much as a couple of thousand dollars a year. That's why you need a reasonably large amount of money in the trust to really make the trust worthwhile. Here's how it works.

There are three different parties involved in a trust arrangement. The *beneficiaries* are the people who will receive distributions from the trust in the form of income and/or capital receipts on a predetermined or discretionary basis. The *trustee* is the manager of the trust and is responsible for maintaining the trust, following the rules of the trust agreement, managing the investments within the trust, and paying the distributions from the trust. The trustees interact with the lawyers and accountants who help create and maintain the trust. The third party is the *settlor*, who is the party or person responsible for setting up the trust and making the initial deposit of cash or assets to the trust.

Here is an example of how a trust would be established: The grandparent would be the settlor of the trust and would work with a lawyer to draft a trust document that outlines the operations of the trust in the future. The trust document can be made ironclad, able to survive any future marriage breakdowns, deaths, or bankruptcies. In the trust document, the grandparent would specify how the assets will be managed, who the trustees and beneficiaries are, how the assets and the income will be distributed to the beneficiaries and when, and ultimately when the trust will be finally wound up and the capital distributed to the beneficiaries. The trust can be set up to follow any kinds of wishes the settlor wants. Almost anything is possible.

Once the trust is set up and the money deposited to an investment account in the name of the trust, the settlor's role is over. In other words, the grandparent no longer has any say in the trust operation. The trustees now take over and will follow the rules that the grandparent established when the trust was set up. Perhaps in this question, the grandparent could dictate that the money deposited into the trust will be invested conservatively by the trustees, and the investment income will be paid out to the children each year until they are age 25; at that time all the capital assets inside the trust will be flowed out to the beneficiary granddaughter and the trust collapsed.

There are a couple of important things to note about this trust:

- Any income earned and retained inside this "living trust" will be taxed at the top marginal tax rate for individuals in Canada (this differs from a testamentary trust created after death, which is taxed at the regular graduated marginal rates for individuals); income flowed out to beneficiaries each year will be taxed in the hands of the beneficiaries at their graduated tax rates and it is generally advantageous to do this with a living or inter vivos trust.
- Once the money is put inside this trust, the grandparent permanently loses control over this money, although the grandparent could be one of the beneficiaries as well. This type of living trust is not created as a tax minimization trust—it is generally created for non-tax planning purposes such as asset protection against an irresponsible child. There are many different trust uses possible so it is important to explore whether a trust could be used in your personal finance situation.

The use of trusts in your finances can be very helpful to accomplish a number of different goals. Whether it is for tax planning, creditor proofing, asset protection, or for other reasons, discuss the use of trusts in your situation with a qualified tax lawyer or accountant.

# 68

## Should I make my assets jointly owned with my children to help them avoid probate fees on my death?

I am not a fan of making assets jointly owned with children. There are many issues to examine (legal issues and tax issues, to name two) before making assets jointly owned with anyone.

There are *tax* implications of making assets jointly owned, and there are separate *legal* implications. Many Canadians don't realize that there are these two different factors, and often just see one or, worse, none. Let me examine specific tax and legal issues of making assets jointly owned. (I will assume that there is a transfer of legal and beneficial ownership of the asset in making it jointly owned.) The table below contains just a few examples of the complicated rules that surround simple joint ownership.

Here are the key points to remember about making assets jointly owned:

- Taxation of investment income in Canada is guided by attribution rules in the Income Tax Act. Attribution means taxation of income and capital gains is based on who created the pool of investments. If the person who purchased the investments changes the name on the investments to another family member, the original purchaser may still pay tax on the investments.

- Making assets legally jointly owned with your children can expose your life savings to loss from marriage breakdowns and other costly events that happen to your children or grandchildren. No matter how much you trust your children, and no matter what age they are, you cannot determine what will happen in their lives. Take steps to protect your assets.

- If you want to give your children control over your accounts to assist you with managing your finances in old age, consider giving them a power of attorney over the money instead of joint ownership. This way the money remains legally yours (and safe from loss from a child's divorce, for example), but they can have some control over the funds to be able to help you out.

- Making assets jointly owned with your children may or may not allow you to avoid probate fees. It depends on whether you transfer beneficial ownership of the assets. Transferring beneficial ownership means you are really giving some of the asset to your children for their ownership and use. This differs from just putting their name on the account to help you complete transactions while it is really still all your money. If you transfer beneficial ownership by making an asset jointly owned, then you will avoid probate fees on death on this asset. But at the same time, changing beneficial ownership will result in a partial deemed disposition of the assets you are making jointly owned. This may result in taxes due at the time of the joint assign-

## Some Joint Asset Ownership Rules

| Situation | Legal Issues | Taxation Issues |
|---|---|---|
| Dad makes a bank account of cash jointly owned with mom. | Each parent would now have a legal entitlement to the proceeds of the account; so if mom goes bankrupt after getting in a car accident and being sued, half the proceeds are exposed to loss to creditors. | If dad contributed all of the funds in the account, he must always continue to pay tax on all interest earnings from the account, regardless of whose name is on the account. |
| Mom makes a bank account of cash jointly owned with her 16-year-old son. | If her son gets married in the future, and then divorced, the son's half interest in mom's account is exposed to loss on divorce. | Since mom contributed the cash for all of the investments, she will continue to pay taxes on and interest on the entire account. |
| Dad makes a bank account of cash jointly owned with adult daughter. Adult children are aged 18 or older. | Half of the money is now exposed to possible excess spending, bankruptcy, and divorce by the daughter, among other things. | If dad is gifting half of the account to the daughter, then the adult daughter will now have to claim one-half of investment income on the account. Generally, gifts to adult children result in no attribution of taxable income back to a parent. |
| Mom makes an investment account holding equity funds with large unrealized gains jointly owned with her adult daughter. Mom makes the family cottage jointly owned with her adult daughter. | Same as above. | If Mom is gifting half of the assets to the daughter, the adult daughter will now have to claim one-half of any investment income on account in the future. Also, there is a deemed disposition on half of the existing capital gain on the assets immediately that mom must pay tax on in the current year. |

ment if there are any existing capital gains on the assets, and may not be desirable if the gain is large (say if you make a cottage property jointly owned). But if you make an asset jointly owned and don't intend to transfer beneficial ownership, not only do you not trigger a deemed disposition and tax on a portion of a built-up gain, but you also don't avoid probate fees. Simply put, you can't have your cake and eat it too.

- Even more important is the cost-and-benefit analysis that should be done before making an asset jointly owned to avoid future probate fees. If you make the family cottage jointly owned (or gifted completely) to your children, this could immediately trigger the realization of the tax bill that has been accumulating on your cottage gain since you purchased it. It does not make sense to trigger a $100,000 tax bill today to save $2,500 of probate fees in 20 years. Don't rush to rearrange your affairs without evaluating the common sense of the strategy.

The tax and legal issues around joint ownership and gifting of assets to your children are significant. With tax alone, there are different rules depending on the type of asset made jointly owned, the type of income generated by the asset, and the person you make an asset jointly owned with. For example, tax issues around making a cottage jointly owned are different than rules for making a bank account jointly owned. Interest income can cause different tax results than capital gains. And joint ownership with your spouse has tax implications that are different from joint ownership with your adult child or your minor children. Before you make any significant assets jointly owned or give them away, talk to a qualified professional about all the tax and legal issues that need to be planned for to accommodate your wishes.

# 69

## What is a power of attorney? Do I really need one?

Rather than making assets jointly owned to permit your family to assist you to manage your life in old age, consider giving your family power of attorney over some of your assets. A *power of attorney* (POA) is a document that authorizes another person or persons (your family or your lawyer or someone else) to act on your behalf. The POA can be very general in nature, authorizing the stated persons to do almost anything you can do. Or the POA can be restricted, limiting the stated person's authority in a number of ways.

Below are some of the ways that POAs can be limited:

- You can give someone POA to close the sale of your new home on your behalf while you take an extended vacation out of the country.
- You can give someone POA on your behalf for a specific time frame.
- You can give someone POA on your behalf if something happens to you, such as if you become incapable of managing your own affairs after having a stroke.

It is important to consider using a continuing POA, otherwise a POA will be automatically revoked if you become mentally incapacitated. This would leave you with no POA at all.

As well, consider appointing all of your children together ("joint and several") on your POA to ensure that they communicate with each other and agree on all aspects of managing your affairs. Many times using only one child can cause disagreements among all the children.

If you already signed a continuing POA at your bank, be aware that it may only be limited to business that you have at that bank and will not relate to your assets and wishes beyond that institution. You may need another POA to cover all the affairs intended.

Have your lawyer review and update your POA forms if you haven't had them examined in several years. Legal forms change, new legal precedence is established, and your goals can shift, requiring an update to your POA forms.

If you own property or assets outside of the province you live in, you should talk to your lawyer about the need for a separate POA (and a separate will) to cover your wishes for those assets. They may not be covered by the POA (or will) for your province.

A continuing POA deals with matters related to your property, but not your health and physical well-being. To have someone make decisions on proposed medical treatments on your behalf, you need a separate document called a POA for personal care. Personal care includes your safety, health care, clothing, nutrition, hygiene, and shelter.

When you die, all of your POAs cease to apply. At that time, the executor of your estate takes responsibility for managing the affairs of your estate until they are finalized.

Every Canadian would be well served by having some form of POA in place. Work with a professional financial advisor to review your POA preferences.

# 70

**Are there things I should be doing now to prevent a large tax bill on the family cottage on my death?**

There are many financial issues surrounding cottage ownership and passing it on to the next generation of family. Consider the following example:

Mom and Dad bought a cottage in 1975 for $20,000. In 1981 the market value was still only $20,000. In 1985 an additional bedroom was added for $20,000. In 1994 the fair market value of the cottage was $175,000. In 1998 the value of the cottage was appraised at $210,000. In 1998, Dad made the cottage jointly owned with their adult child to avoid probate fees on death and to gift the child half the interest in the property. Mom died in 1999. Dad died in late 2000. After both parents died, the child inherited the cottage. The estimated value at that time was $340,000.

Now let's examine all the financial issues surrounding the cottage and the family through the years.

- It is important to keep track of the cost base of the cottage right back to the beginning because this information will eventually be needed to calculate the taxable capital gain on sale or on death. In this case, the cost base or "ACB" is $40,000, consisting of the original cost plus the cost of additions throughout time. It is a good idea to keep receipts to back this up.
- Since the cottage was purchased before 1981, there may be an opportunity to shelter the gain up to this point with something called the principal residence exemption. Before 1981, each Canadian was entitled to own one property on a permanently tax-free basis. In 1981, the rules were changed to permit only one tax-free residence per family. On capital gains earned before 1981, it would be possible to still apply two exemptions so that two spouses can shelter accrued gains on a house and a cottage. In this case, there was no gain in this early period, but for many Canadians this would be an extra tax-saving opportunity.
- Also on the cost base, before 1994, there was the opportunity to use a capital gains exemption on the cottage and other assets to shelter another $100,000 of gain that existed at that time. In our example, this would have permitted the cost base on the family cottage to be increased from $40,000 to $140,000, avoiding tax of more than $25,000 for someone in the top tax bracket in Canada. If you missed taking advantage of this stepup a few years ago, you lost out on an easy tax saving.
- When Dad made the cottage jointly owned with the child in 1998, he transferred beneficial ownership of half the cottage property and, with that, triggered half of the accrued capital gain that existed on the cottage. This capital gain amounted to ($210,000 less $140,000) $70,000 x $\frac{1}{2}$ = $35,000. For a top-tax-bracket individual,

that amounts to an immediate tax bill in 1998 of roughly $13,000! Making assets jointly owned with your children is not always a smart move! In addition to tax now owing, Dad has also now given the son some control over the cottage, and may expose the property to the son's credit risks and marriage breakdown risks.

- When Mom died there was no tax to pay on the cottage because she did not legally own the cottage nor did she own the cottage for tax purposes since she didn't contribute any of her own money at any time to buy the cottage. Even if she had, on the death of the first spouse it is possible to transfer assets to the second spouse without triggering any tax on accrued gains that exist to that point. This is the case for all Canadians. A family typically only faces a tax bill on family assets with accrued capital gains on the death of the last spouse.
- On Dad's death, all family assets that remained were taxable all at once: all of dad's (and Mom's former) RRIFs or RRSPs and all assets with accrued gains. Cash is not taxable on death, by the way. In this case, there was more tax to pay on the cottage since the value had increased again after it was made jointly owned. The final tax on Dad's share of the cottage gain amounted to $340,000 less $140,000 = a $200,000 gain times half ownership = $100,000 capital gain to claim on Dad's final tax return. This will result in a tax liability of $25,000.

So now we get to the question at hand: If Dad's estate doesn't have the $25,000 to pay CCRA, or if the father doesn't like the idea of losing so much to taxes, can anything be done to eliminate or reduce the payment? You can't eliminate this payment. This is tax due, no way around it. But you can take steps to plan to offset the impact of this result. Here are some options:

- The child can negotiate with CCRA to set up a repayment schedule (like a loan) to pay the taxes due. CCRA will be fair with the child in this regard. Interest will also be due, of course.
- The child could get a loan from a financial institution to pay CCRA.
- The child could sell the cottage and use some of the cash proceeds to pay the tax bill. But this may not be a desirable result.
- Mom and Dad and child could have purchased a life insurance policy before the parents' deaths that would have paid out a tax-free death benefit that could have been used by the estate to pay the tax bill. The child could have paid the life insurance premiums when the parents were alive so that Mom and Dad wouldn't be burdened with the cash flow requirements.

As you can see, there are many complicated twists to dealing with a cottage property on death, even when you make it jointly owned with others. If you own any asset with significant value built up in it, like a cottage or a family business, ensure that you talk to a qualified lawyer or tax accountant about planning for the future.

# 71

## Can probate fees be avoided by purchasing segregated mutual funds?

Segregated funds (seg funds) are fund investments offered through life insurance companies. They are like regular mutual funds, with a few important differences. One of the attractive characteristics of seg funds is that probate fees can be avoided when the seg funds are passed to the heirs—this is not possible with regular mutual funds. Probate fees are a tax on the market value of assets in your estate at death and, depending on the province, can amount to more than 1% of the value of your estate as a one-time hit. Generally, avoiding probate fees is desirable and can be achieved with proper planning.

## Seg funds protect against probate fees

Seg funds are much like life insurance or your RRSP when it comes to estate planning. In all three of these products, you can designate a beneficiary as part of your planning process for buying the product. Designating a beneficiary allows this asset to pass directly to the beneficiary on death, bypassing your estate entirely. By avoiding the estate, probate fees are not charged on the value of the seg funds, and this is a savings. If you own regular mutual funds, you cannot designate a beneficiary and thus the probate fee avoidance strategy is not possible.

## The rest of the story

In exchange for the probate savings (and other seg fund benefits such as guarantee of original principal), you pay a higher annual fee in the form of a higher management expense ratio (MER) of the seg fund. In some cases, the MER of a seg fund will be double or triple the cost of a similar plain mutual fund.

So let's re-evaluate the use of seg funds for probate avoidance. You may want to think twice about buying seg funds for probate avoidance purposes for the following reason: In some cases, you will be paying 2% or more each year you are alive (in the form of higher annual fund MER) to save a one-time payment of 1.5% on your death. Put another way, if you buy seg funds today, and don't die for 20 years, you will pay an extra cost of 40% (20 years times 2% MER each year) to save a one-time probate fee of 1.5% or less!

Seg funds are not a wise buy for probate avoidance alone. It can get even worse for seg funds and estate planning. Here's another potential disadvantage with seg funds for estate planning.

## Seg funds and death of a spouse

When you die owning regular mutual funds, you can defer any taxation owed on these investments by leaving them to your surviving spouse. It is important to know that with seg funds it is not that straightforward. Depending on how the seg fund is set up with the annuitant and the contract holder (investor), you may or may not achieve a similar tax deferral on the death of the first spouse. If not structured appropriately, the seg fund may face taxation on the death of the first spouse. This is usually highly undesirable. Speak to a financial advisor about how to structure seg fund ownership to ensure that no surprising tax hits arise.

## One advantage to using seg funds for estate planning...maybe

One of the most attractive features of seg funds is the guarantees they provide against loss of your original investment amount. This is by far the greatest reason seg funds are purchased. This guarantee can offer comfort to many, including seniors. Many seg funds normally only offer the guarantee of capital if you hold their seg fund for ten years straight. However, in old age the seg fund guarantees apply within the ten-year period if you die. For many seniors interested in pursuing above-average returns in the stock market without the risk of losing money, seg funds can be attractive. One point to consider, however, is that recently the cost of owning seg funds has risen significantly. Evaluate the cost and benefit of owning seg funds based on these new higher costs against the reasons that you originally needed this product.

Be very cautious about the purchase of seg funds for estate-planning purposes for your portfolio in general. Seg funds do have good attributes (protection from creditors in some cases, guaranteed principal in some cases), but clearly they are not an investment product for everyone.

# RULE 9

**Explore insurance carefully for effective net worth preservation and enhancement.**

The insurance industry has changed dramatically since the days of insurance agents knocking on your door to sell you simple life insurance. Today, there are many different types of insurance for sale: life insurance (such as term, permanent, and universal), disability insurance (with a variety of bells and whistles), and critical illness insurance, among others. And insurance is purchased for a variety of uses today: risk protection, liquidity, and net worth enhancement. Many financial advisors are able to speak to the complexities of insurance products and their uses.

Here are just a few of the common uses of various types of insurance:

**RISK PROTECTION.** Basic protection against income loss for any wage earner with dependants who is killed or becomes physically disabled and unable to work to generate an income to live on.

**LIQUIDITY.** Insurance for shareholders of large private companies as part of their estate planning/company exit strategy. Insurance proceeds received on death can provide cash to the family, remaining shareholders, or to the company to enable the parties to buy out the deceased shareholder.

**PROTECTION AGAINST TAX LIABILITY.** Insurance for families with cottages that have greatly appreciated in value during ownership such that a large amount of tax will be due on the death of the last spouse. Insurance proceeds received on death can often provide the cash flow to pay the tax liability.

**CASH FLOW DURING ILLNESS.** Insurance for critically ill people who require cash flow to purchase expensive drugs or pay for medical procedures to treat their condition.

**NET WORTH OR CASH FLOW ENHANCEMENT.** Insurance for families with large RRSPs that want to use the tax-free insurance payout on death to offset the taxes due on the RRSP or RRIF on the death of the last surviving spouse.

**TAX SHELTER OPPORTUNITIES.** Insurance for more affluent individuals who want to take advantage of the tax sheltering of income that insurance offers in some products. This tax sheltering can defer taxation and result in a larger net worth.

Insurance products are complicated and more people than ever before are selling them. You can buy life insurance through your employer, directly from banks and insurance companies, over the Internet, from your broker, and from a wide variety of financial advisors. Each one of these sources can offer insurance products from a variety of insurance companies. Some of these companies have built their own insurance products. The choice can be overwhelming.

Insurance products can be great products to own, but like most things, they are not suitable for everyone. There are specific reasons to purchase insurance. Some insurance is essential (such as protection against income loss when you have dependants) while other insurance is nonessential (such as buying insurance for medical treatment on a disease you might or might not get or buying insurance to offset tax on death). Ensure that you buy insurance first for essential needs. Then look more carefully at buying insurance for nonessential needs. Is this the best use of your money? Take time to evaluate needs and products and consider a second opinion before you buy.

# 72

## Should I purchase critical illness insurance to cover medical costs in case I develop a serious disease or medical condition?

I call critical illness insurance "Cadillac insurance" because it is a luxury form of insurance that is nice to have, but it is not an essential insurance product.

Critical illness insurance is insurance where you pay premiums from the date of purchase, and the insurance will pay you a tax-free lump sum of cash if you get a specific disease like cancer, heart disease, or a stroke. The idea is that the insurance proceeds will assist you to pay for expensive medical treatments and drugs, and will cover pain and suffering and lost income while you battle the illness. Critical illness insurance is being sold as the cash solution to cover all these costs including private nursing care, rehabilitation, child care, and continuing expenses such as mortgages and other expenses. All cost money while you are battling your illness.

Purchasing critical illness insurance can be difficult given there are unpredictable variables that affect you when you have an illness. For example, how much cash will you need should you get sick? It may be very hard to accurately forecast what it will cost for drugs or treatment, especially if you have to visit the U.S. for treatment, where costs can skyrocket. Purchasing too little critical illness insurance may be ineffective while purchasing too much can be hard on your finances today.

Then there is the matter of the particular disease you may get and what exactly is covered. Upon review of critical insurance policies of four major insurance companies in Canada, I noted the following interesting characteristics:

- Each company had variations on the type of insurance product it offered as its critical illness policy (for example, variations on the cost and on the length of time premiums are paid).
- Each company covered different aspects of a particular disease; for example, one company offered to pay proceeds to a client after a stroke only if there was a measurable neurological deficit 60 days after the stroke; another company said they would pay after only 30 days.
- All the insurance companies I reviewed included cancer as a basic core coverage, but upon further research I discovered that didn't include stage A prostate cancer. Beware exceptions!
- All the insurance companies I reviewed included cancer, stroke, and heart disease under the basic coverage. Additional coverage for many other diseases was possible through the purchase of additional insurance "riders." This means that you either have to guess correctly what illness you will get in the future or face having no coverage when you get a disease that your critical illness insurance doesn't cover.

Be careful with this insurance. It is being aggressively sold to many Canadians, particularly older Canadians. Don't be afraid to ask hard questions and always get a second opinion before buying. Critical illness insurance can be a great tool in specific cases, but it is not for everyone.

# 73

## Should I buy universal life insurance to avoid my estate having to pay up to half of my RRIF or RRSP in taxes?

On the death of the last remaining spouse (you or your husband/wife), all family assets where you have been able to defer taxes are finally taxable all at once. This means your RRSPs or RRIFs, for example, which have been tax sheltered so far, are now fully taxable in most cases. This will mean that up to 50% of the value of the plan may be lost to taxes on death. You can't stop the Canada Customs and Revenue Agency (CCRA) from getting their fair share, but you can offset the taxes with life insurance that will pay out tax free on death.

There are several variables you need to consider before you buy life insurance for death planning purposes. What are your goals? If you are strongly motivated to maximize the value of your estate, you may want to consider life insurance as one means to do that. Do your kids really care whether they get more cash after you are dead, or would they prefer to see you live your life more fully with greater cash flow now instead of paying insurance premiums? Maybe they are prepared to pay the insurance cost for you? Or maybe they are not. Have a heart-to-heart discussion with the family before you go out and spend a lot of money on an estate-planning insurance policy.

Can you afford the insurance? Since the cost of insurance premiums is going to come out of your cash flow, are you prepared to sacrifice your current standard of living to contribute towards a policy that will pay out a benefit after you are dead? If you are a low-income pensioner, perhaps you should not be buying life insurance just to be able to leave your kids more money on your death. You may face rising health care costs and inflation over the years that will cause you to need all of your savings.

Have you taken advantage of other forms of savings first? Don't consider an insurance policy for death planning until after you have fully maximized your RRSPs each year. It is generally considered more advantageous to contribute to an RRSP where the accumulated tax-sheltered savings will lead to more money than an insurance policy payout.

Have you paid off all non-tax-deductible debt first? Generally, you should pay off your mortgage or other personal debt long before considering an insurance policy for your estate. Typically, the cost of debt after tax is hurting you more than an insurance policy would help you.

Does this insurance suit your particular situation? People with high income levels, people who own small businesses that they want to keep in the family, and people with cottages they have held in the family for decades are some of the categories of individuals who are well suited to life insurance as an estate planning tool.

Once you decide that you are going to buy, decide how much insurance and what type you need. It will depend on what you can afford, what your goals are, what your family wants, and what makes sense according to your financial situation. Further, if you decide that you are going to buy a lot of insurance, think about how solvent the insurance company may be. In other words, will they survive another 20 years to be able to pay out the policy on your death?

Pay attention to cost! When it comes down to it, you are still buying risk management protection, no matter how much you are now thinking of insurance as a tax-deferred investment. For that protection, you will have to pay an annual fee inside the insurance product that will take away from your investment returns. Make sure you understand the amount of fees taken each year, how these fees can fluctuate, and so on. The growth of your investment pool inside the insurance policy may also be affected by dividends credited to your pool by the insurance company, and this may be affected annually by the company's costs. Look at historical costs and dividends credited to the policy. Compare these among insurance companies. Stay away from variable costs that can rise and fall each year, leaving you uncertain as to what is actually going on within your policy.

Some factors are undesirable but essentially unavoidable. It is possible that you could buy an insurance policy where you agree to pay premiums for ten years, and after ten years the company says you will likely have to pay for another four years. The payment of unexpected and additional premiums can be a function of inaccurate forecasting of reserve requirements (for example, dividends paid to you) within the policy, inaccurate forecasting of investment returns earned within the policy over time, or other inaccurate assumptions made long ago when your policy was set up. All you can do is ensure that you are comfortable with the cost variables of your policy when you buy and understand what may or may not lead to additional future costs.

The results of life insurance product forecasts are assumptions made by the agent and the insurance company. Make sure the assumptions are reasonable with respect to investment returns, costs, dividends, bonuses, and other variables that affect long-term performance. Unreasonable expectations can leave you with a rosy view of the future that may not be accurate. Always examine worst-case scenarios as part of your evaluation process.

Universal life insurance is popular today as an estate-planning product sold to offset death taxes. It is important to remember, however, that this is a nonessential insurance need for most Canadians. Ensure there is good logic and a strong financial case supporting your need to buy.

# 74

## Should I buy universal life insurance, which pays out tax free on death?

This is a case of buying insurance as a savings plan instead of for risk-management purposes. In other words, the insurance policy is not required to guard against unexpected loss; instead, the tax-free payout on death is being contemplated as a net worth enhancement tool.

There are varying opinions on the appropriateness of buying insurance for savings reasons. Some parties say that insurance should only be purchased for risk-management reasons because the cost of pure insurance cannot be separated from the savings component, making this an expensive way to invest. However, other parties will state that given the right kind of insurance, the right conditions, and the right kind of individual, insurance can in fact enhance net worth more than a regular taxable savings plan. Since insurance payouts on death are tax free and large amounts of investment savings can accrue within the policy, the potential exists to create a large savings pool that can be realized on death in a tax-free manner. Typically, universal life insurance policies are used for this type of planning.

Here are some thoughts to consider about this tax-deferred income savings strategy:

- Only consider this strategy if you have a strong desire to maximize your estate, have already maximized your RRSPs, have no non-tax-deductible debt, and have the cash flow to fund the policy premiums. This product and strategy is not for most Canadians, who struggle just to maximize their RRSPs.
- A universal insurance policy consists of the cost of insurance and a savings component. Compare the pure cost of insurance in the universal life policy with competing products to judge value—in other words, shop around. Also ensure that the savings component offers broad investment choices, not just fixed-income investments.
- If you are healthy and expect to live beyond age 85, consider buying term-to-100 insurance as the insurance component; that way your premium levels are guaranteed for life. Other forms of insurance can get extremely expensive the longer you live, making the funding of a universal policy difficult to keep up in your old age.
- Some investors have been going one step further and borrowing against the cash value of the policy in retirement. Investors who have built up a cash value in a universal life policy over time can access this value without triggering tax. In some cases, the cash surrender value of a policy can be used as collateral for a bank loan. The insurance policy owner can take out a loan from a bank and use the funds to live on in retirement. A loan is not taxable income so it provides a lot of additional cash flow. Interest is charged on the loan and accumulated by the bank, and the loan

is not paid off until the insurance policy holder dies. The policy proceeds are then used to pay off the loan and outstanding interest, and any remaining insurance proceeds go to the estate and heirs.

While this strategy sounds great, there are pitfalls: First, there has been talk for years that the CCRA doesn't like this borrowing strategy and might shut down this quasi-tax-avoidance plan. Second, the whole strategy will collapse if you live long and borrow so much that the loan and interest use up the insurance policy money, or if the collateral value of the policy falls below the value of the bank loan.

Most Canadians are interested in maximizing the value of their estate. Life insurance, particularly universal life insurance, is being aggressively marketed as a product that can enhance net worth on death. While this is possible given the right circumstances, most Canadians either cannot afford it or simply don't need insurance for death planning. Ensure that if you buy estate-planning insurance, you examine all options with your eyes wide open.

# 75

## I'm 30 years old and single, with no dependants. What type of insurance should I buy?

If you ask a couple of different insurance professionals you may get different recommendations about what insurance you need in your situation. Let me give you my opinion (as a non-product licensed insurance advisor) on your lifetime insurance needs. The chart below summarizes my thoughts, and I encourage you to seek professional advice based on your specific situation.

| Situation | Insurance Required | Purpose of the Insurance |
| --- | --- | --- |
| Before age 25 | None | You have no dependants, no debts, no one who will suffer should you die. |
| Get married | None | You were both fine before marriage, why would you all of a sudden need insurance? |
| Buy a home | None | Without you, does your spouse need a big house alone? If the spouse cannot fund the mortgage payments, consider a sale of the property, assuming there are no children. |
| Have children | $1.5 million of term insurance (more or less, depending on your needs) from the child's birth to age 21 | Now you have dependants. You need enough insurance that if you died, the insurance proceeds could be invested to generate adequate after-tax income to replace what is needed to take care of your dependants. If your spouse returns to a career, you may need far less insurance. |
| Spouse stays home to raise children | Same as above | You now need insurance to provide an income in the event of your untimely death. |
| Getting a new job | You will likely get group term insurance from the employer | Group policies can be expensive and poorly crafted with inadequate amounts, and are non-transferable if you leave your job. Look for your own insurance to fill in the gaps. |
| You have specific estate-planning goals, and you can afford to maximize the estate | Universal life insurance; purchase it in your 40s, 50s, or 60s | Offset taxes on death to preserve or enhance estate value by using an insurance policy that pays out tax free on death. |
| Own a successful family business that you want to pass on to the next generation | Universal life insurance purchased on the lives of the business owners | To permit shareholders to transfer share ownership by using the proceeds to buy out the shares of the deceased owner. |

| | | |
|---|---|---|
| Own a long-time family cottage with a large accrued capital gain; few other family assets of value exist | Universal life insurance purchased by the parents or children who will get the cottage | If there is no cash available to pay the death taxes on the cottage, insurance can be used to generate needed cash. |
| Concerned about getting certain diseases | Could consider critical illness insurance | Provides money for medical treatment. |
| Concerned about disability | Disability insurance; your employer may provide coverage; consider another personally owned policy to fill the shortcomings of the employer's policy | Your employer's policy may be a good start but likely needs a top up policy to ensure the coverage matches your needs. |

In the above table I have generalized as much as possible, and that is not practical for specific situations. Understanding your insurance needs and product solutions to match your needs can become tremendously confusing. Don't rush into buying insurance. Take time to understand the variables and shop around.

# RULE 10

## Factor your children into your net worth growth.

When it comes to thinking about children and financial planning, most parents only go so far as to think about how to save for a child's future education. While this is an important planning aspect, it is only the start of planning that should involve children. Every individual with little ones around needs to step back and re-examine their finances from the point of view of including the children more closely.

Take the time to understand the variety of financial issues and strategies that evolve as a child ages and as you age. The impact on your family's bottom line can be tremendous.

Here are some examples of what I mean:

- The idea of saving for a child is popular today. Should a parent use an RESP or an in-trust account? In-trust accounts were popular five years ago. RESPs are hot today. Much has been written on both. What is the right answer for you? I will examine these issues in the next strategy. The more important question is, do you know how much money your child will need for a future education?

- Involving children in your tax planning is a must. There are many opportunities to shift income into the hands of minor children and reduce family income tax. Yes, family income tax. Every family should think of their taxes in the context of what the entire family pays, and how to minimize the total family tax bill. Planning becomes easier when looked at this way.

There is a tremendous amount of planning that can be accomplished involving children or grandchildren.

# 76

## Should I use an RESP, an in-trust account, or a formal trust as the vehicle to save for my children's future?

Today there are three different vehicles you can use to save for your children.

1. RESPs (Registered Educational Savings Plans)
2. In-trust accounts
3. Formal trusts created by lawyers and accountants

The right vehicle for you and your family to use will depend on several factors: the purpose of the savings; your desire to create the largest savings pool of money possible; and your desired control over the money.

Many financial advisors would lead you to believe that you should choose one or the other type of vehicle for tax or investment reasons. That is not the case. You can achieve roughly equal tax results from all three types of savings plans mentioned above: all provide ways to income split and shift taxation of the income onto the children for tax savings. As well, under all three plans, you can defer taxation on the capital gains earned. You can also own similar types of investments (for example, mutual funds) in all three of these structures.

Let's now examine the different criteria that will help you decide how to save for your children or grandchildren:

**THE PURPOSE OF THE SAVINGS.** The purpose of the savings is critical to deciding what method to use for children's savings. An RESP can only be used to save for a child's postsecondary education (university or college), so if the child decides not to go to university and instead opens a small business, major penalties may be incurred if RESP savings are in place based on the current rules. An in-trust account can be used as a savings vehicle for any purpose and is very flexible due to its simplicity. A formal trust is equally flexible and can be used for any purpose.

**CREATING THE LARGEST POOL OF MONEY.** Since all plans can provide similar tax breaks and similar investment options, they can provide similar results over time. This would always be the case, except that RESPs now offer an additional registered educational savings grant of up to $400 per child per year. This extra cash gives RESPs an advantage over the other two plans and should result in the most money over time, assuming you put the same amount of money into each vehicle.

**DESIRED CONTROL OVER THE MONEY.** In my opinion, having control over the proceeds is the most important aspect of deciding how to save for children and grandchildren. With an RESP the children must go to university or college, or financial penalties can ensue. Parents as contributors don't have a lot of control over the proceeds since the use of the money is limited to funding the child's education.

In-trust accounts provide the least amount of control over the money. Because many in-trust account agreements are very simple documents, they don't deal with the complexity of issues that may arise. There is little guidance on what would happen with this money if one of the parents dies, if the child dies, or if the parents divorce. When the child turns 18, he or she is entitled to free and complete access to the money—all of it—and may decide to spend $100,000 on a car or a trip. So be aware that when you put money into an in-trust account, you give up complete legal control over that money once the child turns 18. Further, many in-trust agreements are so full of holes that there is much uncertainty about what happens should the family or the child have certain issues. Should the child marry and divorce at an early age (teens and twenties), the money may be subject to division in a settlement.

Formal trusts may be more expensive to implement due to legal and accounting fees paid to establish and maintain the trust, but they are also the strongest vehicle—they can withstand deaths, marriage breakdowns, and most other of life's issues. They can be used for any kind of spending that the contributing family find acceptable. The principal is guarded against a child's bad habits. Simply put, there is no better method for dictating how and when anyone should have access to money and assets in general. The tradeoff for this superb protection is annual professional fees.

Overall, an RESP will provide the most money but the children must attend a post-secondary educational institution. The formal trust is the vehicle that is most flexible and easiest to control. Most parents or grandparents should consider an RESP first; if the savings become very large (maybe due to an inheritance) then instead consider a formal trust. As a rule of thumb, if the savings for a child will amount to $60,000 or more, the cost of the formal trust can become worthwhile for the extra protection.

# 77

## I'm 50 years old and financially comfortable. Should I give $100,000 to my daughter and her husband to help pay off their large mortgage?

"Gifting" children money for the mortgage on their family residence can be very dangerous to the best interests of your family net worth. In most provinces, any money put into the family home, from any source, will be subject to division between spouses in the event of a breakdown of the marriage. This means you may stand to lose half of your gift should your daughter's marriage fizzle (you can never know what will happen!).

Generally I try to discourage people from gifting assets to their children, or at least encourage them talk to a lawyer to ensure that it is done with as much protection as possible against loss from marriage breakdowns, bankruptcies, and spendthrift periods (again, you cannot know what will happen).

People often say, "Kurt, I have good kids, I can trust my kids," or "My kids will always be there for me if I need the money back." I say to them, " I know you trust your kids, but…." You can't control whom your kids marry. No matter how much you trust your kids, you never can predict what will happen in their futures. This exposes your gifts to them to loss from marriage breakdowns, bankruptcies, and spendthrift habits.

Also, don't expect the kids to be able to return the gift to you later in your life. If you gift your kids money, they are likely going to spend it, or apply it against debt, or put it into their RRSPs. None of these three options are very liquid in a way that they could easily get the money out should you need it in an emergency—for life-saving surgery in the United States, for example.

Finally, you may need the money in the future for yourself! No one knows what the cost of health care will be in Canada in the coming years. We are seeing more and more user fees already, so having more money in your grasp is a great safety net.

Still, if you truly want to help out your kids by giving them cash, try these ideas:

- Give them small amounts at a time, and only what you can truly afford to lose.
- Thoroughly document all gifts to your child and maintain these documents as an audit trail should the child's family break up.
- Consider loaning the money instead of gifting; this can help to ensure the return of your loan should your child get divorced.
- Give your kids money, but don't let them put it into the mortgage or use it as a deposit for the family home. There is a greater likelihood that your child can get this money back if it is not used for the family home.
- Get advice from a lawyer with expertise in gifting and marriage breakdown issues.
- Be cautious about the tax implications related to your gift. If you gift cash to your adult children, there are no tax implications to you. However, if you gift an asset

with an appreciated value—such as a stock or equity mutual fund or a piece of real estate—the gift triggers the realization of the accrued capital gain, and it is taxable on your next personal tax return. Imagine if you gifted the family cottage to your child and unintentionally triggered a whopping capital gain that had been building for 30 years. The tax liability you created could be in the hundreds of thousands of dollars. All due next April!

The simple act of gifting assets to family members can have tremendous tax and legal implications. Speak to a professional financial advisor before gifting any major assets.

# 78

## What are some of the other financial issues related to children? I rarely think about my children with respect to complicating my finances—is that correct?

Children and grandchildren have dozens of financial issues that can become quite complicated but cannot be ignored, since they affect the finances of parents and grandparents.

Parts of this question has been discussed elsewhere, but it might be useful to summarize the many financial issues relevant to children, just to demonstrate how much there is to think about. No doubt about it, ignoring your children's role within your finances will cost you money. Here are a few of the issues that affect children:

- Registered Educational Savings Plans (RESPs) are a government-created savings plan for children's future education. Parents and grandparents need to carefully consider whether these plans are appropriate for them and how much money to put in the plan. There are also individual and group RESP plans to evaluate. Parents feeling a cash crunch may also face decisions about whether to contribute to an RESP or their own RRSP.
- Parents should think about filing a tax return for teenagers, even though they have very little taxable income. Filing a tax return will commence tracking of their RRSP contribution room.
- There are many costs associated with raising children that qualify as tax deductions and tax credits:
  - Tuition for qualifying schools is a tax credit.
  - Qualifying child care costs are a tax deduction.
  - Child maintenance costs paid between divorced parents have complicated tax implications depending on the situation.
  - Braces on a child's teeth may qualify as a medical tax credit.
- Investments owned by minor children that generate capital gains are taxed in their hands, not the parent's or grandparent's. This is not the case with interest income and dividends where taxation is retained by the gifting parent. Putting investments in the hands of minor children, if carefully planned, can reduce family taxation.
- Making assets or investments jointly owned with children has complicated tax and legal implications, as discussed in Rule 68.
- Gifting assets to children also has tax and legal implications. Even further, the tax issues for joint ownership and gifting will also differ if the child is a minor, or 18 years of age or older. On the legal side, putting assets of yours into a child's name can expose your assets to the risks of the child's life. If the child marries and then

divorces, it is unlikely that you will want the child's half interest in your house to be included in his or her divorced assets.

- Death and estate planning is a huge area where children and grandchildren are greatly integrated within your finances. Since children are typically the beneficiaries of an estate, often sophisticated attention needs to be paid to the tax, legal, and many other issues surrounding estate planning.
- If minor children are your dependants, there are likely needs for life and disability insurance that you would not have if you had no children.
- Having children makes you plan for guardianship, should something happen to you.
- Should you have life insurance on the life of a child? Likely not. Money would be better spent on building a savings plan for the child.
- Having children will greatly affect your retirement plans, as significant amounts of money will be diverted from your retirement savings to raise the children. This greatly complicates retirement planning and needs to be thought through regularly. It may not be wise for you to pay their costs of going to university, because your retirement finances will be harmed.
- You may want to establish a formal trust to hold assets for the benefit of your children. Or you may want to use an in-trust account for children's savings after an analysis of the pros and cons of each structure. If your children will receive substantial inheritances from a relative, you may want to explore more complicated vehicles like trusts for holding this money with greater controls built in.
- As children grow from tots to teenagers to young adults, their financial issues change, and the way these issues affect you also changes. Regular review and analysis of family financial issues is important to ensure that opportunities are not missed.
- Children are often in lower tax brackets, and throughout their lives there are many opportunities to implement income-splitting strategies to save tax. Re-evaluate these opportunities regularly.
- If your children live in different provinces or countries, there are different issues and strategies to be considered.
- If your children have debt (student loans, car loans, mortgages, etc.), it may be more appropriate for you to pay off their debts, to increase overall family wealth.
- If your children are all different ages, a variety of strategies must again be considered. Tax rules, for example, differ for children of different ages.
- As your children have children of their own, the number of issues and opportunities grows even larger.
- And what about grandpa and grandma? Often they are in the best positions to share money with the family. Often inter-generational planning can greatly increase family wealth.

If you have children, your personal financial analysis must include detailed analysis of children's issues. It must also explore all the opportunities to enhance family wealth by including children more formally in your plans when thinking about money.

# RULE 11
## Re-engineer your retirement finances today for a better tomorrow.

Wake up, Canada! Twenty years from now there may be no paid health care, no Canada Pension Plan, no Old Age Security benefits. You may be on your own. Yet many of us continue to take a nonchalant attitude towards our financial future. We can no longer assume that the government will take care of us.

Many people have lived a good life but have failed to save appropriately. Then, on their first day of retirement, they are shocked to find that they have to live on one-third the income that they have lived on for the last 20 years. They no longer have enough money to take fancy vacations or to buy a new car. And if they retire now, it is too late to change things.

It's a good idea to get control over your finances long before you retire. This section of the book is designed to provide some guidance on retirement planning.

Your working time may last 40 years—these are your wealth-accumulation years. Take advantage of this time period to plan for the final 30 years of your life in retirement.

Planning for retirement during your working years is hard. Saving for the future is often the lowest priority behind paying the mortgage, paying for children's needs, and just keeping up with the Joneses. But it is essential to put some money away for retirement. It is also important to constantly review the financial characteristics of your current life to ensure that all planning opportunities are maximized for a richer lifestyle when you retire.

Here are a few of the issues that should be addressed by most Canadians during their income-earning years. Many of these questions require thorough analysis, so ensure you take the time to examine the options and make well-thought-out decisions.

- Should you contribute any spare money you get to pay down your mortgage or to top up your RRSP?
- Should you borrow to invest? Should you borrow to make an RRSP contribution?
- Should you bother to contribute to an RRSP anymore?
- Should you save for your child's future using an RESP or just pay as you go out of your cash flow?
- What is the best age to buy a house? Is a home a good investment at all?
- Should you buy a car, lease a car, or take a loan to buy a car?
- Are you saving enough to provide the retirement you desire? How do you know?

- Do you have the right investment portfolio mix for your personal situation?
- Do you own the right kind of investments for your personal situation?
- Do you have too little or too much life and disability insurance? Do you have the right kind of insurance?
- How much money are you saving each year, and what is the logic behind the chosen amount you are saving?
- Are you doing all you can to minimize your taxes each year? Have you had a tax-planning opportunity review in the last two years?
- Are you doing all you can to minimize your family tax bill?
- Is your employment situation structured tax effectively?

It is essential that you take responsibility for building the retirement lifestyle you want. Your retirement may equal one-third of your life—will you be financially prepared?

# 79

## How can I factor inflation increases into my retirement planning?

It is necessary to consider inflation when it comes to retirement planning. Many of us know someone who retired years ago on a fixed pension. That means the pension benefits are not indexed for inflation over the years. If they retired 20 years ago on a pension of $20,000 a year, today they are trying to survive on exactly the same amount. In this last 20 years, inflation has destroyed their purchasing power and taken them from a comfortable retirement to one of near poverty. Their pension stayed flat, while the price of stamps, milk, cars, and everything else continued to rise. They lost ground because they forgot about inflation.

People who have purchased many GICs in the last 20 years may have been pushing themselves into poverty right in front of their eyes. With inflation, they may have been taking economic steps backwards with each GIC purchase! Look at this example:

| | |
|---|---|
| Interest rate paid on a GIC: | 6% |
| Tax paid on the interest income (assume 50% tax rate): | –3% |
| Net return: | 3% |
| Subtract the impact of inflation: | –4% |
| What you actually earned/lost: | –1% |

## Inflation strategies

There are several different ways to counter the impact of inflation on your money and lifestyle:

- Put some high-dividend-yielding equities or equity mutual funds inside your investment portfolio since dividends have a tendency to be raised over time, and this will counter the impact of inflation.
- Get some real estate investments (rental property, real estate investment trusts—REITs—for example) since rents tend to rise over the years with inflation and these raised rents can be passed on to you in the form of higher returns.
- Be on the lookout for investments that offer an inflation-adjusted return. Some bonds, called real return bonds, offer a rate of return that gives some consideration to inflation each year.
- Put at least a small amount of well-diversified equities or equity mutual funds in your investment portfolio to offer you the potential for a total rate of return that will far exceed inflation for the year. Equity investments offer the potential of 7% to 12% average returns over the long term. Ensure, however, that any equities you purchase fit with your overall investment program. This last strategy is likely the easiest to implement and advisable for all long-term investors.

In the last few years, inflation in Canada has been very low (1% or so), making the need for inflation-fighting investments less important. Looking back over the last 50 years or so, however, we see that inflation has averaged more like 5% a year. This means that the cost of living rose, on average, 5% a year. Because we don't know what inflation will be like in the future, it is wise to include some element of inflation-fighting investments in your portfolio to ensure that you are well positioned against rises in the cost of living.

# 80

## Should I contribute to my RRSP or pay down my mortgage? I can't afford to do both.

The answer for your particular situation involves some analysis of your specific facts. To determine whether you should contribute to your RRSP or pay down your mortgage, the following variables, among others, need to be considered in the analysis:

- Your mortgage interest rate (present and future expected rates), the size of your mortgage, and the mortgage amortization period;
- The size of your RRSP today, your planned RRSP savings per year, your expected rate of return in the future, what you do with any tax refunds, your marginal tax bracket in the future, and the size of RRSP you will need for a successful retirement.

As you can see, the analysis of RRSP versus mortgage is not straightforward, as many of the variables to consider must contain best estimates. This makes any analysis only an approximation at best. However, here are some general rules of thumb:

- The younger you are, the more sense it makes to maximize your RRSP since the success of an RRSP depends on putting a lot of money inside the plan early in life and leaving it there for a long time. In other words, a long period of time for growth to compound and compound again is critical to amassing wealth. If you shortcut this process at any time, you will harm your chances of having a large RRSP for retirement purposes. Therefore, you should do anything you can to avoid interfering with RRSP contributions while you are in your 20s, 30s, and 40s.
  1. Maximize your contributions each year.
  2. Reinvest tax refunds.
  3. Borrow to contribute, if you must, but repay the loan quickly.
  4. Do not use your RRSP for a home purchase or other reasons while you are young. You need to leave the money alone to grow for several decades.
- If you have a mortgage with a very high interest rate, or if you have an RRSP where the investments inside it earn very little, the argument may start to sway to the other side, and you may want to consider paying down the mortgage first. It comes down to a comparison of the after-tax cost of debt versus the after-tax returns of the money invested within the RRSP. What makes this analysis tricky, however, is that the RRSP is tax-sheltered money while the mortgage is after-tax money. As well, the RRSP has the added benefit of a refund that is generated with an RRSP deduction. All of these variables have to be looked at together to determine what is the better route for your money.

## A win–win situation

You can, however, have the best of both worlds by contributing as much as you can afford to your RRSP each year and then taking the tax refund resulting from the RRSP tax deduction and applying it against your mortgage as a lump-sum payment each year. This approach allows you to work on building your savings and paying off your debt at the same time, and will result in elimination of the mortgage years earlier.

# 81

## I want to buy a new home. Should I borrow from my RRSP to make the down payment?

To answer this question properly you really need to sit down with a financial advisor and do the number crunching with all the relevant variables, such as estimated investment returns within your RRSP, your age, the interest cost of the mortgage today and in the future, your estimated tax bracket in the future, estimated lengths of debt repayment, and so on. But for this book I'm going to try to cut to the chase and make some assumptions to try to give you a rule of thumb on the right approach.

The dilemma involves two separate goals that are unfortunately tied together: You want to reduce the amount of your debt while permitting you to buy a home, and you want to maximize your RRSP savings for your retirement down the road. Of course you want to accomplish both, but if you must choose one or the other, which one should it be?

Practically, you could analyze the pre-tax cost of the debt (say a mortgage with a 6% interest cost) for the new home, grossed up by a tax factor of 50% (since debt is paid from after-tax cash flow.) Gross it up by your tax bracket to equate to a pre-tax cost, which equals a pre-tax cost of debt of 12%. Compare this with the pre-tax cost of your RRSP investments (remember, your RRSP is tax sheltered, making this a pre-tax amount of money already).

If you are earning greater than 12% pre-tax on your investment returns, you should not take money from your RRSP since, arguably, it is doing better for you inside the RRSP. A word of caution about this overly simplistic analysis: The above tax gross-up factor of 50% will vary according to your own marginal tax rate and could be far less than 50%. Also, don't forget about the value of annual RRSP refunds, which can be reinvested to make the RRSP option more valuable.

I generally recommend leaving your RRSPs alone when it comes to buying a home. Either find the money somewhere else or don't buy the home yet, recognizing that you just don't have enough money. The key to success with the RRSP system is to start to contribute young and to contribute often. If you just get started and then yank out all the money to buy a home, you have just harmed the most valuable growing years of your RRSP—the early years.

Contribute to your RRSP each year as much as you can, and perhaps save your refunds towards the contribution for your home. Maybe get an additional loan from mom and dad, if feasible, to make up the shortage in your home deposit. I know it may be hard to ignore the desires of owning a nice home with a yard and the like, but if it will mean devastating your RRSP savings for the next 15 years, maybe you should think about renting for a while longer. If you did borrow from your RRSP to buy a home, you would have up to 15 years to repay the loan to your RRSP. Assuming you bought a home this way at age 30 and then took the full 15 years to repay the loan, you would be 45 years old before the capital in your RRSP would be restored to where it was at age 30. By then, it is likely too late to build a significant retirement nest egg since there are not enough years left for compounding to build real wealth.

## High-ratio mortgages

I'm also not a big fan of buying a home on a high-ratio mortgage, where you put down as little as 5% of the purchase price. Again, the actual results depend on your personal scenario; however, mortgaging 95% of the value of the home can amount to a tremendous amount of debt. For example, if you end up with a $200,000 mortgage, at 6% interest that would be an annual interest cost of $12,000 in the early years. That is more than $1,000 of interest alone each month of the year. You may have been better off to continue to rent for less than $1,000 a month, and save the difference towards a bigger deposit on a home.

Take a hard look at the economics behind your financial decisions to ensure that you make educated decisions about what to do with your money. Consult a financial advisor to aid with any sophisticated number crunching.

# 82
## What other risks do I face in my personal finances?

There are many risks in personal finance that an individual needs to plan for. Often you hear about investment risk, but the varieties of risk throughout your personal finances are many. This section provides a partial list of risks that need to be addressed in your finances. In answer to a previous question, I addressed investment risk as defined by short-term volatility, and will build upon that here.

**INFLATION RISK.** There is risk that the constantly rising cost of living will rise beyond what you have planned for. Each year the price of stamps, milk, and gasoline rises. This is the result of inflation. It is important that your income sources throughout your life account for the impact of inflation. This means that your paycheque raise each year should factor in inflation. It also means that your savings need to account for inflation. Failing to plan for inflation leaves you with less and less purchasing power each year, effectively making you poorer.

**RETIREMENT RISK.** There is the risk that you will not have the retirement you dream of. Retirement risk can also be described as having insufficient money to live off in retirement. Being forced to live a substandard retirement is caused by poor planning during your working years. Perhaps you didn't save enough. Maybe you retired too early. Many different factors affect your retirement, and all of them need to be regularly evaluated before you retire.

**FAMILY DISRUPTION RISK.** Lack of proper financial planning can result in fights that effectively destroy a family. A good example is the death of a parent that leaves the children to sort out the estate and their inheritances. Without substantial planning, entire families can be shattered forever, because there was no clarity about financial issues. Similar problems can occur when money is given to children as a gift, or when assets are held in joint ownership with children. It is essential that any issues involving money be periodically examined from the point of view of the family.

**INTERRUPTED INCOME RISK.** If you have dependants who count on you to provide an income for them, any disruption to this income source can leave your dependants in a difficult position. Planning for disability or death is rarely high on anyone's agenda, but it is critically important, given the terrible consequences. This is one risk that must be planned for, because the cost is great if it is not.

**GOAL RISK.** Everyone has financial goals. Whether it is a retirement plan or a special vacation next year, increasing the likelihood that your goal will be reached requires planning and evaluation of all variables. It also requires revisiting your plan as you progress towards your goal, to provide for necessary changes.

**LEGAL RISK.** All of us face legal threats to our net worth regularly. Cause a car accident tomorrow, and you may find yourself at the wrong end of a lawsuit that leaves you bankrupt. Divorce by your only child may see your large wedding gift half disappear. Owe any debt, and you have creditors with claims on your assets. Legal risk is everywhere and requires proper planning.

**INVISIBLE RISK.** There is risk associated with what you don't know. Lack of information about something that may benefit you, hurts you. For example, if you complete your own tax return each year, it is unlikely that you will find tax-planning opportunities that could save you money. You are not a tax expert, and further, you have not decided to hire a tax expert to review your situation. But you should. A second example of invisible risk occurs in purchasing an investment. Today you may buy a mutual fund from financial advisor A. However, you may never know that the same product was available from financial advisor B at a lower cost, with greater value attached as well. In this case, unless you shopped around, you may have been taken advantage of.

Invisible risk is one of the most important types of risk overall. Blindly accepting situations based on what you see doesn't allow you to benefit from what you don't see. Invisible risk can be reduced by being proactive in your personal finances, asking many questions, shopping around, and getting second opinions.

Overall, focusing on risk planning is a whole separate area of financial planning that warrants regular attention. Risk is not limited to investing, and all areas of your finances should be explored annually for their risk consequences.

# RULE 12
## Optimize retirement cash flow to enjoy the golden years.

Generally, I think that Canadians don't spend enough time planning their retirement cash flows and their retirement issues. But how else will you know if you will have enough money to last the rest of your life? You may be left with very little, and will need to look for ways to stretch every last dollar you have. On the other hand, you may have ample resources to live on, but be overly burdened with taxation. There are many things that can be done to help in both cases. This section of the book deals with a few select retirement issues relevant to both categories.

For example, here are a variety of retirement issues that many Canadians would need to address in retirement:

- Should you start receiving Canada Pension Plan payments as early as age 60 or as late as age 70? What factors are relevant in the decision? Should you split CPP with your spouse?
- At what age should you convert your RRSP to an RRIF and start drawing from it? Everyone hears that you must do this by age 69, but maybe you should start as early as age 60 or 55 in your case? What is the right answer for your situation and what are the relevant decision factors?
- How should your investment portfolio change composition once you retire? Should it change again once you start drawing on the money?
- If you need an income from your investments in retirement, how should that income be structured? What kinds of investments should you own to generate the income you need? Have you examined the various choices you have for income sources? Should you take income from your RRSP or RRIF, or should you take income from your taxable savings?
- Have you done all you can to minimize income taxes in retirement? Is your retirement cash flow structured tax effectively? Do you own tax-smart investments? Have you taken advantage of income splitting opportunities between you and your spouse?
- If you have a company pension plan, group RRSP, or DPSP, have you reviewed the various benefits and income options within these plans and selected the options most suitable for your situation?
- Have you taken steps to maximize government benefits as a senior?

- Are all of your assets set up to minimize fees and taxes on the death of the first spouse? Are your financial affairs set up so that the surviving spouse will be able to manage the family finances after you are gone? Does he or she even want to?
- Do you know what you can spend each year out of your savings in order to have enough money to last the rest of your life? Do you know if you have enough income to last your lifetime?
- Have you examined the tax and legal implications of giving assets and investments to your children in old age? Do you know if you can afford to give them anything at all?
- Have you reviewed the merits of using life insurance for various net worth enhancement strategies in old age?
- Has your will been updated since you retired?
- Have you explored ways to financially assist your children or grandchildren without exposing your money to undesirable loss? Can you lower the family tax bill by implementing these strategies?

As you can see, there are many retirement issues to deal with. There are also many strategies and planning opportunities to enhance retirement. Advice on retirement matters can be complicated since the advice must be integrated across various aspects of your personal finances. For example, advice on tax planning affects investing, cash flow, tax levels, and financial goals.

# 83

## What can I do to manage my retirement cash flow more effectively?

I'm often contacted by retirees who are surprised at the amount of tax they continue to pay in retirement and those looking to maximize their after-tax retirement cash flow by reducing taxation. Let's examine solutions for both of these concerns by looking at a sample scenario.

**Retired senior, age 70**

| | |
|---|---|
| Annual pension income | $50,000 |
| Annual Canada Pension Plan income | $9,300 |
| Annual Old Age Security income | $5,000 |
| RRIF income  this year and more each year as per RRIF mandatory withdrawal requirements (approximated) | $8,000 |
| Interest income  this year (5% times taxable savings below) | $20,000 |
| Total income | $92,300 |
| RRIF savings balance | $200,000 |
| Taxable savings | $400,000 |

**Retired spouse, age 67**

| | |
|---|---|
| CPP | $2,000 |
| Old Age Security | $5,000 |
| Savings | Nil |

Based on the basic scenario above, let's now examine several different retirement issues:

1. How can you reduce your income taxes?
2. How can you enhance your after-tax income?
3. What happens when the first spouse dies?

The following strategies are not a comprehensive list of options but are merely some specific thoughts on these issues. Consult a financial advisor for a more thorough review of strategies.

## How can you reduce your income taxes?

- Apply to the government to have your Canada Pension Plan payments split between the two spouses. This is as simple as filling out a government form once. But recognize that it is forever. Equalizing the CPP payments will shift some income from the higher-earning spouse to the lower-earning spouse. This is generally a desirable strategy as long as the two spouses get along!

- Decide how much income you need to live on versus how much income you are earning. If you are earning more than you need for day-to-day cash flow, restructure your income streams. In the case above, the RRIF income and interest income are the only two types of income that are controllable.
- RRIF withdrawals must be made according to a pre-set schedule that is based on your age or your spouse's age. Therefore, you can minimize all RRIF withdrawals by basing them on the age of the younger spouse. This will maximize a continued tax deferral within the tax-sheltered plan. Also, consider making larger RRIF withdrawals in years when your taxable income is lower for one reason or another. This would allow you to remove more from the RRIF at a lower tax cost. This strategy is not effective in the above case since the guaranteed pension income ensures that the taxpayer will always be in a higher tax bracket. However, there may be opportunities to take advantage of this strategy after the first taxpayer's death, depending on what happens to the pension income.
- Replace the investment generating the interest income with another type of investment that will generate a more tax-smart investment income. For example, purchasing a low turnover Canadian equity investment will generate an annual return that is largely deferred capital appreciation. This form of return is only taxable on sale, thereby deferring taxation into the future. This maximizes after-tax wealth far better than a fixed-income investment.
- Consider whether there are any assets that the lower-income spouse can sell to the higher-income spouse in order to legitimately transfer taxable wealth into the hands of the lower-taxed spouse. For example, if the lower-income spouse has jewelry that can be sold to the other spouse for cash, this will allow the lower-income spouse to invest the sale proceeds and earn a return at a much lower tax rate. This strategy can also work for cottages, vehicles, and other assets of value that the lower-income person brought into the relationship.
- Get a professional tax-planning review done by a qualified tax professional to ensure that both spouses are maximizing their tax deductions and tax credits each year.
- Use the income of the higher-earning spouse to live on. The lower-income spouse can save his or her income for investment. That way any investment income generated by the lower-earning spouse will be less taxable.
- Move to Alberta where taxes are lower on personal income.
- Move out of the country to a lower-taxed jurisdiction where Canadian income sources can be preserved in Canada but will face less taxation overall. Ensure that you talk to a tax specialist who can help you to evaluate all the pros and cons of emigration.

## How can you enhance your after-tax income?

This can be accomplished in two ways in this case: Increase total income, and decrease taxation. Above we have dealt with reducing taxation. Here are some ways to increase total income:

- Arrange your taxable savings portfolio and RRIF to own investments with the potential of generating higher long-term portfolio returns. Generally, equity investments outperform fixed-income investments over the long term. Any portfolio change should be examined in the context of your entire investment program, however.
- Preserve your government benefits. In the above example, your high income is causing a clawback (partial) of Old Age Security benefits. This can be avoided by transferring the taxable savings portfolio into a new holding company owned by the taxpayer. All the income generated on this money will now be held inside the holding company (and taxed there) until it is decided to release this income from the company and put it into your own hands. Because this income is moved off of your personal tax return, it is legitimately "hidden" for purposes of calculating taxable income leading to clawback of benefits. Evaluate all of the pros and cons of putting a holding company in place before doing so.
- Get a part-time job in retirement. Something you enjoy. Beats watching TV all day. In my opinion, you should be working until age 65 before considering retirement. When you consider that you will live another 30 years or so beyond that, you will need as much savings as you can get to account for that time.

## What happens when the first spouse dies?

On the death of the first spouse, generally no tax implications arise if the surviving spouse inherits the net worth of the deceased. Under the Income Tax Act, assets can transfer to another spouse "at cost," deferring taxation on any taxable assets until the death of the second spouse or until the second spouse sells the assets. This will not be the case, however, if assets are left to children or other heirs.

Here is a brief summary of the taxation of some common assets on death:

**YOUR PRINCIPAL RESIDENCE (HOME).** CCRA allows your main home to be sold tax free no matter how much it is worth. If you have more than one piece of real estate, talk to a tax specialist about how to plan for this appropriately.

**CASH.** Any form of cash investments such as GICs or Canada Savings Bonds are not taxable on death, since their fair market value equals their cost. Any interest income they generate is taxable, but pure cash simply passes to the heir untaxed from an income tax point of view.

**RRSPS/RRIFS.** RRSPs and RRIFs are tax sheltered, so on the death of the surviving spouse they become fully taxable all at once. This can result in a significant tax liability if you have a large RRSP or RRIF.

**APPRECIATED STOCKS OR EQUITY MUTUAL FUNDS IN A TAXABLE PORTFOLIO.** The appreciated capital gain on these investments is fully taxable in the year of death.

**FAMILY COTTAGE OR FAMILY BUSINESS.** The appreciated capital gain on these assets is fully taxable in the year of death. It is wise to seek professional assistance in reviewing the potential tax liability around these two types of assets long before death.

# 84

## Should we consider moving to a condo closer to our kids in a different part of the country?

There are many things to think about before you sell and move away from the family homestead. These types of decisions are about more than just money. While the rest of this answer will focus on the financial aspect of the decision, I feel it is important to mention that I rarely recommend that people move away from their communities, their backyards, and their life-long friends. These non-financial factors are often more important than a few more bucks in your pocket. Living in a condo where you may never know your neighbors, and where you can't walk on the grass in your backyard in your bare feet is hardly a step up for many Canadians. Also, reconsider following your children around the country to live close to them. Chances are you won't see them any more often, and you may just end up baby-sitting the grandchildren. Is that the way you wanted to spend your retirement?

Now let's examine the financial aspects. At first glance, it appears that you should downsize the home since it appears that you are in a cash flow crunch, with little extra cash lying around. This could also be getting worse if you have a fixed-level pension and rising inflation is lowering your standard of living each year.

People with a lot of money tied up in assets such as a home or land and also having little cash flow to live on are called "asset rich, cash poor." All of their wealth is tied up in assets that don't generate any income. Holding on to a big home worth a lot of money while at the same time having only a small annual income doesn't make sense.

Let's look at an example of how much cash flow can be freed up.

A retired couple live in a home in Toronto that they have owned for 35 years and is worth $460,000. This is their only home, and they are thinking about selling and moving into a small home in the suburbs that costs only $160,000. If they sold and repurchased, how much money would that add to their cash flow?

Since this is their only home, the capital gain would be tax free. The couple would be able to invest $460,000 less $160,000, or $300,000 cash. Investing $300,000 at 6% annually would add $18,000 a year to the couple's pre-tax income. That would likely amount to more than $12,000 a year of after-tax cash flow. That's an extra $1,000 to spend each month as long as they live! And I used a relatively conservative return of 6%!

With such a big boost to cash flow, this has a substantial impact. Adding this much cash flow gives them the freedom to do so much more in their lives. This can provide an improvement in their quality of life that that they would not have had otherwise.

Selling your lifelong home is never an easy decision. But where a tremendous amount of net worth is locked within one asset, the increase in your standard of living from accessing the cash may be too significant to ignore.

# 85

## I just turned 70 and I'm still in the top tax bracket. Is there anything I can do to get my RRIF money back at a lower tax rate?

Some seniors have saved for 30 years and the time has come to turn their RRSPs into RRIFs and start making withdrawals. But many of them are not in a lower tax bracket and they end up paying tax at the top marginal rate on their RRIF withdrawals. Yet they had thought they would be able to withdraw the money and pay less tax! What happened?

Your RRSP savings and other savings worked as good as or better than expected, resulting in a high enough income to remain in the top tax bracket beyond your working years and well into retirement. If you are in this situation, here are a few ideas on how to get more money out of your RRIF:

- Leave Canada permanently. In other words, emigrate. If you do this and leave your RRIF in place after you leave, you can likely get your money out of your RRIF slowly each year while paying minimum withholding taxes—likely no more than 25%, or even less, depending on where you move to.
- Withdraw the minimum out of your RRIF each year, and don't make the withdrawals until the last possible moment. This will continue to maximize the deferral of money inside your plan. When you turn 69, you have to convert your RRSP to an RRIF that year, but your first withdrawal doesn't have to be made until December of the year in which you turn 70, effectively permitting another year of tax deferral.
- Base your RRIF withdrawals on the age of the younger spouse, if you are married. RRIF withdrawals are calculated according to age and by using a younger age you can continue to minimize withdrawals from the plan. This continues to defer tax.
- Make withdrawals from your RRSP or RRIF in years where your total income is less than usual, even before you retire. Anytime after age 50, if your total taxable income drops, consider withdrawing money from your RRSP or RRIF. This is not always the best approach, and really depends on the amount of tax you pay, what you do with the money after you withdraw it, and future investment returns you earn. Generally, if you make the withdrawals early, reinvest all after-tax proceeds. Have a financial advisor examine your total financial picture to see if you can truly benefit from reducing your RRSP or RRIF early.
- Find deductions on your tax return that will offset your income inclusions from the RRIF withdrawals you make. For example, interest expense from investment loans can be tax deductible in many cases. If you borrow to invest in a taxable account, the tax-deductible interest cost can offset an RRIF income inclusion, resulting in a reduced tax position.

If you can't find a way to reduce the tax you pay on RRIF withdrawals, maybe I can cheer you up with this comment: When you think about it, it's a nice problem to have.

## Alternatives to an RRIF

When you turn 69, you are required to collapse your RRSP. Up until then your RRSP is a wealth accumulation tool, but at age 69 it must be converted into a wealth distribution tool. You actually have three options to choose from regarding the money from your RRSP:

1. Convert the RRSP to a RRIF and start taking minimum withdrawal amounts or more based on government-provided formulas. This is by far the most popular choice with Canadians as it provides the most flexibility over your money.
2. Buy an annuity with your RRSP proceeds. This is rarely a good choice today due to the limitations on annuities as an investment.
3. Collapse the RRSP and collect the cash. This is a very unwise thing to do. Withdrawing all the money from an RRSP makes the entire plan taxable in one year, subjecting the funds to the highest rates of taxation all at once. This is generally not desirable.

# 86

## Should I enter into a reverse mortgage?

Reverse mortgages can be useful for seniors who live in a mortgage-free home and are looking for more cash flow to live on, yet they are not ready to sell their home to free the locked-up cash value. With a reverse mortgage, a lending company offers to loan the home owners money on a regular basis to supplement their existing cash flow. The loan is based on their home value as collateral and is typically some percentage of the market value of the home.

The lending company keeps track of the loan payments made to the seniors, charges interest on the loan, and doesn't collect repayment of the loan and interest until the elderly couple dies. At that time, the company will have first claim on the couple's home, and will apply the proceeds from the sale against the outstanding loan and accrued interest. Using this reverse mortgage strategy, the elderly couple can receive monthly payments from the loan company that they can use to supplement their income and enhance their lifestyle in a way that they couldn't otherwise.

The advantage of a reverse mortgage is the additional cash flow to live on without having to move out of your beloved home. The disadvantage of reverse mortgages is that you are supplementing your retirement with borrowed money, and all borrowed money comes with a cost. This may be an expensive price to pay for a bit more cash flow. Further, you may be concerned about what will happen if you outlive the loan. The loan payments to you will stop because the loan value and interest have gotten so big that the maximum loan value based on the collateral value of your home has been reached. The debt will continue to grow as long as you live, potentially surpassing the value of your estate or forcing the sale of your home while you are still alive. Both of these possibilities are scary, and you may find yourself with a monster debt that eats up your net worth.

Reverse mortgages can be useful for some Canadians, but I would prefer to see seniors look for alternative ways to supplement their retirement income. Perhaps you could downsize your existing home and invest the spare cash to supplement your earnings. Call me a conservative accountant. At a minimum, ensure you investigate reverse mortgages closely.

# 87

## Is it wise to borrow against the cash value of my life insurance policy to boost my income?

There are instances with some insurance policies and banks whereby you can remove money from the policy by effectively taking out a loan against the accumulated cash value. Since this is a loan and not income, these amounts received would not be taxable in your hands. Banks that permit this borrowing will charge you an interest rate on the loan, and compound the interest as long as the loan is outstanding. On death, the insurance company will offset the loan against the insurance proceeds payout, leaving the estate with the net.

There are several variables to consider before embarking on this strategy:

- If the insurance proceeds on your death are designated for a specific purpose, any loan you take today that will be repaid out of the death proceeds could harm your original goal for the insurance. In other words, why did you buy the insurance in the first place, and will borrowing against your policy harm your ability to reach your goal? For example, if you need the policy to pay out $500,000 on death to offset death taxes, a growing loan against the insurance payout will reduce this estate goal.
- Do you really need the additional retirement cash flow? If not, why take on a loan with non-tax-deductible interest expense to generate a cash flow?
- Have you explored other strategies to enhance your retirement income before resorting to borrowing?
- If you really need to borrow to generate retirement cash flow, explore how a reverse mortgage on your house or other debt would compare to the cost of debt against the insurance policy loan.
- Shop around among insurance companies and banks that offer the ability to borrow against an insurance policy before you buy. There are a number of factors (loan interest rate, lending value, collateral value, etc.) that will affect the success of this strategy and all of them should be explained thoroughly. Further, sensitivity analysis should be performed around these variables to see what results could occur should the product not perform as expected. Seek a second opinion.
- Find out what would happen if you live long enough that the bank cuts off your regular cash flow loans because the loan and accrued interest now exceed the value of your insurance policy.
- Understand the tax risks of this strategy. There has been talk for a number of years that the CCRA will shut down this strategy all together.

Most Canadians, in my opinion, should not borrow against a life insurance policy in their retirement years to boost cash flow. Evaluate your needs cautiously with a financial advisor.

# 88

## Should I sell my bond investments to buy royalty trusts since cash flow yield for the trusts is so much higher?

No. A lot of people mistakenly compare royalty trust returns to the returns of their fixed-income investments (such as bonds and GICs), and the comparison is not equal. It could be disastrous to replace bonds with royalty trusts.

Royalty trusts are typically an indirect investment in oil and gas properties, coal, or propane, or some other investment. These investments are typically owned through a trust. These specialty investments often qualify for lucrative tax breaks under the Canadian tax system, and these tax breaks can be flowed out to the investors. This means that often you can receive tax-deductible losses from these investments, or you can receive cash flow distributions with a minimum amount of tax.

In the 1990s, as GIC returns plummeted, many Canadian seniors looked to new alternative investments to provide their retirement income. Many royalty trusts have offered high distributions with minimal taxation—it seemed perfect for seniors. But it isn't.

First, let's analyze the cash flow obtained from a royalty trust. Royalty trust cash flow is not a return entirely. It is a distribution composed of some earnings on the investment and perhaps some of your own original investment being given back to you by the money manager. It is a cash-flow distribution, and it should not be compared to the return of a bond or GIC, which is a real return on investment.

Now, let's examine the tax impact of royalty trusts. There are two reasons why the annual taxation is lower on royalty trust distributions. First, some of the cash flow distribution to you can be a return of your original investment. When you receive your own money back, it is not taxable. Second, some of the lucrative tax breaks available to royalty trusts are tax deferral breaks. This means that the tax breaks you get in the beginning of owning the investment may be recaptured in the form of a larger capital gain when you ultimately sell the investment. Talk to a tax specialist about this further to avoid surprises.

Finally, let's look at the investment aspects of what you are buying. A royalty trust can be an investment in some of the most risky natural resources investments in the world. They are far from being a safe and guaranteed investment. Therefore, you shouldn't substitute them for your bonds or GICs since you are not comparing apples with apples. Bonds and GICs are very conservative, low-risk investments. Royalty trusts are not. Know what you are buying before you dive in. And ensure that you understand the tax implications of any investment you hold.

# 89

## Should I take possession of my elderly parents' assets so that they do not have to pay a high share of their nursing home costs?

In some provinces if you move into a health care nursing home, the province will charge you a fee to live there, based on your income level. To calculate what you should be charged, the province may examine your most recent federal tax return and base your fee on taxable income. The higher your income, the higher your cost, since the province feels that people with higher incomes are in a better position to pay a higher amount. Each province has their own system.

Because the system is set up this way on an income-tested format, it has made it easy for some Canadians to "beat the system." Simply by reducing their elderly parents' total income in the years before and during entry into the nursing home, families can make their parents look "poor" and thereby make it possible to pay less to the government for nursing home costs. The elderly parents can be made to look poor by stripping away their net worth and income sources by transferring this wealth to their children before death. This is the process that I see used most often, but there are other methods as well.

However, I have a problem with this approach to net worth maximization:

- It is unethical, unprofessional, shameful, and embarrassing. If you do this, don't go bragging about it at the next party you attend. Most people know that if you cheat the system it is costing them more in taxes.
- Transferring wealth to the next generation before death will expose the elderly person's net worth to their children's potentially wasteful spending. Also, if the children get divorced or go bankrupt, the parent's net worth (that the children now own) may just disappear as well. This would be a terrible result. And it can be naive to think that your kids will magically come up with extra money to give you a wonderful old age.
- However, if you are set on maximizing government coverage of nursing home costs, consider transferring an elderly parent's assets into a trust or a holding company instead of gifting them to kids. Using a trust that is appropriately set up can minimize the parent's net worth and total income in the desired way. It can also allow parents to preserve their assets since a trust is a separate legal entity. Talk to a professional financial advisor about the many powerful uses of trusts in family planning.
- There can be tremendous tax costs to gifting assets to children or making them jointly owned with children in order to move ownership out of the parents' hands. Think twice before going the joint-ownership route.

## Old age security clawback

You can also maximize government benefits through income control. For example, if an elderly Canadian has significant taxable income, he or she will be facing a clawback of their Old Age Security pension since OAS is reduced for seniors who have high income levels.

To see if there is a way around this, let's examine an example of a senior's taxable income:

- $25,000 pension income from previous employer
- $10,000 Canada Pension Plan
- $50,000 investment income from mutual funds and bonds

If we transferred the investment portfolio causing the $50,000 income into a holding company owned by the senior, we could then control the future taxation of the investment income in the hands of the senior. This is because a holding company (and a trust) are separate legal entities; and a separate tax return must be filed on income earned within the corporation or trust. This means that the elderly Canadian's taxable income will drop to $35,000, and he or she will be entitled to keep all of the OAS. This strategy assumes that the senior doesn't need the full $85,000 of income to live on. If the senior does need the full amount then this strategy may not be effective for preserving the OAS benefits.

Consult a professional advisor about implementing a trust or a holding company. These are both complicated tax-planning tools, warranting thorough understanding of the costs and benefits applicable to your situation.

# 90

**In my retirement I spend about six months a year in Texas. I even bought a condo there. What are the financial implications of this, if any?**

If you are spending substantial amounts of time in the U.S., I hope you are counting the number of days you spend there each year. That's because if your days add up to 183 or more each year (talk to a tax professional about the exact formula to calculate days), you may be qualifying as a U.S. resident and have to file a U.S. tax return! That is not something you likely want to happen, and spending six months a year in Texas is dangerously close to the threshold.

## U.S. real estate complications

The situation becomes even more complicated if you have purchased U.S. real estate. This gives rise to even more U.S. tax consequences. For example, if you sell the real estate, your U.S. lawyer should withhold income tax off the proceeds on the sale and send it to the IRS. You also will have to file a U.S. tax return to report the sale and pay tax in the U.S. You'll also have to report the same capital gain on the sale on your Canadian tax return, converted into Canadian currency. The U.S. tax you pay will be included on your Canadian tax return as a foreign tax credit, ensuring that you don't face double taxation on the sale of the property.

If you die with the real estate still in your hands, and if it is an expensive property, your estate may have to pay U.S. estate taxes at rates up to 55% on the market value of the property. You wouldn't have thought your estate would be writing a cheque to the IRS!

And finally, if you legally rent out the U.S. property while you own it, you will have to file a U.S. tax return to report the rental revenue, any tax deductions, etc. You would be wise to consult a U.S. tax expert at this point.

## U.S. tax planning

If you want to spend some time in the U.S. or other countries, I suggest that you follow these basic guidelines to avoid having to pay any kind of U.S. income or estate taxes:

- Don't buy a U.S. real estate property. Just rent one instead.
- Don't rent out your U.S. property.
- Make sure you don't spend more than six months in the U.S. in any given year.
- Don't own significant amounts of U.S. stocks. If you do, hold them inside a Canadian holding company or a Canadian mutual fund. These vehicles are exempt from U.S. estate taxes.

- Get rid of large amounts of U.S. assets before you die.
- Get an opinion from a qualified U.S./Canadian tax expert that everything you are doing is legal under the latest tax rules of both countries. Canadian and U.S. cross-border tax issues are some of the most complicated forms of tax planning, so talk to a cross-border tax expert about your issues.

These suggestions will help to ensure that you preserve your net worth while enjoying your time south of the border.

# 91
## What are annuities? Are they still around?

Annuities still exist. An *annuity* is a financial product in which you give a financial institution a lump sum amount of money today and the company agrees to pay you a rate of return on your money over a multi-year period and also to return to you a regular cash flow that is composed of an investment return and a return of some of your own capital. Annuities are attractive for seniors who want a very simple investment solution (all money is managed on your behalf and you just get a cheque in the mail each month) and for seniors who want to ensure they never run out of money (you can buy annuities that will guarantee a payment to you until you die). They are also attractive because the taxes you pay can be lower since the cash flow you get from the annuity is a mix of earnings and a return of your original investment.

The reason you don't hear as much about annuities anymore is that they were more popular when long-term interest rates in Canada were much higher than they have been in the last decade or so. The rate of return and the payments you will receive over the life of the annuity are based on the interest rates that exist when you buy it. In other words, if you buy an annuity that is designed to fund your entire retirement cash flows, the amount of money you will get over that entire period will be based on future expected interest rates on the day of your purchase only. Then you lock it in.

I would recommend that someone consider annuities only if they match the scenarios below:

- You are incapable of taking care of your money due to illness, incapacity, old age, or unusual circumstances. In these cases, annuities can provide a guaranteed easy cash flow stream forever.
- You want to take advantage of the $1,000 pension tax credit that is available for all Canadians who have qualifying pension or annuity income.
- You want to make your investments very simple because you would prefer to enjoy life not worrying about your finances.

If you do look into buying annuities, there are some factors you will need to consider when deciding on the type of annuity:

- How long should the annuity pay you an income stream?
- Do you want the cash flows to be adjusted over time for inflation, or not?
- When do you want the annuity payments to start?
- Do you want your estate on your death to get any remaining annuity money, or not?

If you want the largest payments to result from your annuity purchase, keep it simple. The fancier the annuity, generally the less money you will get.

Most Canadians should explore all other investment management options before considering annuities. Despite their simplicity, annuities lack the flexibility that most investors demand today. Add to this a less than stellar internal rate of return, and it's no wonder that annuities are not too popular. If someone is trying to sell you an annuity, get a second opinion on your annuity needs and make sure you shop around.

# 92

## Should I stop contributing to my RRSPs and put money into non-tax-sheltered investments instead? Will my estate get more money when I die?

There is no simple answer to this question. In order to determine what is appropriate for you to do, you have to do a mathematical calculation and forecast under both scenarios: contributing to an RRSP for your entire life, and saving in a non-tax-sheltered open investment account instead. This will involve making a lot of assumptions that may or may not happen, such as future tax rates, future investment returns, future reinvestment amounts, future savings amounts, your spending needs, and so on. Using all of these assumptions, you need to make an educated guess as to which approach will be better. If you are not up for all this work, and you don't want a financial advisor to do the calculations for you, consider contributing to both an RRSP and a taxable savings account over time.

Let's compare the two scenarios below.

**CONTRIBUTE PRIMARILY TO AN RRSP.** Assume that a Canadian investor will deposit $5,000 a year into an RRSP for 30 years in a row. This will give rise to a tax deduction and tax refund of half of the contribution, or $2,500 a year. Assume too that the refund is reinvested in a taxable savings account, and both this money and the RRSP money will earn an annual compounded return of 8% a year, consisting of 6% interest and 2% deferred capital gains. At the end of the 30 years, the RRSP is liquidated to trigger built-up taxes all at once. The interest income will be taxed at 50% annually and the 2% deferred return will be taxed at 25% all at once at the end of year 30.

*Under this scenario, an investor will have approximately $470,000 at the end of 30 years, after tax.*

**SAVE TO A NON-RRSP ACCOUNT ONLY.** The same $5,000 savings amount is invested in a taxable account, earning 8% a year in the same proportion as above. The annual return on these investments will be taxed at the top marginal rates of 0% for deferred capital gains (assume buy and hold, whereby capital gains are only taxable when sold) and 50% tax on interest. Assume that all the capital gains return (2% a year) wouldn't be taxed until the end of the 30 years. At that time, the realized capital gains will be subject to tax at 25%.

*Under this scenario, an investor will have $328,000 at the end of 30 years.*

The RRSP option resulted in more money in these two comparisons. Note, however, that one of the factors that helps to sway this argument is the amount of deferred investment return in the taxable portfolios in both examples. The greater the amount of deferred return, the less tax that is paid until the very last year, and the greater the wealth accumulated in the open account. Generally, it would be wiser from an after-tax wealth accumulation point of view to prefer deferred growth in your taxable investment portfolio instead of annually taxable returns such as interest and dividends.

The Canadian RRSP system is one of the greatest tax shelters remaining in the western world. It will usually result in greater net worth to you than if you hadn't used it. There are exceptions, however. I encourage you to invest in both if possible: Contribute to your RRSP and create a taxable savings pool as well. That way, you have a combined investment portfolio that can offer the benefits of both. You can see from the above example that many variables must be examined in order to devise the right strategy for you.

# 93

## There are so many different kinds of fixed income investments. What types are suitable for my retirement portfolio?

Seniors often search for the highest return on their investments but with little risk. More specifically, they relate these criteria to their fixed-income investments.

This strategy will review a variety of investments that older Canadians may consider for their investment portfolio income. We will not discuss equity investments in this strategy, or how they fit within a portfolio. We will discuss these primarily fixed-income investments according to the following criteria: return potential, volatility risk, fees, flexibility, and taxes. It is important to note that this is not a complete list of possible fixed-income investments that seniors could consider, nor are the criteria above all the factors that need to be considered before purchase.

### RRIF versus Open/Taxable Accounts

This analysis of fixed-income products will ignore whether they are best suited for ownership within your RRIF/RRSP or within a taxable account. Clearly, income earned from these products situated within a tax sheltered vehicle is deferred until withdrawal from the plan. In an open account, taxation of investment income is annual, based on a calendar year.

For purposes of the analysis below, the tax consequences will be reviewed for products that are owned in an open, taxable account only. Speak to a financial advisor about the extra level of planning that must be considered to determine whether to own fixed-income products within an RRSP or within an open account.

### GICs (Guaranteed Investment Certificates)

GICs are largely offered by a bank in exchange for your money, and you receive a fixed interest rate for a fixed period of time. Maturities range from 30 days to five years, and your money is locked in for that period. Your money is usually protected against loss of up to $60,000 by the Canadian Deposit Insurance Corporation. Interest income is the kind of return you can earn, taxable at your personal marginal tax rate.

**THE GOOD:** GICs have been around for many years and seniors are comfortable with them. Easily available at the bank down the street.

**THE BAD:** Returns may not be as high as other fixed-income investments. GIC interest is highly taxed. Investors are insured up to $60,000 only, when other investments are not capped in this way. Investors are locked in, with no flexibility. Interest income is provided annually and/or on maturity.

**RECOMMENDATION:** Not worth purchasing.

## Canada Savings Bonds (CSBs)

Debt issued by the federal government, providing a fixed interest rate in exchange for your bond purchase. Available in a variety of denominations but with a fixed maturity. Cashable on the first day of any month. Available through many institutions. Generates interest income.

**THE GOOD:** Cashable whenever you want. Easily available.

**THE BAD:** Better returns available from other products. Some interest may be lost if cashed in at the wrong time. Generates highly taxed interest income. Provides interest income annually.

**RECOMMENDATION:** Not worth purchasing.

## Government of Canada Bonds (bonds traded on the bond markets daily)

Debt issued by the federal government providing a fixed interest rate in exchange for your money. Available in a variety of denominations and a variety of maturities. Cashable every business day. Generates interest income if held to maturity and interest and capital gain/losses if sold actively, since market value fluctuates daily, depending on market interest rate movements.

**THE GOOD:** Maturities of one day to 30 years available. Fully government guaranteed. Cashable at any time. Better returns possible compared to other fixed-income investments. Potential to generate capital gains return in addition to interest. Provides interest income quarterly, semi-annually, or annually.

**THE BAD:** Minimum investment of $5,000. Available for purchase primarily through financial advisor with full securities licensing. Can result in a capital loss if sold after market interest rates rise.

**RECOMMENDATION:** Every investor would be well served owning Government of Canada bonds and holding them to maturity.

## Government of Canada Stripped Bonds

Regular Government of Canada bonds in which the interest-paying component has been separated from the bond capital, and each sells separately as an investment. Stripped bonds sell at a discount from their future maturity, based on an implicit interest rate that will be earned annually. No interest payments are ever received. The value of the investment simply rises until it reaches the face value at maturity. Taxation occurs annually, based on a calculated implicit rate of return.

**THE GOOD:** Better returns than regular Government of Canada bonds. Cashable at any time. A variety of maturities available. Possibility to earn capital gains on top of the interest return, if they are sold prior to maturity after interest rates decline.

**THE BAD:** They provide no income stream, yet they are taxed annually on the return they earn. Possible to generate a capital loss if sold prior to maturity, after interest rates go up.

**RECOMMENDATION:** Fantastic fixed income investment for an RRIF or RRSP prior to retirement.

## Government of Canada Treasury Bills

Short term debt obligations of the federal government that are fully guaranteed. Maturities range from 30 days to one year. Cashable at any time. Generate interest income but can add capital gains or losses if sold prior to maturity. Minimum investment of $5,000. Available through fully licensed financial advisors. T-bills are sold at a discount to their face value and mature at their face value. This means that no interest is paid during ownership.

**THE GOOD:** Cashable at any time. Reasonable interest rates.

**THE BAD:** Only available up to one year maturity. For sale only through fully licensed financial advisors. Not good for a regular income stream.

**RECOMMENDATION:** May be a good short-term investment versus a GIC. Shop the rates to see which is better. Not useful for a retirement income stream.

## Money Market Funds

A mutual fund consisting of a pool of short-term, very liquid investments that are actively managed by a professional money manager for an annual fee. Access to your money is usually within 24 hours. Some mutual funds charge fees to buy and sell. The investments usually owned by money market funds consist of Treasury Bills and short-term bonds of governments and corporations. Fund generates interest income monthly, quarterly, or at other intervals.

**THE GOOD:** Mutual funds are widely available. Minimum investments is as low as $25, which buys a share of the entire pool of investments. The professional money manager takes care of the buying and selling of investments on your behalf. You can buy and sell the fund any business day.

**THE BAD:** Some money market funds may own investments you would never own personally. Some money market funds charge high annual fees and high fees to buy and sell.

**RECOMMENDATION:** Great investments for a variety of purposes but buyers should become comfortable with the kinds of investments that the fund owns and should shop around for low fees.

## Bond Funds

A mutual fund consisting of a pool of short-term, medium-term, or long-term market traded bonds that are actively managed by a professional money manager for an annual fee. Access to your money is usually within 24 hours. Some mutual funds charge fees to buy and sell. Fund generates interest income monthly, quarterly or at other intervals. Managers actively trade the bonds based on interest rate changes, to try to generate additional capital gains returns on top of the interest earnings.

**THE GOOD:** Over the long term, actively traded funds have generated rates of return on an after-tax basis that are far superior to most other fixed-income investments. They are a flexible investment that can provide a regular retirement income stream. Choice for varieties of bond funds is broad, and they are easily available at many institutions.

**THE BAD:** In the short term (over only a few years) it is possible to lose money with a bond fund, as a result of the active trading by the money manager. Annual bond fees and the commissions for buying and selling can be high.

**RECOMMENDATION:** Bond funds can play an important role in the longer-term portion of your fixed income portfolio. Shop around on fees. Verify that the holdings of the fund suit your liking.

## High-Yield Funds

A mutual fund consisting of a pool of more aggressive cash-flow generating investments, such as preferred shares, royalty trusts, convertible securities, lower quality corporate bonds and debentures, among others. These are riskier investments that will offer greater return in exchange for taking on greater risk. High-yield funds are actively managed by a professional money manager for an annual fee. Access to your money is usually within 24 hours. Some mutual funds charge fees to buy and fees to sell. Funds generate interest income monthly, quarterly, or at other intervals. Managers actively trade the investments based on interest rates and stock market changes, to try to generate additional capital gains returns on top of the interest earnings.

**THE GOOD:** Higher returns are possible. Potential to earn tax-friendly capital-gains returns on top of interest income. Can be purchased with small amounts of money. Cashable at any time.

**THE BAD:** These are not blue chip investments and may have very high risk levels. May have high annual fees and commissions to buy and sell.

**RECOMMENDATION:** Suitable only for the aggressive fixed-income portion of your portfolio, or not at all.

## Royalty Trusts

Royalty trusts are flow-through investments that allow an investor to invest indirectly in industries like oil and gas and to benefit from tax breaks offered to companies in this sector. Cash-flow yield can be tax advantaged as a result of these tax breaks. Cash-flow yield can be preset and quite high.

**THE GOOD:** Tax-advantaged cash flow that can be higher than traditional fixed-income investments.

**THE BAD:** For sale by fully licensed advisors only. Risky investments that can have a very volatile value in the short term. Annual fees to own and to buy and sell. The tax-advantaged income is misleading, because often the cash flows consist of a return of your own capital (which is not taxed). The tax breaks are often just deferrals rather than outright tax savings.

**RECOMMENDATION:** These investments are not a substitute for a traditional fixed-income investment, yet many seniors treat them that way. These investments act more like an equity and carry the risk beyond even many safe equities! It is inappropriate to compare a royalty trust cash-flow yield to the return of a bond or GIC, since the royalty trust cash-flow yield may contain non-investment return components. If you buy royalty trusts, take time to fully understand the risks and tax implications.

There are many more investments that investors can consider to provide them with cash flow. Here I have discussed only a few. As you shop around for fixed-income investment alternatives, ensure that you consistently compare them by return potential, fees, risk, liquidity, and tax efficiency.

# RULE 13
## Carefully explore using debt to grow your net worth.

It is almost impossible to get through life without borrowing money for a variety of purposes. For example, home purchasers use a bank's money through a mortgage. Most Canadians have credit cards, which is another form of borrowing. Many students take out loans to pay for their university education. And don't forget car loans, margin accounts at brokerages, and so on. Users of debt are everywhere, it seems. In this section of the book I discuss the prudent uses of debt.

There are two different types of debt: essential debt, which lets you live your life, and optional debt, which may enhance your life. Existence without the items obtained through essential debt, some argue, would leave the individual with a less fulfilling life. These items would include a family home and student loans. Items obtained through optional debt (a speedboat or investments held outside of an RRSP) could enhance your lifestyle and your net worth.

It is important to prioritize debt and manage your total debt load. And all Canadians should explore prudent uses of optional debt. Borrowing to invest—backed by a sound investment strategy—can be a financial windfall for many Canadians over the long term.

# 94

## Should I borrow against the equity in my home to invest in the stock market?

Borrowing to invest is called many things: leverage, margin, or just plain borrowing to invest. Borrowing to invest consists of using someone else's money to build your wealth faster. Because you are adding someone else's money to your money and earning a taxable return on both, the potential exists to accelerate the growth of your assets as long as the cost of debt is not too high. When you think about it, this is the same strategy you may already be practising on your own home—if you have a mortgage. This strategy can be aggressive, but can add significant wealth to your bottom line if it works. Here are some of the aspects to consider before borrowing to invest:

If you have never borrowed to invest before, put your toe in the water before you dive off the deep end! Try a little bit of leveraged investing instead of taking a large investment loan—because it can be very scary if the markets don't go up! Use, say, $5,000 as a starter loan.

### Why your leveraged portfolio needs to be invested in equities, not bonds

If you take out a loan to invest in a taxable portfolio, the interest expense on the loan may be tax deductible to you. So, for example, if your cost of borrowing is 6% and you are in a 50% tax bracket, your true cost of debt is only 3% after tax. However, we need to examine the investments purchased with the borrowed money as well, and give them a tax-affected return. For example, if you invest the borrowed money in bonds that are safe but only return 5% a year, in a 50% tax bracket you will only keep 2.5% after tax. This is less than the cost of debt, and doesn't make borrowing to invest a very smart thing for you to do.

If, however, you invest the borrowed money in some equity investments that offer the long-term return potential of 10% a year on average, borrowing to invest becomes more feasible. A 10% pre-tax return can be a 7.5%(or more) after-tax return if you earn realized capital gains on your equities. In this case, borrowing to invest is making you money since the after-tax return exceeds the after-tax debt costs each year.

### Time horizon is critical

It is also important to remember that if you are going to buy equities with borrowed money, you should plan to invest for at least ten years. If your time period is shorter, you may be exposed to some volatile and negative returns that can result from equity investing, and this may not make leveraging to invest very worthwhile. In fact, it can be even worse than if you had just invested your own money. See the example below.

## Tax treatment of interest expense on borrowed money

Interest expense on money borrowed to invest in a taxable portfolio of stocks, bonds, mutual funds, or a small business you are starting will generally be tax deductible. Interest expense on money borrowed to invest in your RRSP, a car, or your home is not tax deductible. In order to keep the interest tax deductible it is important to leave the investments in place untouched. Any reduction of the invested capital amount may see a corresponding reduction in the interest expense amount.

## An example of the power of leverage

An investor borrows $90,000 at 6% to invest in a portfolio of equity mutual funds. This is on top of $10,000 of the investor's own money that is also invested. What is the overall return if the investor achieves the following actual investment returns on the invested money?

1. If the investor earns 10% on the investment in one year, the return will be 10% of $100,000, or $10,000, less interest cost on the debt of $5,400, for a net return of $4,600. Only $10,000 of the investor's own money was used, so the overall return is 46% ($4,600 / $10,000). This is very good.
2. If the investor loses 10% on the investments in one year, the return will be –$10,000, plus the cost of interest of $5,400, for a total cost of $15,400. Only $10,000 of the investor's own money was used, so the overall return is –154%: That's negative 154%!

Be warned, folks. Leveraged investing works well when the market goes up. As you can see from this example, the downside is worse than the upside is good. When you lose money on the investment, you have lost the investment and you still have to repay interest and a loan.

If you are considering leveraged investing, start out with a small loan amount and have a long time horizon. Ensure your investments reflect your investor profile as defined by your Statement of Investment Policy and Guidelines. Evaluate the after-tax cost of your debt against the after-tax returns you hope to make to see if the economics of the strategy make sense. If you stay true to a plan, leveraging can be very effective as an enhanced investment strategy.

# 95

## Should I take out a loan to maximize my RRSP contributions?

Borrowing to contribute to your RRSP can make sense, but only if you pay off the loan within a few years, and if you don't borrow year after year.

To evaluate the pros and cons of this strategy, you need to compare the cost of the debt with the investment returns you make. But this is not easy to do because the loan interest is paid with after-tax dollars (your bottom line paycheque) while the investment earnings grow tax sheltered inside your RRSP (pre-tax dollars).

If we assume that you can get an RRSP loan today at 6% and you purchase investments inside your RRSP paying 9%, is it wise to borrow to contribute? Maybe, maybe not. You have to compare the pre-tax cost of both the debt cost and the asset growth to see whether you are getting ahead. Within the RRSP, your pre-tax earnings are 9%. However, the loan at 6% must be grossed up by a tax factor to convert it into a pre-tax cost of debt. If we assume your marginal tax rate is 20%, your interest expense on the debt, pre-tax, is really 6% divided by one minus your marginal tax rate of 20%, which equals 7.5%. This means your tax-sheltered return of 9% exceeds the pre-tax cost of debt of 7.5% in this case.

However, something else to take into account in the example above is that the cost of debt will last only as long as the loan exists—perhaps a few years at most—while the benefit from the investment will last the life of the RRSP—maybe 40 years. Also, what about the refund from the RRSP contribution and deduction? Reinvesting the tax refund supports borrowing to invest as well. However, only some Canadians actually reinvest their refund cheques, and also the value of the tax deduction that led to the refund reverses itself when money is ultimately drawn out of the RRSP and becomes taxable. But clearly there is a time value of money advantage here that pads the argument for contributing to your RRSP any way you can.

But let me focus again on the pure argument of borrowing to invest in an RRSP. Two points are worth making:

1. If you don't earn an RRSP tax-sheltered return each year that exceeds your pre-tax cost of debt, borrowing to invest may be unwise for you. Historically, it has been shown that in order to get a high investment return, a large amount of money has to be invested in equity investments. Ensure that this approach would match your SIP&G before borrowing.
2. If you borrow for your RRSP and pay it off within a year, you don't have to worry about the cost of debt exceeding the investment returns each year. However, the types of Canadians who typically borrow to contribute to their RRSPs are cash-strapped individuals who will need to borrow next year, and the following year, and the year after that. This means they may never escape the debt burden of their RRSP

loans, so borrowing to invest for their RRSPs may always be a losing strategy. It is important that you pay off the loan fast, and don't borrow each year.

Borrowing to invest can be a good strategy for many Canadians, but the appropriateness of this approach needs to be evaluated according to your unique financial situation. If you don't earn enough investment returns over the long term, of if you lengthen the loan payments over several years, the only person that may end up making money is the financial institution that made you the loans!

# 96

## I have several different kinds of debt. Which ones should I pay down first?

When you have several different types of debt (for example, a mortgage, student loan, car loan, investment margin account, credit card) that you (and potentially your spouse) are trying to pay down, it is important that you prioritize the costs of each of your debts and pay down the most expensive ones first.

Let's look at an example to better understand how to pay down debt in an effective manner.

You have the following types of debt currently:

- a mortgage for $150,000 at 6%,
- a car loan for $10,000 for 6.5%,
- an investment margin account with a negative balance of $22,000 at 8%,
- a student loan of $3,000 at 9%, and
- a credit card that has been overdue by $4,000 at 15% for two months.

Assume that you are in a 50% marginal tax bracket. What is the best way for you to tackle your debt problems?

To answer this question we need to calculate the after-tax cost of debt in all cases, in order to permit us to compare apples with apples. You can't just look at interest rates and pay down the lowest, since some of the loan interest is tax deductible in some cases. This changes things.

1. Pay down the credit card debt first. At an after-tax cost (meaning you pay this out of your net pay after tax) of 15%, this is outrageously high. Just by paying down this debt you can essentially earn a *return* of 15% by wiping out a *cost* of 15%!
2. Next focus on the student debt at 9% since the next most expensive after-tax cost of debt.
3. Then the car loan at 6.5%.
4. Then the mortgage at 6.0%.
5. Last, pay down the investment loan or margin account. Its after-tax cost of debt is only 4% since the 8% interest cost is tax deductible (at a 50% tax rate), reducing the real cost to only 4%.

If you can't afford to pay down these debts quickly, consider at least refinancing the most expensive debts. For example, you could have your local financial institution pay off your credit card bills for you and set up a term loan to repay at a lower interest rate. A debt still remains but the interest cost will likely be one-half to one-third of what many credit card companies charge. Take the reduced interest cost and pay down the debt faster.

Another option, if you have the choice, is to have your parents pay off your debts through a gift to you or with a loan to you. No doubt your family will give you more favourable interest rates on debt than a credit card company. I encourage you to consider a loan instead of a substantial gift in case your marriage breaks down. With a loan, there is more protection of your parents' money against this type of life risk.

# RULE 14

## Understand what wealth management means and whether it is right for you.

The world of Canadian financial services is changing today. The 1990s were about mutual funds. While mutual funds will always play a significant role in investor portfolios, the shift today is towards greater focus on service and advice. More specifically, the concept of wealth management has entered the Canadian financial services scene in a mass-market kind of way.

Wealth management may be defined as the management of your personal finance issues by a professional financial advisor. Wealth management is generally only available to individuals and families with a large net worth or large income. Many financial institutions in Canada now offer some version of wealth management services (also called private client services or private wealth services, among other terms) that cater to the more affluent client.

When you shop around for wealth management services and products, you will quickly realize that comparison shopping is not easy. Few financial services institutions and financial advisors define wealth management the same way, nor do they identify the same kind of client for their wealth management services.

Wealth management is a complicated and highly competitive industry. Every institution you talk to will have its own variation on products, services, and fees. Some may not even want you as a client. Before you start to shop around, first decide if you really need wealth management services. The strategies in this section will help you with that.

Here are three examples of wealth management providers in Canada today and what they offer for their business line:

**INSTITUTION A.** Here wealth management means that new investors buy a mutual fund wrap investment program instead of regular mutual funds. This entitles the investor to enhanced monthly reporting and automatic re-balancing of accounts if desired. Minimum client investment is $100,000. Fees are charged within the investments and start at 2.5% before declining downward with larger investments. Some informal asset allocation is also completed as part of the initial process of sorting out a client's investment mix. Your financial advisor's title is "private client consultant," and all consultants are salaried. This is the extent of this institution's wealth management services.

**INSTITUTION B.** Here, wealth management means building an individual account of stocks and bonds, charging an investment counsel fee that is directly deductible on your tax return, and meeting with you quarterly to review results. Minimum client investment is $1 million and fees start at 2% and decline downward. Fees are charged as a percentage of assets invested. Your advisor's title is "financial consultant," and he or she earns a living from commissions generated from your account. As part of this company's service package, it will also do your tax return each year.

**INSTITUTION C.** For this institution, wealth management means tax and estate planning services, cash flow management in retirement, and investment counsel. The organization helps you to hire professional money managers and supervises them, but does not manage your money itself. Advisors are called "personal wealth managers," and fees are a combination of hourly advisory charges and asset-based investment counsel fees.

Wealth management has been around for a hundred years in Canada, but only now is it becoming mainstream. Wealth management continues to evolve in Canada today, but many people don't know what it really means. I hope my more than ten years of experience dealing with wealth management clients and money managers can assist you to become informed about this interesting line of financial services.

# 97

## Do I qualify for wealth management services?

Determining whether you qualify for wealth management services may sound funny, but it is based on some fundamentally sound logic by the institutions providing the services and products. The main reason there are client standards for acceptance is the cost of providing extra services to a client. When the institution provides services to pamper rich clients, this must be paid for. The more services, the greater the cost potentially. One way that institutions can avoid raising the fees is to only accept more wealthy clients who will generate enough revenue to the institution to cover the costs of providing the service. In other words, the institution will collect more investment counselling fee revenue from a million dollar account than from a hundred thousand dollar account.

Another way that institutions deal with costs is to extra-bill for certain services. In other words, the institution may provide a core amount of service to their affluent clients, but charge extra for additional services. For example, they may charge an extra fee to prepare your tax return. For some people, this "user pay" approach may be attractive since it affords them the ability to decline extra services. Other people may find one all-encompassing fee preferable.

So what gets you in the door to be a wealth management client?

## Investable wealth

Most institutions will charge you an annual fee that is a percentage of your investments held with them. In some cases, this is the only fee you get charged—its level varies with the amount of service you sign up for. Generally, there are four different levels of wealth management services by investable wealth offered in Canada:

1. $100,000 of total investments
2. $500,000 of total investments
3. $1 million of total investments
4. $5 million+ of total investments

The amount of service and communication (a.k.a. pampering) you get from these institutions may vary widely if their service fees are linked to your investments. This is important to note, as many individuals sign up for wealth management services with $100,000, but expect a service level appropriate for someone with $1 million. Clients need to match expectations with economic realities of the institutions. A typical wealth management client wants a lot of service and is willing to pay professionals to take care of them the way they want to be taken care of. Rarely does this come cheaply.

## What if I have a lot of money?

If you have investment assets that total a few million dollars or you are a multimillionaire, the range of wealth management providers and money management solutions available to you is extensive. Mutual funds and brokers are now a thing of the past. As a multimillionaire you should be considering solutions placed with money managers from around the world evaluated through a sophisticated investment consulting process. Your should have a team of specialist advisors for tax, investing, and legal issues at a minimum. Investment fees should be tiered and cost you a fraction of the fee percentages applicable to smaller investors.

At higher wealth levels, you definitely need wealth management services and should be dealing with advanced specialists on all of your personal finance matters. Having increased wealth opens the door to a variety of new financial issues (particularly legal and tax issues) that require special attention not often affordable at lower wealth levels. Investing on your own or with an unsophisticated provider can be costly and financially dangerous if they are not set up to deal with the differentiated issues of a wealthy individual.

If you shop around, you will see that it is easy to qualify for some form of wealth management services. As you now know from this strategy, however, that pampering can take many forms. Ensure that the services you will be getting are the ones you need before signing on.

# 98

## Do I need wealth management services?

To answer this question, we need to define what services wealth management includes. This is difficult since most institutions define it slightly differently, and since individuals will define their needs differently as well. However, wealth management services may include some or all of the following items:

**INVESTMENT CONSULTING.** Every wealth management institution will include investment advice and portfolio management in their services. Many institutions offer only this and no other services. Your fees are often derived from the investment assets as well. It is safe to say that for many institutions, managing investments is the centrepiece of their wealth management service offering. Within wealth management services, investment products are rarely mutual funds, as higher wealth levels open up a whole new world of investment products for consideration.

**BASIC FINANCIAL PLANNING.** Most wealth management institutions will offer some element of basic retirement planning and cash flow management. This is usually done using some form of software tool and requires annual or regular review and updating.

**TAX PLANNING AND TAX RETURN PREPARATION.** Few institutions will offer detailed tax planning and preparation of your returns as part of their core service package. I believe that more institutions should, as I view tax planning as essential to all areas of personal finance including any investment decisions.

**ESTATE PLANNING AND ESTATE MANAGEMENT.** Many institutions will help you to plan for your estate but few of them will actually assist in the professional management of your estate after you die. Managing your estate includes preparing and filing several tax returns in the year of death, dealing with the estate assets, assisting the executor, handling legal matters, completing sales of assets, and so on.

**OTHER SERVICES.** There are a variety of other possible wealth management services such as bill payment, offshore planning, contract negotiations, legal services, personal assistant services, bookkeeping, and family office services.

Only you can decide if you need wealth management services. If your account is large enough, you may be able to find one institution willing to offer all these extra services for the same fee that you are already paying another company that doesn't supply them. If so, and all other factors being equal, you should jump at the chance.

The bottom line is that most of us require assistance with investing, taxes, estate, and financial planning and would be well served by experts assisting with these areas of our finances for a fee. There is also value to having coordination among all your personal finance needs, as discussed earlier in the book. A wealth management institution that can manage all your needs may offer an attractive time and cost savings.

Be sensitive to the total cost of what is being provided in terms of wealth management services. Once you have a million dollars of investable wealth, you are an attractive client to most wealth management institutions in Canada today. At that wealth level, you can obtain a variety of services included with your investment management, often at no extra cost. Once again, it is important to define your needs, do proper research, and consistently comparison shop.

# 99

## I've heard about trusts. Do I need one?

We grow up thinking that trusts are tools for the sole use of the rich and famous. Not so anymore—trusts have become more mainstream. In fact, most Canadians could benefit from using a formal trust in their financial affairs. Here I will explain the basics of trusts and encourage readers to explore trusts for their own use.

What is a trust? A trust is a planning instrument commonly used for tax planning, legal planning, cash-flow planning, risk management, and other applications that relate to personal and corporate finance where it is desirable to separate the legal ownership and control over property from the use of the property. Effectively, a specific amount of money or assets is set aside to become part of the trust and then used for a specific purpose.

A trust is a binding relationship between three different parties: a trustee (who is the person or parties that control the assets of the trust); the beneficiaries (who are the recipients of the income or capital paid out of the trust); and the settlor (who is the person or parties that contribute the contents of the trust and set the rules of the trust). A formal trust document names the beneficiaries and the trustee, and lays out plans for the assets in the trust. The trust document sets out the rules for the trust that will be followed by the trustees, and it is often created with the assistance of a lawyer.

It is possible for the same person to carry more than one of the three roles within a trust (e.g., a trustee may also be a beneficiary); however the roles of a person or party need to be carefully planned, because they may affect the tax treatment of the trust.

The settlor who sets up the trust is similar to an architect: he or she designs it but does nothing more. The beneficiary simply benefits from the income or capital from the trust. However, the trustee is the trust's manager, responsible for executing the wishes of the trust document, paying out income needs, hiring and firing money managers to manage the trust's money, dealing with upkeep of assets within the trust, paying trust expenses, filing trust tax returns, and so on. Being someone's trustee is a busy and complicated role—a role that can last 21 years!

## Types of trusts

There are two broad types of trusts: *inter vivos* trusts and testamentary trusts.

1. **Inter vivos trusts.** An *inter vivos* trust is a trust created by someone who is still alive. The most distinguishing characteristic of a living trust is that the income earned is taxed at the highest personal tax rates in Canada each year unless the income is paid out to a beneficiary before the end of the year. A trust tax return must be filed for an *inter vivos* trust each calendar year.

2. **Testamentary trusts**. A testamentary trust is created out of the will of a deceased individual and consists of any assets that are placed in it according to the will. Testamentary trusts start the first day after death and can operate on a fiscal year (not a calendar year). It is important to note that testamentary trusts are taxed differently from *inter vivos* trusts. Testamentary trusts are taxed just like people are, meaning that any income earned within the trust benefits from normal graduated tax rates.

## Taxation of trusts

The many specific details of trust taxation are beyond the scope of this book. But there are some important basics to know:

- A trust must file a tax return once a year. Whether or not you must file on a calendar year basis depends on the type of trust you create.
- *Inter vivos* trusts are taxed at tax rates different from testamentary trusts.
- A separate tax return called a T3 must be completed and filed. It is advisable to have an accountant prepare this tax return for you, since the tax return for trusts is different from the return for individuals.
- It is generally possible to avoid all taxation within a trust if all annual income is paid or payable to beneficiaries. In that case, it will be taxed in their hands. This can be advantageous if the beneficiaries are in a lower tax bracket than the trust.
- When assets are initially contributed to the trust they are normally deemed to be disposed of at the point of contribution. That is, any tax liabilities that have accrued on the assets will be due immediately after they are contributed. So putting a valuable 40-year-old family cottage into a trust without proper planning can make things difficult.
- Trusts are fully taxable on trust assets with accrued capital gains every 21 years. Before that time the taxation is deferred until the asset is sold.

## Uses of trusts

There are many uses for different types of trusts:

- *Alter ego* trusts can be set up to hold seniors' investment assets. Since investment income is taxed within the trust, it is not included on seniors' personal tax returns. This reduces their personal taxable income on their tax returns, so it can enhance the amount of Old Age Security benefits they receive or reduce the fees they must pay to a nursing home to live there. It can also be used to avoid probate fees.
- *Inter vivos* trusts can be set up to hold investment assets of a disabled child. Since the investment income is taxed within the trust, it is not included on the child's personal tax return. This reduces the child's personal taxable income on his or her own tax

return, possibly enhancing the disabled child's government benefits. *Inter vivos* trusts can also be used to provide direction over the finances of a disabled child after supporting parents have died. A trustee can pay the child's bills, provide money for food, and otherwise provide support.

- Trusts can be established in Canada or offshore to guard against undesirable loss of assets from creditors. Trusts are considered separate legal entities, so they protect assets against challenges to your personal net worth: If you cause a car accident and someone files a lawsuit against you, a trust shields your assets from loss. If you are in a high-risk profession, a trust shields your assets from potential lawsuits. If you are faced with bankruptcy, a trust shields your assets from being taken.
- Trusts can be an excellent way to keep your assets confidential. We have all read about the confidentiality of offshore trusts and Swiss bank accounts.
- Trusts can be set up to take care of seniors. Perhaps one spouse is the family's money manager. When he or she dies, the other spouse may be left to manage the family finances but may lack the skill or motivation to do so. A trust can manage the family affairs while also providing an income to the surviving spouse, as though your family finances were on autopilot. Children with one remaining parent in another province may also find this solution comforting.
- The primary use of trusts is for tax planning. Trusts can provide significant tax breaks. For example, a testamentary trust created on death to hold assets that would otherwise be transferred directly to beneficiary children benefits from taxation of income at graduated tax rates and may pay less tax on income than for those children who take their inheritance immediately and invest it personally. Since the trust has no other income (while a child beneficiary may already have a large salary), the trust is in a lower tax bracket than the beneficiary. The result can be tremendous annual tax savings to the beneficiary.
- Trusts can reduce taxes when grandparents would like to leave some money for grandchildren or set aside some money today for their grandchildren's futures.
- Trusts can avoid probate fees on death. Probate fees are a tax on assets held within your estate on death. The tax rate varies by province.

Trusts are a very powerful planning tool for financial advisors. As you can see, there are many situations where trusts can benefit the average Canadian. Talk to an expert who is familiar with the rules about trusts. Carefully evaluate the costs and benefits to determine whether a trust would help to preserve or enhance your net worth.

# 100
**Do I need my own investment holding company?**

Have you ever been to a dinner party and overheard someone talk about owning his or her own company and then been confused because that person was an executive with a local company and didn't appear to own the business? That person may have been referring to ownership of a private holding company, which anyone can set up. All it takes is a few hours with a lawyer, and you too can have your own company.

A private corporation is a separate legal entity that you create when you file legal documents to register it with the government. You can pick a name for your company, determine what to use it for, decide who the owners will be and how much stock they will receive, and set other parameters. Some companies are used to operate businesses such as restaurants or dry cleaners. Other corporations are simply empty shells that own shares in other companies. Private companies differ from public companies in that private company stock is not traded on a public stock exchange. There are many other differences as well, like tax treatment, that are beyond the scope of this book.

## Taxation of a corporation

Corporations must file an annual tax return based on a 12-month period you pick. It does not have to be a calendar year end. A corporation has its own set of tax rules that are much different from personal tax rules. You will almost certainly need an accountant to prepare your annual tax return for the company.

## Investment holding companies

A private investment holding company is a corporation that exists solely to hold your taxable investment portfolio (excluding RRSPs, RRIFs, and all tax-sheltered assets). There is no active business operated by the company, because the investment holdings are not considered an active business. If you have a corporation that operates an active business or that blends investments with business interests, consult a tax professional about the specific tax characteristics.

A discussion about general corporation tax rules is beyond the scope of this book, but there are a few important details worth mentioning:

- In many cases, private companies are subject to tax rules different from those for public companies.
- The first $500,000 of capital gains that you earn on the sale of your private company shares is tax free, provided you qualify and the company is an active business. Talk to a tax specialist about how to qualify.

- The investment holding company will be taxed annually on dividend income, interest income, and capital gains income. All investment income that the company earns on the investment portfolio is taxable, but taxed at a rate that is different from the rate for personal investments.
- Generally the tax rates applicable to investment income within a corporation are set by the governments so that there is little or no difference overall from rates for investments held in your name and taxed personally. This equalization is called integration, and the government has regularly adjusted tax rates to keep this integration fairly equal. Integration ensures that there is no undue benefit to holding an investment within a corporation instead of holding it personally. The extent of integration varies by province.
- Assets can be transferred to a corporation on a tax-deferred basis. This means that you can move your entire investment account into a new corporation without triggering any taxes. Be careful, though—it doesn't work the same way when you try to get it out.
- Shareholders can remove earnings from their company in two main ways: They can pay themselves a justifiable salary or pay dividends based on shares owned. Both methods have tax implications.
- Each year financial statements should be prepared for the company, showing income less expenses. This information is necessary for the tax filings. A bookkeeper may need to be hired for the accounting work. Usually the accountant who does the tax work can also do the accounting, depending on the complexity. An accountant can also tell you how to get a GST number and a PST number.
- A corporation must file a corporate tax return and perhaps also a capital tax return, depending on the province of residence.

## Why have a private investment holding company?

After reading the previous section you may be thinking that a holding company is too complicated to own. Yes, there are a lot of rules, but usually hiring an accountant can take care of all the filings and day-to-day work, leaving you with little else to do except manage the cash flow and the needs of the investment portfolio.

In the past, if you asked someone why he or she had a holding company, the reply was most likely "for tax reasons." In the past, it was likely that your after-tax return was greater if you owned your investments through a holding company than if you owned the investments personally. Those days are gone. In many cases there are no tax savings. If you have had a corporation for several years, you may want to revisit the reasons for having it, if originally they were for taxes alone. Today, there are new and different reasons to own a holding company:

- Private corporations can be set up to hold investment assets of seniors. Since the investment income is taxed within the corporation, it is not included on seniors' personal tax returns. This will reduce their personal taxable income on their own tax returns, possibly increasing their Old Age Security benefits or reducing the fees they have to pay to a nursing home to live there.
- Private corporations can be set up to hold the investment assets of a disabled child. Since the investment income is taxed within the corporation, it is not included on the child's personal tax return. This reduces the child's personal tax on his or her own tax return, possibly enhancing the disabled child's government benefits.
- Private corporations can be established in Canada or offshore to guard against undesirable loss of assets to creditors. Corporations are considered separate legal entities, so they protect assets against challenges to your personal net worth. If you are in a high-risk profession, a corporation could shield your personal assets from potential lawsuits. If you are faced with corporate bankruptcy, a corporation could shield your personal assets from being taken.
- Private corporations can provide confidentiality. A public company must publish financial statements and even the salaries of key employees, but private corporations have no such obligations. Many of Canada's largest companies are privately owned, and the public never sees the financial details of their successes.
- Private corporations can hold foreign real estate and foreign stock portfolios. Few are aware that their U.S. condo in Florida and their U.S. stock portfolio may be subject to U.S. estate taxes on their death, subject to the qualifying rules, so your executor will have to pay taxes to the IRS shortly thereafter. Holding these assets within a corporate structure that you own protects you against this IRS threat, since U.S. estate taxes do not apply to qualifying corporations. If you have substantial U.S. assets, ensure that you talk to a U.S. estate tax specialist.
- Private corporations can be used to hold assets from your net worth and avoid probate fees on death because private companies can be passed through a second will that does not require probate.

Private investment holding companies can be a very effective planning tool. The rules for corporations, are complicated and any discussion about holding companies should involve a lawyer or an accountant familiar with how they work.

**Active management** Management of investments by professional money managers who actively buy and sell investments using available information, research, and forecasting techniques in an attempt to produce a better rate of return than the broad market does. The opposite of passive management.

**After-tax rate of return** The remaining return on a taxable investment's gross return after any income tax is taken away. After-tax return is the bottom line return that remains, similar to the after-tax portion of your pay cheque.

**Aggressive** Describes an investment with a lot of risk. An aggressive portfolio is one with investments that have an overall greater than average risk.

**Asset** A possession that has value; anything that is owned.

**Asset allocation** The process of determining the amounts and combinations of various investments to invest in when building an investment portfolio. *See* strategic capital allocation.

**Asset class** A category of assets, such as stocks, bonds, and real estate. Cash, fixed income, and equity are three basic types of classes for consideration within an investment portfolio. Others include geographic classes such as Canadian equity and U.S. equity. Sectors can also be a form of asset class (such as technology and health care).

**Balanced mutual fund** A mutual fund in which the money manager decides on the blend of stocks, bonds, and cash to buy based on market conditions (market timing). From day to day, the proportion of what is invested in each of the asset classes may vary. Also called a balanced fund.

**Blue-chip stock** Public stock of companies having strong investment qualities; these are large, diversified, established companies that are considered safer than many other equities for investment purposes. Such companies are nationally and internationally known for the quality and wide acceptance of their products or services and for their ability to thrive and grow. These companies may be better able to weather a poor economy than smaller and weaker companies.

**Bond** A financial contract between an issuer and holder to loan money to the issuer for a period of time with a cost of borrowing attached. An issuer may be a corporation or federal, provincial, or municipal governments using bonds as a means of raising capital. The issuer guarantees to pay a specified amount of interest to the holder for a specified length of time, and repay the original loan at maturity. This is an example of a fixed-income investment. From an investor's point of view, bonds can offer more certainty of income (but less income) than equity investments over time.

**Bond funds/bond mutual funds** *See* fixed-income fund.

**Broker** An investment advisor who is paid a commission for executing a client's buy and sell orders on investment products. A broker may offer little or no service in the form of personal financial planning.

**Canada Customs and Revenue Agency**  The Canada Customs and Revenue Agency (formerly Revenue Canada) is the department of the federal government that administers and enforces the laws outlined in the Income Tax Act.

**Canada Pension Plan (CPP)**  A social insurance and retirement savings plan operated by the federal government of Canada. Ensures a measure of protection for working Canadians (employees and self-employed individuals) who contribute to the plan. In retirement, benefits are received in the form of regular payments for themselves or their families to provide income, or against disability or death.

**Canadian Deposit Insurance Corporation (CDIC)**  This organization, established by the federal government, guarantees to insure a basic amount of money deposited in a bank account or a GIC (but not a mutual fund) at a member institution. Members of the CDIC include many of the major financial institutions in Canada.

**Capital gain**  Any profit received from the sale of a capital asset (certain types of assets such as stocks) over its acquisition cost. A taxable capital gain is an amount to be included as income on an income tax return, and is calculated at 50% of net capital gains (capital gains minus capital losses for the year).

**Capital loss**  The opposite of a capital gain. An allowable capital loss is calculated at 50% of net capital losses (capital losses minus capital gains). A capital loss may not otherwise be used to reduce regular income. Capital losses can be carried back three years or carried forward indefinitely to apply against taxable capital gains in order to reduce tax.

**Cash flow forecast**  An exercise of predicting your financial future income and expense levels by examining the interaction of financial variables in your life over time. For example, a common cash flow forecast looks at the savings you have today and how much you are saving regularly, then estimates a rate of return on this money and forecasts into the future how much money you will have. There are many varieties of forecasts possible, all of which require assumptions and facts about your financial circumstances today and in the future.

**CCRA**  *See* Canada Customs and Revenue Agency.

**CDIC**  *See* Canadian Deposit Insurance Corporation.

**Certified financial planner (CFP)**  A professional designation licensed by the Financial Planner Standards Council of Canada and provided to individuals who have completed an educational requirement to practice financial planning. The CFP designation is becoming widely recognized as the designation of choice for financial planners in Canada and worldwide. Note that a CFP designation does not mean that the planner has experience working as a financial planner—it is only an academic designation.

**CFP**  *See* certified financial planner.

**Clone funds**  A mutual fund that uses derivatives to mirror or replicate the return in an existing underlying fund, usually a foreign equity fund. A clone fund qualifies as 100% Canadian content for an RRSP or RRIF, while providing a return that is linked to a foreign investment. This serves to increase the foreign content above the allowed 30% limit while still following the foreign content rules. Also called a 100% RRSP-eligible fund.

**Commission**  The fee charged by a licensed financial advisor to buy or sell investments for a client. This fee may be a flat fee or a percentage based on the size of the transaction.

**Critical illness insurance**  This type of insurance provides cash flow to the insured person upon diagnosis of certain types of illnesses. The coverage amount may be used to replace lost income and to pay for medical expenses, medication, etc.

**Deemed disposition**  A notional disposition (not a real sale) of an asset resulting in a realization of any accrued capital gains or losses and triggering any resulting tax. A deemed disposition occurs, for example, upon a death when the deceased's assets are deemed to be disposed of at fair market value, and tax may be due on any gains realized.

**Deferral of tax** The process of delaying the payment of tax until a point in the future. RRSPs and RRIFs defer tax since no tax is paid on income earned in the plan until the proceeds are withdrawn (usually in retirement). Deferral of tax permits assets to continue to earn income on a pre-tax basis, enhancing the growth rate.

**Derivative** A financial instrument, such as an option or future contract, that derives its value from another asset or investment. For example, an option contract to buy stock at a future date for a fixed price is a derivative. If the value of the stock goes up, so does the value of the option in some proportion. On that future date, if the market price of the stock is greater than the option price to purchase, the derivative holder can exercise the option, purchase the shares at the option price, then sell those shares at the higher market price and make a profit on the difference. Derivatives are complicated financial instruments warranting sophisticated expertise.

**Discretionary investing** A client gives written authorization to a qualified money manager to trade securities or manage a portfolio on his or her behalf. The client enjoys the freedom of not having to be consulted at all, knowing that reasonable decisions will be made in keeping with his or her investment goals. An example of this would be owning a mutual fund.

**Distribution** Money allocated or directed to a unit holder of a mutual fund as a result of investing activity within the fund. A distribution may be interest, dividends, capital gains, or foreign income that is generated from investments and trading. Distributions are made at regular intervals during a calendar year to unit holders of record on the distribution dates.

**Diversification** Diversification is investing in a combination of assets of various characteristics such that overall volatility of a portfolio is reduced without reducing expected returns. There are many ways to diversify an investment portfolio, such as investing in cash, equities, and bonds. One can also diversify geographically by investing in Canadian equities and U.S. equities. These are only a few examples of diversification.

**Dividend** An after-tax monetary distribution paid to shareholders of a company in proportion to the number of shares they hold. Dividends may or may not be paid regularly, and the amount paid may vary.

**Dividend-yielding stock** Stock of a company that issues dividends to shareholders. Only some stocks issue dividends at all, and the level of dividend varies by company.

**Equity** Stock issued by a company, representing ownership in that company. *See also* stock; equity mutual fund.

**Equity mutual fund** A mutual fund investing in equities or stocks of companies. There are several categories of equity mutual funds, including Canadian and international.

**Estate planning** The process of making legal, tax, and other decisions relating to an individual's net worth and personal circumstances that will be applied upon and after death. Planning may involve preparation of a will, creation of a trust, implementation of powers of attorney, and choosing an estate executor, among other responsibilities.

**Executor** A person appointed by an individual to carry out the provisions of his or her will and manage the deceased's estate.

**Fair market value** The amount that a buyer and seller would agree on in relation to the purchase and sale of an item, where the market is unrestricted and the buyer and seller are not connected in any way.

**Financial advisor** A highly trained and experienced professional who offers personal financial advice to clients for a fee and/or commission.

**Financial plan** Advice, or a document summarizing advice, on an individual's financial affairs, including goals, net worth, cash flow, and strategies to reach goals in areas that may include retirement, estate, insurance, investing, employment, children's savings, and others.

**Financial planner** A financial advisor who follows a six-step financial planning process as outlined by the Canadian Association of Financial Planners. A financial planner focuses on broad financial advice in addition to product solutions and often provides broader financial advice than a broker, who simply sells products. *See* certified financial planner.

**Financial planning** A process of developing and prioritizing financial goals, and developing strategies to meet those goals. The process involves collecting information about a client's current personal and financial situation, identifying goals, developing alternatives and recommendations to meet goals, providing assistance with implementing goals, and monitoring the client's achievements of those goals over time.

**Fixed-income investment** An agreement between a debtor and a lender (investor) whereby the investor agrees to lend an amount of money to the debtor for an amount of interest over a period of time. There are many different types of fixed-income investments with varying characteristics. Examples include GICs, Canada Savings Bonds, Government of Canada bonds, and bond mutual funds.

**Fixed-income fund** A mutual fund that invests primarily in bonds, mortgages, and/or other forms of debt. Bond funds are a form of fixed-income fund. The money manager of a fixed-income fund may actively trade bonds in the markets, making bond funds more volatile than owning bonds directly.

**Foreign content** The portion of an investment portfolio that is invested outside Canada. For an individual's RRSP, the maximum allowable foreign content level is 30% of the book value or original cost of the investment. This level may be legally increased well beyond the 30% level when clone funds are used, while still adhering to the rules in the Income Tax Act.

**Formal trust** A legal relationship, evidenced by an agreement created when a person (settlor) transfers property to another (trustee) who is responsible for dealing with the property for the benefit of persons known as beneficiaries. The fundamental characteristic of a trust is the separation of management of the property from entitlement to it. A trust is a separate taxpayer and must file a tax return annually. Trusts may aid in many different situations such as tax planning, creditor proofing, and asset protection.

**Forward contract** A form of derivative. *See* derivative.

**Fragmentation** My term for the phenomenon whereby people spread their investments around and fail to disclose the entirety of their investments to a single financial advisor or institution. Therefore, they are not building an integrated and comprehensive investment program. There is also a tendency to concentrate only on the investments, rather than on the way they interrelate within the entire financial picture.

**GIC** *See* Guaranteed Investment Certificate.

**Growth stock** A company with a record of growth in earnings at a relatively rapid rate. Instead of paying out dividends, the corporate profits are put back into the company to pay for expansion.

**Guaranteed Investment Certificate** A fixed-income investment in which an investor deposits funds in an institution such as a bank for a specified period of time (during which the investment is usually locked in) with a guaranteed rate of return. At the end of the term, the investor is repaid the principal amount plus the interest income.

**Hot fund**  A fund for which the money manager has produced very good returns recently, compared with similar investments.

**Income-splitting strategies**  Certain methods of tax planning involving the legal shifting of taxable income and assets between family members to reduce the family's overall tax burden.

**Income Tax Act of Canada**  The federal statute that contains the income tax laws and regulations governing the taxation of individuals, corporations, and trusts in Canada. Such laws are created and amended federally by the Minister of Finance. The CCRA (Canada Customs and Revenue Agency, formerly Revenue Canada) is the federal government department that administers the Income Tax Act and deals with Canadians and their federal taxes.

**Index**  An indicator of broad market performance within an economy. In Canada, the Toronto Stock Exchange Composite Index (the TSE 300 Composite Index) includes stocks of 300 large and established Canadian companies. In the U.S., Standard & Poor's 500 Index (S&P 500) includes 500 U.S. companies that are representative of major industry groups.

**Index fund**  A mutual fund that invests in the same securities included in a broad market index such as the TSE 300 Composite in Canada or Standard & Poor's 500 in the United States. The holdings of the fund try to mirror the index and produce a rate of return similar to it, so there is no need for an active manager. This type of fund management is called passive or indexed management.

**Index-linked GIC**  A type of GIC in which the original investment amount is guaranteed and that pays an investment return that is "linked" to the return of a stock market, for example, the TSE 300. An amount reflecting the actual annual stock market return, or part of it, would be earned, but without the risk of loss of the original investment.

**Inflation**  A measure of the increase in cost of living over time within an economy. An example of the impact of inflation has been the rising price of the postage stamp over the years. As the cost of living increases through inflation, a person's income should also grow in order to prevent a decrease in the standard of living through a loss of purchasing power.

**Integration**  I utilize this term for the concept of considering all aspects of one's personal finances, not just investments, in order to properly view and strategize the larger financial picture.

**In-trust account**  An informal account where funds are held in trust by someone (the trustee) for a child (the beneficiary). This type of arrangement, without the related documentation and process involved in the creation of a formal trust, is available from many Canadian financial institutions.

**Investment management style**  Money managers take different approaches to picking stocks and bonds. Two such styles, among many, are growth and value. Long-term money management performance is tied to a style's interaction with market conditions at a point in time and over time.

**Investment Policy Statement (IPS)**  *See* Statement of Investment Policy and Guidelines.

**Investment time horizon**  The period of time available to investors for investment purposes in order to achieve their financial goals.

**Investment turnover**  The frequency at which investments are bought or sold within an investment account or mutual fund. Less turnover can result in less frequent annual taxation and a greater after-tax net worth. Zero portfolio turnover in a year means no investments were sold or bought in the year; 100% turnover means that all investments were effectively sold once within the year; 500% turnover means that the contents of a portfolio were effectively bought and sold five times in a calendar year.

**IPS**  *See* Statement of Investment Policy and Guidelines.

**Labour fund** A specialty investment, similar to a mutual fund, that offers significant tax credits to the investor in exchange for investing in private businesses looking for investment capital. A labour fund is a relatively risky investment and requires a multi-year investment period before you can sell.

**Life insurance** Upon loss of life of an insured individual, a designated beneficiary is paid a specific sum (which may be tax free) as stipulated by the policy contract. The insurance premium depends on variables such as amount of coverage, age, gender, state of health, and whether the insured is a smoker.

**Liquidity** The ease with which an investment can be converted into cash.

**Load** For a mutual fund, the fee charged upon initial investment (front load) or redemption (rear load or deferred sales charge, DSC) according to a published schedule. The charges go towards paying the advisors and may range from 0% to 8% if units are redeemed within a designated length of time, such as one year.

**Loss carryforward** A tax benefit that allows tax losses from investments to be used to reduce taxable income and capital gains in future years.

**Management expense ratio (MER)** A representation of costs of operating a mutual fund, including management expenses, all expressed as a percentage of the total market value of the fund. For example, a typical Canadian equity mutual fund might charge a management expense ratio of approximately 2.25% annually of the market value of the fund.

**Management style** *See* investment management style.

**Marginal tax rate** The tax rate applicable to the next dollar of taxable income to be earned by a person. In Canada, taxable income is taxed according to a progressive tax rate system, whereby income is taxed at higher rates as you add more income, up to a point. The marginal tax rate is the tax rate applicable to each of these tax brackets and the amount of income that falls within the bracket.

**Market timing** An approach where an investor attempts to invest according to predicted increases or decreases in particular market sectors based on theories about market conditions and investment performance. This type of guessing is not a good long-term investment solution.

**Market-traded bond** A bond that is traded daily in the Canadian and world bond markets. Market-traded bonds such as Government of Canada Bonds fluctuate in value with changes in market interest rates. GICs and Canada Savings Bonds are not market-traded bonds.

**MER** *See* management expense ratio.

**Momentum investor** A money manager who tries to guess the next hot area of the market and then ride the wave of investors as they invest in that area or industry.

**Money manager** A person, group of people, or company that trades investments on behalf of others. The manager buys or sells investments on behalf of the investors. Similar terms are investment manager or portfolio manager.

**Mutual fund** A professionally managed pool of investments, such as stocks and bonds, owned by a group of investors together. By buying units in a fund, an individual investor can invest in a wide range of Canadian or international stocks, bonds, and other investments that otherwise might not be affordable to that investor. Mutual funds are legally structured as trusts or corporations.

**Net worth** The value of an individual's total assets less the value of total liabilities equals the net worth of an individual. Success in an individual's personal finances is measured by an increase in net worth with time.

**Net worth approach** Instead of using income level to evaluate personal wealth, I advocate the approach of preparing a net worth statement that includes all aspects of an individual's personal finances at least once each year. This results in a better evaluation of success and may be easily viewed for future comparisons.

**Net worth statement**  A statement that lists all of an individual's assets at fair market value and then subtracts the value of any debts to arrive at net personal worth.

**No load**  A mutual fund with no initial purchase fee or fee for redemption.

**Nondiscretionary investing**  An investment approach in which a money manager must consult the client and be sure of the client's understanding and approval before carrying out any investment trading transactions for the client.

**Old Age Security**  The Old Age Security program provides a modest pension in the form of monthly benefits to most Canadian applicants 65 years of age or over. Employment history is not a factor in determining eligibility, nor does the applicant need to be retired. The amount of pension is determined by how long the person has lived in Canada. OAS benefits are reduced if your income is above a certain threshold.

**Passive management**  An investment management style that is associated with index mutual funds. The opposite of active management.

**POA**  *See* power of attorney.

**Pooled fund**  A fund investment similar in structure to a mutual fund, except that minimum investment amounts are much higher ($85,000 to $150,000) and MERs tend to be in the range of 1% lower than those of mutual funds. There is no sales fee involved in buying or selling a pooled fund.

**Portfolio**  Collection of investments or securities held by an individual or an institution. A portfolio may contain bonds, mutual funds, preferred stocks, common stocks, and other investments.

**Portfolio rebalancing**  Periodically realigning the proportions of assets in a portfolio as needed, when the levels of some assets increase beyond desired ranges. This ensures that everything is in keeping with the original permitted ranges in the Statement of Investment Policy and Guidelines and prevents the portfolio from developing too much or too little risk according to investor tolerances.

**Portfolio turnover**  *See* investment turnover.

**Power of attorney**  A power of attorney, or POA, is a legal document that authorizes another person or persons to act on behalf of the person who appointed them as a substitute decision maker. This allows a person to plan ahead and have confidence that their plans will be carried out.

**Probate fee**  A fee/tax imposed for the processing and validation of authenticity of a deceased person's will. Calculation of this fee is based on the value of assets in an estate, and varies from province to province.

**Protected fund**  A mutual fund that offers a guarantee of principal, ensuring no loss of original investment over a fixed period of time.

**Registered Education Savings Plan (RESP)**  A savings plan created by the federal government that allows accumulated contributions to grow on a tax-deferred basis and to be withdrawn by a named beneficiary (child) for funding qualified postsecondary education. The contributions are not tax deductible. The funds are taxable upon withdrawal for educational purposes in the hands of the student, and the taxes would likely be minimal or nil for a student.

**Registered Retirement Income Fund (RRIF)**  An individual retirement account registered with the federal government, the assets of which have been transferred from an RRSP or registered pension plan. Contributions are not made to an RRIF; instead, minimum sums must be withdrawn from it each year according to government-determined levels, and these withdrawals are taxable. There are no maximum withdrawal amounts. Funds inside the RRIF can continue to be invested as desired and remain tax-deferred until withdrawn. An individual may convert an RRSP to an RRIF at any age up to 70, but no later than the year in which they turn 69. The first withdrawal can be deferred until the person's 70th year.

**Registered Retirement Savings Plan (RRSP)** A savings plan registered with the federal government. Contributions to an RRSP are based on limits determined with reference to earned income and benefits accruing under employer-sponsored registered pension plans and deferred profit-sharing plans. Contributions are tax deductible, and income inside the plan grows tax deferred. Individuals can contribute to their own RRSP or to a spousal RRSP. For a spousal RRSP, the contributor gets the tax deduction and the spouse withdraws the investment at least three years in the future, at which time the withdrawals would be subject to tax.

**RESP** *See* Registered Education Savings Plan.

**Revenue Canada** *See* Canada Customs and Revenue Agency.

**Reverse mortgage** An agreement allowing homeowners to borrow against the paid up value in a home they own, up to a point. The loan can be paid to them as a lump sum or in periodic payments. Interest is charged on the loan, and the total amount of the loan and interest may be collected on the owners' death and ultimate sale of the home by the estate.

**Risk** The degree of volatility of return on an investment or uncertainty in meeting your financial goals. It is important to know the level of risk associated with a particular type of investment before purchasing. Usually, an investment with a higher potential rate of return has a higher risk associated with achievement of that return.

**Risk-adjusted return** A rate of return on an investment where the level of risk associated with the investment is acknowledged in measuring the return.

**Risk-managed investing/risk-managed approach** By identifying and evaluating various financial risks, unnecessary risk may be avoided through proper planning of your finances. A risk-managed investment portfolio is one in which the investor's risk tolerance has been taken into consideration to put together a portfolio having only as much risk as is needed. Portfolio risk can be managed in a variety of ways, including the setting of target returns and through portfolio diversification.

**Risk profile** Consideration of an individual investor's understanding and tolerance of volatility and fear of loss, as well as historical experience with risk for investment purposes.

**Risk tolerance** A measure of an individual's willingness or ability to endure volatility and loss.

**RRIF** *See* Registered Retirement Income Fund.

**RRSP** *See* Registered Retirement Savings Plan.

**SCA** *See* strategic capital allocation.

**Sector** An asset class, industry, geographic region, or other specific type of investment (for example, technology sector).

**Sector rotator** A money manager who jumps from one market sector to another trying to guess which sector will be the next to outperform.

**Seg fund** *See* segregated fund.

**Segregated fund** A variable annuity contract offered by a life insurance institution, whereby the underlying investment is guaranteed if certain rules are met. Seg funds are available only through life insurance companies.

**Sensitivity analysis** A risk-managed approach to investing, which considers and analyzes different combinations of possibilities—a worst-case scenario, where something such as an undesirable investment return may occur; a best-case scenario; and a most-likely scenario—leading to a healthier understanding of the outcome of your financial objectives.

**Settlor** An individual who contributes the initial investment capital to a trust.

**SIP&G** *See* Statement of Investment Policy and Guidelines.

**Statement of Investment Policy and Guidelines (SIP&G)** A three-part document that acts as a blueprint for building a professional investment program and purchasing investment products. It is one of the most important documents an investor can have. Also called an Investment Policy Statement (IPS).

**Stock** A stock or share is a representation of equity ownership in a company or corporation. Stock may be common or preferred, each type having different rights attached, such as voting ability and dividend entitlement.

**Stock option** A contract whereby employees are permitted to purchase their company's shares at a specified exercise price within a specified time period.

**Strategic capital allocation (SCA)** A process for building and maintaining an investment portfolio specific to an individual investor, by giving consideration to unique financial and nonfinancial characteristics of investors and resulting in the creation of a personal Statement of Investment Policy and Guidelines.

**Tactical asset allocation** A money manager who predicts changes in market conditions and invests in areas that may be positively affected.

**Target annual return** Desired or necessary annual rate of return on an investment or portfolio in order to meet financial goals.

**Tax-adjusted basis** The examination of an asset or investment after giving consideration to the tax implications associated with it.

**Tax bracket** A specified range of taxable income to which a given tax rate applies. In Canada, rate of tax generally increases as income increases, up to a point.

**Tax compliance** The process of reporting tax information required by statute, including completing a tax return. This differs from tax planning, which provides strategies to save and defer tax.

**Tax planning** The process of applying tax minimization and tax-deferral strategies, within the rules of the Income Tax Act of Canada, to help a taxpayer minimize the taxes paid. This is potentially of great value to individuals, trusts, and companies.

**Tax-smart investing** Giving consideration to the impact of taxes on the return of an investment before it is purchased and before it is sold, in an attempt to maximize after-tax returns.

**Term insurance** Temporary insurance that provides guaranteed death benefit coverage for a specific period of time. Premiums increase when you renew but overall are inexpensive when you are young. No cash value accumulation is possible as it is with universal life insurance. This is ideal coverage for large obligations over a fixed period of time.

**Term-to-100 insurance**  Insurance in which level premiums are paid to provide a death benefit up to age 100. These policies don't build a cash value.

**Testamentary trust**  A trust that is created on the day a person dies, usually based on instructions from the deceased's will. A testamentary trust may be used as a tax planning strategy to take advantage of a lower tax rate than might be available to the beneficiary of an estate.

**Time value of money**  The value of a pool of money varies over time due to a rate of return that could be earned on the money, and the amount of time involved. The longer the time period, the greater the fluctuation possible in the value of the money.

**Trailer fee**  A fee paid to a licensed financial advisor by a mutual fund company when one of its qualifying funds has been purchased by a client through that financial advisor. The financial advisor may receive trailer fees as long as the financial advisor is used by the client to hold the investments. The trailer pays for ongoing service provided to the client by the financial advisor.

**Treasury bill**  Short-term debt issued by the government at a discount, to mature at face value. There is no interest paid; rather, the difference between the purchase price and maturing value is taxed as interest income. T-bills are fixed-income investments.

**Trust**  *See* formal trust.

**Trustee**  As the administrator of a trust, the trustee is responsible for making sure that the trust is maintained and operated properly as outlined in the trust document.

**TSE 300 Composite Index**  A Canadian index of public company stocks representing 300 of the largest companies in Canada trading on the Toronto Stock Exchange. The TSE 300 is widely used as a measure of the performance of the stock market and the economy in Canada.

**Unit holder**  An investor who owns units in an open-ended mutual fund.

**Universal life insurance**  A permanent interest-sensitive life insurance policy that allows the accumulation of a cash value. It is divided into basic insurance and an investment account. You can decide how much goes into the savings component, and it grows tax sheltered until the payout on death.

**Well-diversified portfolio**  A portfolio that includes investments in a variety of asset classes, money management styles, and investment in different sizes and types of companies within Canada and internationally. Money is carefully spread as far and wide as possible to reduce the risk of excessive volatility from any one particular piece of the portfolio.

**Wrapped program**  Investment program in which a collection of professional money managers have been selected to manage money for investors according to specific mandates. A wrapped product might consist of mutual funds, pooled funds, or segregated money management. The cost of advice and management is "wrapped" into one comprehensive fee that is charged regularly to the investor based on assets invested within the program.

**Zero load**  A regularly loaded mutual fund sold at zero commission to buy.

Kurt Rosentreter is a chartered accountant who specializes in the field of income taxation planning. He is also a certified financial planner and a tax and estate practitioner, and he holds an honours finance degree from the University of Manitoba. Most recently, he became a certified investment management analyst, a designation he received from the Investment Management Consulting Association in affiliation with Wharton Business School in the United States.

Kurt has spent almost a decade with one of the world's largest professional services firms, Ernst & Young, working in affluent client financial affairs. In the late 1990s, he co-founded a start-up investment counselling and financial planning practice within Ernst & Young that exceeded $1 billion in little over one year of operation. Currently, Kurt is Vice President, Private Client Services, at a major financial services institution in Toronto.

Beyond his day job, Kurt Rosentreter is regularly called on by Canada's media to comment on personal financial issues. He has contributed to *Canada AM*, CBC's *NewsWorld*, numerous national radio shows and most of Canada's major newspapers and financial magazines. Kurt Rosentreter's first book, *50 Tax-Smart Investing Strategies*, is a Canadian bestseller and has led to extensive public speaking engagements.

Kurt Rosentreter sits, or has sat on, several committees within different national associations, including the Canadian Association of Financial Planners, the Financial Planners Standards Council, and the Canadian Institute of Chartered Accountants.

## Books

Kurt Rosentreter's first book, *50 Tax-Smart Investing Strategies*, can be purchased in most Canadian bookstores or directly from the author by calling 416-988-8900.

## Speaking engagements

Kurt Rosentreter is available for corporate or group conferences, seminars, workshops, and other educational and promotional events. To arrange a speaking engagement, contact Kurt directly at 416-988-8900 or write to:

Kurt Rosentreter
P.O. Box 5264, Station A
Toronto, ON  M5W 1N5
Canada

E-mail: kurtrosentreter@hotmail.com
Website: www.kurtrosentreter.com